A
R) 834 ^X

from
Barbara & Hugh

17 September 1993

The COUNTRYSIDE COMPANION

Compiled by Sam Elder

Introduction by
ROBERT HARDY

MICHAEL O'MARA BOOKS LIMITED

First published in Great Britain by
Michael O'Mara Books Ltd
20 Queen Anne Street
London W1N 9FB

The Countryside Companion © 1989 by
Michael O'Mara Books Ltd

A CIP catalogue record for this book is available from
the British Library.

ISBN 0-948397-99-3

Reader: Diana Vowles
Design: Mick Keates

Typeset by Florencetype Ltd, Kewstoke, Avon
Printed and bound in Great Britain
by Mackays of Chatham PLC

CONTENTS

PART II COUNTRY PEOPLE

PART III COUNTRY WAYS

INTRODUCTION
BY ROBERT HARDY CBE

The inhabitants of the British Isles have perhaps always written better about their countryside than those of any other land. A few novelists have written and still write about the past of our land, but the best writing that survives was written originally about the present, written sometimes by dwellers in the country, sometimes by travellers to other parts of Britain than their own, sometimes by city dwellers roaming the countryside at leisure, or moving from place to place, before the speed of today's travel meant that the travellers' attention is focussed on the motorway, and very little upon the country through which it roars. What few dare do is predict the future, but standing on the heights of 1989 the distant prospect is not reassuring. We treasure so much of what has gone before, and yet we are constantly driven to acts of destruction which are altering forever the appearance, and diminishing for future generations the beauty of our countryside.

The developers range the land picking any excuse that offers to build new housing estates, not bless you at easy prices for those who still work the land and who, being of the villages from times past, are now being bought out, and priced out by the crowds of fugitives from city noise and pollution. The local authorities, split between wanting new life in their villages, which have been dwindling for a long while and for many reasons, split between repopulating and their hopes of controlling the worst excesses of the speculative builders or the wealthy newcomers, are not helped by the attitude of Government, which seems to be that on the whole development should go ahead unless there is some over-riding reason for preservation. And that of course can be argued until the cows are gone.

Many are now trying to take action to halt the spread of concrete, but seldom with great success. Many, many others with more leisure and swifter transport than ever before roam even the less accessible and wilder parts of these islands so that in some places the march of countless feet is altering the very shape of the ground. Those who tramp the wild places are searching for the peace, the solitude and the beauty that they cannot find in the cities. The cities in fact are spreading out across the land in more ways than by the encroachment of brick and concrete. Those who come from the cities are not always the wisest judges of country matters; and since, wherever humanity turns its attention, the

8

natural world is more or less in danger, the limited surface area of Great Britain is among the least secure land spaces in the world.

Is nostalgia over the past glories of our countryside all that is left to us? If that were true then this collection of writings about British country, country life and country people would be invaluable, as the title suggests, on the bedside table, so that we could conjure up pictures of the past in drifting moments before sleep claims us. But I believe this volume has a much more positive value than that. However much we may regret the changes, in some cases the ravages that are perpetrated upon our country, our country as it is today is what we have to live with, and we must try might and main to save the best of what remains of it; but we cannot decide what is best, what is worth saving, without knowing a good deal about it, about how and why it was as it was, and how and why it is changing. The decisions and actions of the present must be based on a true understanding of the past, and an understanding of the miseries and tragedies of that past as well as its glories. I would say that there are few better, certainly few pleasanter ways of gaining that understanding than by a study of this collection. It is enormously broad in its selection and rich in its choice.

You can of course read about cottage gardens, and the Hens' Domain, but you can be reminded by Oscar Wilde that 'the more we study Art, the less we care for Nature,' which might lead one to believe that we are a nation of art-lovers. I believe we are not.

We are led to the most likely part of Galway in which to find bog-butter (let not my use of the term British Isles offend readers from Eire; this volume naturally includes good writing about your lovely country as well) or the chance of unearthing a 50-foot prehistoric boat, miraculously preserved in bacteria-free, water-logged soil. We hear debate upon the life-span of animals and birds, and learn that creatures of the wild, left in the wild, live longer, barring accidents, than their apparently more fortunate domesticated relations. In the case of the fox, for instance, cunning takes the place of teeth in old age, and elsewhere in the book are at least two marvellous stories of Charlie's brilliance as a hunter. One observed fox at a lakeside pulled out tufts of rush and floated them out towards feeding ducks until suspicion was allayed, and then swam out himself, only his mask above water, camouflaged by another tuft, to catch his bird.

I was particularly glad to read the excellent summary of the poisonous effects of the yew, because as a writer about the long-bow and the timber from which it has always been best made, the

9

whole history of the various yews is a fascination. The berries are harmless to pigs, and deadly to cattle. Sheep, turkeys, deer all seem to survive without harm, after eating the green of yews, either off the living tree, or rotting on the ground, while it has been known for horses to die merely from being tied to a faggot-pile of yew and gnawing at the bark. Jan Morris writes of Wales' 'hallucinatory grandeur' as the lights change and the mists wreathe, and disappear, reminding us how Belloc once wrote that nothing 'so moves me with the awe and majesty of great things as does this mass of the northern Welsh mountains' seen from 'their silent sea.'

There is Giraldus Cambrensis writing about both Wales and Ireland in the middle ages, saying of the latter, 'There is here scarcely any mean between constant health and final death,' in spite of the almost incessant rain. It was Giraldus' description of the Welsh longbowmen and their weapon which has so frequently been misinterpreted as meaning that he found the earliest such bows among the Welsh hills, and thus it has come to be thought that the Welsh invented the longbow. Great as was their prowess with the weapon, it was not their creation.

There is a 1976 piece, 'Without the Elms,' which makes one wonder, as new diseases appear among other species than the almost annihilated *Ulmus campestris*, that unless care is taken, unless more hardwoods are planted, we may look forward to a land of steadily diminishing woods and hangers, coppices and spinneys. Nathaniel Hawthorne writes about the Lake District in the mid-19th century, when it must have been much as it was when I first knew it, and found it melancholy, brooding and wet, as a child in the late 20s and early 30s. He notes that the would-be purchaser of a five-acre plot is referred to a solicitor in Town, and reflects 'the lake country is but a London suburb' – and he had never seen a charabanc, nor a traffic jam in Kendal, nor the coloured lines of fell-walkers across the green and grey and dun landscape. There is Massingham on Cornwall with a memorable description of the mist clearing from 'the armoured hide and warted snout of the Gurnard's Head.'

A lot of what is here may be preaching to the converted, but let those who know little of the country saunter through this remarkable book, like courting couples in May before the arrival of the Cinema, and they will learn much and have much pleasure. I was about to recount my own tale of lambing in the Yorkshire Dales in four feet of snow, but it is high time you began reading. Who knows, you might be the worst kind of developer and you just might change your mind.

PART I

COUNTRY
REFLECTIONS

1

THE HILLSIDE HEDGE
(1879)

Richard Jefferies

A low thick hawthorn hedge runs along some distance below the earthwork just at the foot of the steepest part of the hill. It divides the greensward of the down from the ploughed land of the plain, which stretches two or three miles wide, across to another range opposite. A few stunted ash trees grow at intervals among the bushes, which are the favourite resort of finches and birds that feed upon the seeds and insects they find in the cultivated fields. Most of these cornfields being separated only by a shallow trench and a bank bare of underwood, the birds naturally flock to the few hedges they can find. So that, although but low and small in comparison with the copse-like hedges of the vale, the hawthorn here is often alive with birds: chaffinches and sparrows perhaps in the greatest numbers, also yellowhammers.

The colour of the yellowhammer appears brighter in spring and early summer: the bird is aglow with a beautiful and brilliant yet soft yellow, pleasantly shaded with brown. He perches on the upper boughs of the hawthorn or on a rail, coming up from the corn as if to look around him – for he feeds chiefly on the ground – and uttering two or three short notes. His plumage gives a life and tint to the hedge, contrasting so brightly with the vegetation and with other birds. His song is but a few bars repeated, yet it has a pleasing and soothing effect in the drowsy warmth of summer. Yellowhammers haunt the cornfields principally, though they are not absent from the meadows.

To this hedge the hill-magpie comes: some magpies seem to keep almost entirely to the downs, while others range the vale, though there is no apparent difference between them. His peculiar uneven and, so to say, flickering flight marks him at a distance as he jauntily journeys along beside the slope. He visits every fir copse and beech clump on his way, spending some time, too, in and about the hawthorn hedge, which is a favourite spot. Sometimes in the spring, while the corn is yet short and green, if you glance carefully through an opening in the bushes or round the side of the gateway, you may see him busy on the ground. His restless excitable nature betrays itself in every motion: he walks now to the right a couple of yards, now to the left in a quick zigzag, so working across the field towards you; then with a long rush he makes a lengthy traverse at the top of his speed, turns and darts away again at right angles, and presently up goes his tail and he throws his head down with a jerk of the whole body as if he would thrust his beak deep into the earth. This habit of searching the field apparently for some favourite grub is evidence in his favour that he is not so entirely guilty as he has been represented of innocent blood: no bird could be approached in that way. All is

done in a jerky, nervous manner. As he turns sideways the white feathers show with a flash above the green corn; another movement and he look all black.

It is more difficult to get near the larger birds upon the downs than in the meadows, because of the absence of cover; the hedge here is so low, and the gateway open and bare, without the overhanging oak of the meadows, whose sweeping boughs snatch and retain wisps of the hay from the top of a waggon-load as it passes under. The gate itself is dilapidated – perhaps only a rail, or a couple of 'flakes' fastened together with tar-cord: there are no cattle here to require strong fences.

In the young beans yonder the wood-pigeons are busy – too busy for the farmer; they have a habit, as they rise and hover about their feeding-places, of suddenly shooting up into the air, and as suddenly sinking again to the level of their course, describing a line roughly resembling the outline of a tent if drawn on paper, a cone whose sides droop inward somewhat. They do this too, over the ash woods where they breed, or the fir trees; it is not done when they are travelling straight ahead on a journey.

The odour of the bean-flower lingering on the air in the early summer is delicious; in autumn when cut the stalk and pods are nearly black, so that the shocks on the side of the hills show at a great distance. The sward, where the slope of the down becomes almost level beside the hedge, is short and sweet and thickly strewn with tiny flowers, to which and to the clover the bees come, settling, as it were, on the ground, so that as you walk you nearly step on them, and they rise from under the foot with a shrill, angry buzz.

On the other side the plough has left a narrow strip of green running along the hedge: the horses, requiring some space in which to turn at the end of each furrow, could not draw the share any nearer, and on this narrow strip the weeds and wild flowers flourish. The light-sulphur-coloured charlock is scattered everywhere – out among the corn, too, for no cleaning seems capable of eradicating this plant; the seeds will linger in the earth and retain their germinating power for a length of time, till the plough brings them near enough to the surface, when they are sure to shoot up unless the pigeons find them. Here also may be found the wild garlic, which sometimes gets among the wheat and lends an onion-like flavour to the bread. It grows, too, on the edge of the low chalky banks overhanging the narrow waggon track, whose ruts are deep in the rubble – worn so in winter.

Such places, close to cultivated land yet undisturbed, are the best in which to look for wild flowers; and on the narrow strip beside the hedge and on the crumbling rubble bank of the rough track may be found a greater variety than by searching the broad acres beyond. In the season the large white bell-like flowers of the convolvulus will climb over the hawthorn, and the lesser striped kind will creep along the ground. The pink pimpernel hides on the very verge of the corn, which presently will be strewn with the beautiful 'bluebottle' flower, than whose exquisite hue there is nothing more lovely in our fields. The great scarlet poppy with the black centre, and 'eggs and butter' – curious name for a flower – will, of course, be there: the latter often flourishes on a high elevation, on the very ridges, provided only the plough has been near.

At irregular intervals along the slope there are deep hollows – shallow near the summit, deepening and widening as they sink, till by the hedge at the foot they broaden out into a little valley in themselves. These great green grooves furrow the sides of the downs everywhere, and for that reason it is best to walk either on the ridge or in the plain at the bottom: if you follow the slope halfway up you are continually descending and ascending the steep sides of these gullies, which adds much to the fatigue. At the mouths of the hollows, close to the hedge, the great flint stones and lumps of chalky rubble rolling down from above one by one in the passage of the years have accumulated: so that the turf there is almost hidden as by a stony cascade.

2

GALWAY BOGS
(1945)

Robert Gibbings

For contrast to the wilderness of stones and stone walls of southern Connemara one has only to travel inland a few miles from Galway to find a waste of moorland, with never a fence for mile on mile, and never a stone save the age-worn outcrops of silver granite. The bogs are every shade of brown and gold, the hills are every tint of purple, the only signs of green are a stray holly bush or the twigs of a stunted fir. Black bullocks munch the heather. Wild geese rise from the bog, their steel-grey backs the colour of the wind-swept lakes.

On all sides breathtaking glimpses of hill and pool. A robin sings to running water. Listen. Listen again. Tune your being to the song of streams. Close beside a fir tree three sheep are grazing. Stand by the tree and think yourself into it. Touch it with the tips of your fingers. Lay the palms of your hands on its rough bark and feel the tremor of its fibres. Stretch up your spirit towards its topmost branches following each changing urge of growth. Sense its growth, for growth is immortality. We all are but cells, forming and re-forming in the elemental tissue, momentary manifestations, glimpses in the microscope of God. What does the chlorophyll cell in the blade of grass know of biology? Just as much, perhaps, as we do of eternity.

The robin is now in the brushwood. The wind has dropped. There isn't a breath to stir the rushes, the cloud shadows stand as they fell on the hills. The road curves like the hollow of a thigh, the mountains rise like the swelling of a breast, the pools are clear as kittens' eyes. . . .

Dotted about the bogs are stacks of brown turf. Here and there the dark walls of peat faces rise from pools of black oily water. In the peat face may be seen the stems and branches of trees long buried. *Vir* or bogwood, they call it.'The best kindling in the world.' Almost straight from the bog it will light. A twig when dried will burn as a candle. 'It's the oil that's in it from the turf.'

Turf is cut with a slane, a narrow spade with an ear at right angles to the blade so that two sides of the sod are cut at the same time from the stepped face of the bog. Each newly cut sod is like a large brick, dark and oily. A good slanesman will cut close on three thousand of them in one day, that is to say, about four tons of turf. But this turf is 'raw.' It must be spread to dry as hay is spread, cocked as hay is cocked, and stacked into clamps as hay is built into ricks. Finally it must be thatched with straw even as hayricks are thatched against the weather. A ton of raw turf yields but three hundredweight of fuel. Each year the cutting begins when the winds of March have dried the bogs. If that crop can be saved in time, a second harvest is cut in July.

Bogs hold more than turf and bogwood. It is a commonplace that bronze implements of all kinds have been found in them. Scarcely a museum that has not a specimen of one kind or another, preserved by the bacteria-free soil, of wooden bowls and platters, goblets, spades, spoons, canoes, and paddles; not to mention items of ancient dress such as cloaks and tunics of wool, capes of skin, or shoes of leather. One of the largest dugout canoes ever found in western Europe, fifty-two feet in length, was taken from a bog in County Galway.

But one of the most surprising, though by no means un-common, finds is bog butter. This is not, as one might suspect by the name, some strange fungus akin to the yellow jelly-like growth found on trees, and known as witch's butter, but the genuine churn-made product of the milk of cows, sometimes still edible. Knowing the preservative power of bogs its owners had buried it, to await such time as they were going to market, four, five, or six months ahead. Meanwhile, death or accident intervened, and so the wooden firkin, or the skin or cloth container, with its contents, lay undisturbed, fifty, a hundred, maybe two hundred, years.

3

THE YEW TREE
(1789)

Gilbert White

In the churchyard of this village is a yew tree, whose aspect bespeaks it to be of a great age: it seems to have seen several centuries, and is probably coeval with the church, and therefore may be deemed an antiquity. The body is squat, short, and thick, and measures twenty-three feet in the girth, supporting an head of suitable extent to its bulk. This is a male tree, which in the spring sheds clouds of dust, and fills the atmosphere around with its farina. As far as we have been able to observe, the males of this species become much larger than the females; and it has so fallen out that most of the yew trees in the churchyards of this neigh-bourhood are males. But this must have been matter of mere accident, since men, when they first planted yews, little dreamed that there were sexes in trees.

In the yard, in the midst of the street, till very lately grew a middle-sized female tree of the same species, which commonly bore great crops of berries. By the high winds usually prevailing about the autumnal equinox, these berries, then ripe, were blown down into the road, where the hogs ate them. And it was very remarkable that, though barrow-hogs and young sows found no inconvenience from this food, yet milch-sows often died after such a repast – a circumstance that can be accounted for only by supposing that the latter, being much exhausted and hungry, devoured a larger quantity. While mention is making of the bad effects of yew berries, it may be proper to remind the unwary that the twigs and leaves of yew, though eaten in a very small quantity, are certain death to horses and cows, and that in a few minutes. An horse tied to a yew hedge, or to a faggot-stack of dead yew, shall be found dead before the owner can be aware that any danger is at hand; and the writer has been several times a sorrowful witness to losses of this kind among his friends, and in the island of Ely had once the mortification to see nine young steers or bullocks of his own all lying dead in an heap from browsing a little on an hedge of yew in an old garden, into which they had broken in snowy weather. Even the clippings of a yew hedge have destroyed a whole dairy of cows when thrown inadvertently into a yard. And yet sheep and turkies and, as park-keepers say, deer, will crop these trees with impunity.

Some intelligent persons assert that the branches of yew, while green, are not noxious; and that they will kill only when dead and withered, by lacerating the stomach. But to this assertion we cannot by any means assent because, among the number of cattle that we have known fall victims to this deadly food, not one has been found, when it was opened, but had a lump of green yew in its paunch. True it is, that yew trees stand for twenty years or more in a field, and no bad consequences ensue. But at some time or other cattle, either from wantonness when full, or from hunger when empty (from both which circumstances we have seen them perish) will be meddling, to their certain destruction. The yew seems to be a very improper tree for a pasture field.

Antiquaries seem much at a loss to determine at what period this tree first obtained a place in churchyards. A statute passed AD 1307 and 35 Edward I the title of which is 'Ne rector arbores in cemeterio prosternat.' Now if it is recollected that we seldom see any other very large or ancient tree in a churchyard but yews, this statute must have principally related to this species of tree; and consequently their being planted in churchyards is of much more ancient date than the year 1307. As to the use of these trees, possibly the more respectable parishioners were buried under their shade before the improper custom was introduced of burying within the body of the church, where the living are to assemble. Deborah, Rebekah's nurse, was buried under an oak; the most honourable place of interment probably next to the cave of Machpelah, which seems to have been appropriated to the remains of the patriarchal family alone. The farther use of yew trees might be as a screen to churches, by their thick foliage, from the violence of winds; perhaps also for the purpose of archery, the best long bows being made of that material: and we do not hear that they are planted in the churchyards of other parts of Europe, where long bows were not so much in use. They might also be placed as a shelter to the congregation assembling before the church doors were opened, and as an emblem of mortality by their funereal appearance. In the south of England every church-yard almost has its tree, and some two; but in the north, we understand, few are to be found.

4

HOW LONG DO ANIMALS LIVE?
(1891)

Charles St John

It is not easy to determine the length of years bestowed on any of the wild animals. There are no specific and well-ascertained data on which to form a valid opinion. On all such subjects the most positive assertions are often so ill supported by facts that the naturalist should be most careful and guarded as to the evidence on which he founds his opinion. It seems, however, reasonable to suppose that the age attained by all animals bears a certain proportion to the time which they take in coming to their maturity in size and strength.

Judging by this criterion, the eagle may be set down as one of the longest lived of our British birds, as he certainly does not arrive at the full maturity of his plumage for some years. On the other hand, the swan puts on her white feathers at her first moulting, yet is said to live to a very great age; and there are well-authenticated instances that this is the fact. Geese, too, live to a most patriarchal age. The period of life of tame falcons does not exceed eight to ten years – at least so I am assured by some of my acquaintances who have kept these birds. A wild hawk, barring accidents from shot or trap, has, probably, a better chance of longevity than a domesticated bird, however carefully the latter may be tended, as it is almost impossible to hit upon the exact quantity, quality, and variety of food which best conduces to their health, or to give tame birds as large a share of exercise and bodily exertion as in their wild state they would be constrained to take in pursuit of their daily prey. Common fowls live to the age of ten or twelve years, but become useless and rheumatic after six or eight. Such, also, is the case with pigeons. I knew of a pair who lived for fifteen years, but they were barren for some years before their death. The length of life of small birds is probably less: but it is difficult to form an accurate opinion on this point, inasmuch as any deductions founded on canaries or goldfinches in a state of confinement must be fallacious, as all caged birds are subject to numerous diseases, from over-eating, from improper and too little varied food, and a thousand other causes, which do not affect those who live in a state of natural and healthful liberty.

It is a curious fact that one scarcely ever finds the dead body of a wild bird or animal whose death appears to have been caused by old age or any other natural cause. Nor can this result from the fact of their being consumed immediately by animals of prey, as we constantly meet with the bodies of birds who have been killed by wounds from shot, etc. Either (as donkeys and postboys are said to do) the wild animals on the approach of death creep into hidden corners of the earth, or nearly all of them, before they reach extreme old age, are cut off by their common enemy, mankind, or serve as food to birds and beasts of prey. I have, however, killed both eagles and foxes who bore unmistakeable marks of extreme old age; the plumage of the former being light coloured, thin, and worn; so worn, indeed, as to lead one to suppose that the bird could not have moulted for several seasons, and the faces of the latter being grey and their jaws nearly tooth-less: yet they were still in good, and even fat condition. In animals, age and cunning supply the place of strength and activity; so that the eagle and fox are still able to live well, even when they have arrived at the most advanced age assigned to them.

Very old deer become light-coloured and greyish, especially about the head and neck, and have a bleached and worn-looking appearance over their whole body. Their horns, also, lose much of their rich appearance both as to colour and size, becoming not only smaller but also decreasing in the number of their points. The Highlanders assign a great age to the red deer; indeed they seem to suppose that it has no limit, save a rifle ball; and they tell wonderful stories of famous stags who have been seen and known for a long series of years in certain districts. Though these accounts are doubtless much exaggerated, it is tolerably certain that their life extends to from twenty to thirty years. I do not imagine that in these days stags have much chance of reaching that term. At the age of seven or eight years, the animal having arrived at full perfection as to size and beauty of antler, they are marked down for destruction by the numerous sportsmen who wage war against them in every part of the north

of the island. Their numbers in certain preserved districts have, no doubt, increased to a great extent; but very few of the fine, rugged, and far-stretching antlers, which adorn the halls of many of the old houses in the Highlands, are now to be met with on living deer. Where not brought down by the licensed sportsman, a fine-headed stag has now so high a premium offered on his life in the price given for horns, that he is sure to fall by the gun of some poacher or shepherd. I have known as large a sum as five guineas given for a stag's head; and when this is the case, nothing else can be expected but that every stag whose horns are peculiarly fine will be killed. I have occasionally shot roe-bucks, and still oftener does, showing by their size, colour, length of hoofs etc, that they had reached a tolerable old age. But, like all persecuted animals, the chance of their attaining their full extent of days is so slight as scarcely to give us the means of ascertaining how long they would live if secure from danger.

Sheep after seven or eight years lose their teeth, more or less, and show symptoms of their best days being past. But these, like all other domesticated animals, do not afford a good criterion to judge by, as they are all under an artificial system as to food and manner of living, which makes them, like man, subject to many diseases and causes of decay, which would not affect them if they were in a state of nature.

5

NORFOLK IN SUMMER
(1897)

Clement W. Scott

There are worse moments in the life of a man 'who works and feels he works' than the awakening after ten good hours of re-freshing and unbroken sleep, and the first bright peep of a summer landscape from the open window of a farmhouse by the sea. In this silent corner of East Anglia I appear to be at the very end of the world. It is as lonely as Tintagel, as breezy as Boscastle. Two miles away, over the fern-covered down, away by the ruined ivy-covered church at Overstrand and past the bright white light-house that stands amidst acres of soft velvety turf and yellow sea daisies, the shrimp man and the lobster-catcher are arousing Cromer from its slumbers. The old church clock in the fine old flint tower, common to the county of Norfolk, is doubtless chiming eight, accompanied as an after thought by a few bars from Spohr's 'As pants the hart'; they are taking down the shutters at the popular chemist's where everything is to be obtained, from patent pills to boot-blacking, and from calomel to curry powder. At Cromer they are getting out the early bathing machines; the coastguardmen on the cliff are surveying miles and miles of purple and waveless sea with an everlasting telescope; the crowded lodging houses and hotels are relieving themselves of the restless and the early risers; the market women are bringing in their little store of French beans, plums and greengages. At Cromer already there is a stirring spirit and a suspicion of noise, a clattering of little spades and pails, and a scampering of sea babies to the yellow sands and the beneficent beach.

In the farmhouse garden where I rest there is not a stir and not a sound. The front flower garden, separated from the road and its blackberry hedges by a row of white palings and a brighter white gate, seems revelling in the first touches of the August sunshine. Bees are busy with the lavender, and are coquetting with the brilliant French marigolds and deep purple carnations. The roses are almost over now, save on one low corner bush that will yield a yellow crop of Maréchal Niel from this moment until Christmas Day. A bed of mauve-coloured clarksia – the pride of our village – a rival bed decorated with stocks, verbenas, sedums and the early-flowering asters are visited by bees and butterflies alike; the birds are calling one another from hedge to hedge, and so peaceful and beautiful is the scene that the darting house martens who have built in the eaves of the old farmhouse, although collecting for their departure to sunnier climes, seem disinclined to leave this warm corner of the England that they love. But look beyond the garden enclosure to the fields that slope towards the distant hills. On a small green platform crowning a field of waving barley stands the windmill seen for miles around, the most picturesque feature in this sunny landscape, and to our delight is seen whirling round in its old-fashioned way, careless of the counter advantages of machinery and steam. The good old miller has had no cause to regret the opening weeks of a fickle August. It has blown steadily, fitfully and in gusts. Sometimes dark rain clouds have drifted from sea to hill, scattering spray or rain dust rather than rain. Sometimes a deep indigo thunder cloud has sailed from the west, emptying itself on the parched fields, rejoicing the hearts of the turnips and mangolds, but making little impression ten minutes afterwards on the dry and hungry soil. But whenever there has been sun – and we have not had too much of it this summer – there has been a bright, brisk breeze, bending down the apple trees in the garden, bowing down the corn in the fields, and sending the light fleecy clouds scudding along over the windmill top and away into the heart of the country. The young farmer next door is already out with his gun, stealing quietly by the hedge-side up to the ferny plantation to see if he can catch a rabbit on the feed and help to stock the larder at home. Next month's Michaelmas geese are gobbling in the only field not under cultivation, keeping a respectful distance from a family of young turkeys growing up for next Christmas dinner

THE COUNTRYSIDE COMPANION

and paying no attention to the silent cattle or to the old mare with its young foal, who claim the privilege of eating their breakfast between the same hedges.

So much for the front of the house this quiet summer morning. Let us look out at the back. See, we are only a couple of hundred yards from the cliff's edge, fringed with cornfields and decorated with scarlet poppies and mauve-coloured scabious. It will want another good ten days' sun to ripen the wheat, that now shows a lovely tone between dead green and a deep brownish yellow. From the upper windows I can see a vast expanse of purple ocean covered with herring boats starting on their annual journey to the North Sea, well manned with sailors from the little village yonder, whose wives will not see them again until Christmas time most likely, but every Saturday will punctually trudge to the agents at Cromer to draw their weekly house-money. Soon after Lammas Day they are all off, and cannot wait to give a hand at the on-coming harvest, even if they were wanted, for, to tell the truth, the farmer who is a practical man never calls upon the services of a sailor in the harvest field, unless he is uncommonly hard pressed. For Jack at home is a lazy, indolent fellow. I pass him every evening lolling under the thick-set hedge, I notice him in the morning stretched out among the poppies at the cliff's edge, watching the horizon, eternally looking out to sea, smoking in-numerable pipes, and doing simply nothing in a magnificent manner. He is civil enough is the Norfolk sailor. He has always some pleasant salutation on his lips, he never fails to bid you good morning or good night though you pass him a dozen times a day, but when Jack is ashore he doesn't mean to work. The father of some sixty summers may bend his back in the fields from sunrise to sunset; the old mother may go out cleaning to the nearest farmer's; the wife may go down cliff and bring up pails of sea water for the young lady visitors at the farm; but the muscular young sailor only intends to be ornamental, not useful, when he is at home. His occupation is to stroll up to the lookout by the ruined tower and to watch the sea. How often when he is toiling on the deep must he have watched the land, and on a fine night seen the lights in the cottage windows where the lonely women are praying for the men at sea.

It would be pleasant enough to waste hour after hour in the farmhouse garden to enjoy that first morning pipe under the old mill with some favourite book – we never get newspapers here until they are a day or so old – to trudge among the cornfields with the favourite little terrier at one's heels, who is death to field mice and a terror to moles; but there is the sea that can be reached by crossing only one cornfield, and there is no bathing round the coast of England to be compared to the stretch of deserted virgin sand untraversed by any human foot between the busy watering places of Cromer and Mundesley. But the sea below and the springs above, the beating of the waves, and the land water that pours down in torrents when it rains, are creating havoc with the Norfolk cliffs. Composed mainly of soft blue clay, they yield at the pressure of every storm and are lessened by every tempest. Year follows year and acre after acre slips into the sea. The pathway we trod last year lies sheer down below a ruin of grass and wild flowers. The steps cut down the cliff for the children yesterday is today an impenetrable morass of crumbling clay. So serious has been the cliff fall eastward and westward from Cromer that the frightened villagers of our little hamlet have moved their tiny church a quarter of a mile landward and have left their old tower and their buried dead enclosed in a churchyard doomed for destruction, but making in its loneliness and melancholy one of the most pathetic and picturesque corners of this land. For here there is always poetry and always peace. The seabirds whirl about the old church tower, the reapers reap, the sun falls, and nature is as silent as the grave. From here at night, when the sun has set over Cromer, the bright gleam of the white lighthouse, with its brilliant lamps, contrasts with the primrose tint of the distant sky, and makes nature a poem. Here, sitting on the old church wall later on, we see the bats flitter from the isolated tower, and the

white owls swooping over the sailors' graves, and hear the last song of the reapers as they carry the last load home.

The sun still shines by fits and starts, the breezes are boisterous, but though oats are cut down in some of the fields, the barley and wheat will want a good deal of scorching yet before they are ready for the sickle and the reaping machine. The harvest, which lasts a good month in most of the farms, is anxiously expected everywhere. No one can settle down until harvest is over. Directly the word is given for the men to go into the field a wave of excitement passes over the country. The children, much to their delight, are dismissed from school for a good five or six weeks, and the grave schoolmaster, at the head of the lads, chases the rabbits as they are turned out of the falling wheat and barley. Laughter and song are heard all over the land, louder than the wind that bends the ripening crops or the sea that moans at the foot of the crumbling cliffs. Then is the time for 'largesse.' It is the etiquette of harvest time in the Norfolk lands to demand 'largesse' from every passing stranger. 'Please da us largesse,' say the urchins, boys, and girls, whilst the foreman of the gang of labourers will leave the sickle or the horse and ask the stranger alms for the toilers on the field. Later on, when the harvest is over, the oldest labourer of the village calls round at the various farms and houses and demands a more substantial form of 'largesse,' that is expended on a harvest supper at the village inn. There is a good time coming no doubt, but men and lads alike will have to wait a little longer. Meanwhile the country round about is in its full glory of summer loveliness. The crops are changing from deep green to golden yellow, and the scarlet poppies are not yet faded or dead among the corn. The root crops, lately so parched, are refreshed by the recent rains, and the ferns on the hills, where the rabbits hide, stand out rich and green against a skyline of Eton blue. No moon has yet shone out at night over the churchyard by the sea, or made the farmhouse garden decorated with the pale evening primrose and its stars of midnight bloom as bright as day. But after sunset comes that strange white light of summer time, and the evening breezes bring a scent of ripening corn to the late lingerer over the white farmhouse gate.

6

LANDSCAPES OF WALES
(1984)

Jan Morris

To look at, the nature of Wales is deceptive. Within its small expanse the style of terrain changes so often, the mountainous countryside is so constantly corrugated, this way and that, by ridges, valleys, lakes and passes, the sea appears so often, and so unexpectedly, at the ends of vistas or around the flanks of hills – the scene in short is so cunningly variegated that it sometimes seems not natural at all, but like some elegantly conceived park-land or domain. It is not all of equal beauty, of course, and large parts of Wales have been mutated by tourism and industrial-ization, but in natural terms it is a wonderfully well-proportioned country. Nothing is too big, nothing lasts too long, and there is perpetual variety. It is only some one hundred and thirty miles from the northern coast of Wales to the southern, only forty miles from east to west at the narrowest point – a day's drive one way, a couple of hours the other. Yet within this narrow compass there are places that feel rather like India, and places not at all unlike Australia, and places that remind one of Wyoming or northern Spain, and many places that are, with their especial piquant blend of age, damp, intricacy and surprise, altogether and unmistakably Welsh. Let us survey, for an opening look at organic Wales, three or four textbook specimens from this cheek-by-jowl variety of the rural landscape.

The most famous first: the view of Yr Wyddfa, Snowdon, the highest mountain in Wales, from the waters of Porthmadog Bay, looking over the artificial embankment which there crosses the estuary of the Glaslyn river. This grand prospect is like an ideal landscape, its central feature exquisitely framed, its balance exact, its horizontals and perpendiculars in splendid counterpoint. Cloud generally drifts obligingly around the crags of the mountain, and lies vaporously in its grey gulleys; in the green-and-blue foreground swans swim, cormorants dive, cattle really do stand up to their hocks in the shallows of the estuary, as in old watercolours, and the hussocked grass of the saltings is overlooked by gentle green woods on either side.

It is the classic illumination of Wales, being not much like anywhere else on earth. The bare Welsh mountains have few peers, and the illusory scale of them is peculiarly indigenous. That noble peak before us, one of the most celebrated of mountain forms, is only three thousand five hundred feet high, and you could easily fit the whole landscape, its rocky eminences, its winding river, its woods and its salt-flats, into one of the lesser Alpine glaciers. It is a dream-view. It is as though everything is refracted by the pale, moist quality of the air, so that we see the mountain through a lens, heightened or dramatized. 'There is no corner of Europe that I know,' wrote Hilaire Belloc, wondering at it from the deck of his yacht, 'which so moves me with the awe and majesty of great things as does this mass of the northern Welsh mountains seen from this corner of their silent sea.'

Next to the south, to Pont ar Fynach, Devil's Bridge to the English, a favourite among lovers of the picturesque since Victorian times, and still to be approached, if you arrange things properly, by the antique steam train which puffs in summer up the sinuous valley of the Ystwyth from the coast. We are still within seventy five miles of Yr Wyddfa, but we might be in a different continent – might indeed easily be visiting a lesser-known summer station of the British Raj, high in the Punjab hills perhaps, or among the tea gardens of Sri Lanka, so lush and tumbled is the environment about us now, and so neo-tropical the ambience.

It is true that the Hafod Arms Hotel, with its flamboyantly overhanging eaves, consciously contributes to this effect, and that the refreshment pavilions and picnic sites dotted here and there, though jammed with cars and coaches in the tourist season, would be perfectly compatible with mem-sahibs. The exotic suggestion, though, comes from the site itself, the precipitously wooded slopes of the valley that falls away below, the rich, thick, humid-looking foliage, the smell of pine and damp moss, the brownish hill-ridges protruding above the woods, and far away beyond the rustic fencing and woodland walks, the distant white froth of waterfalls slashing through the forest, so excitingly violent, so apparently remote, that upon their rocks one can almost make out the slender poised figures of aboriginals with fishing-spears.

Only another twenty or thirty miles, and we are in the hinterland they used to call The Great Welsh Desert. There can be a terrific solitude to the bleak and featureless slabs of highland which form the inner massif of this country. Up you climb, from coast or valley, up through the foothill pasture-land, fenced with barbed wire and speckled with sheep, crossing cattle-grids now and then (resonant rattle of wheels, disconcerting vibration of steering wheel) until you reach the crest of the ridge; and there, stopping your car on the stubby beast-nibbled grass at the side of the road, you see before you the gaunt heart of Wales sweeping away ridge after ridge from Gwynedd down to Glamorgan.

It looks immense, and there are dark rectangles of conifer forest here and there, and vast cloud-shadows swing slowly across the counties. No towns show, no villages even, only a few white farmhouses tucked away with their outbuildings in the flanks of hills, and the only sound is the steady drone of a tractor somewhere out of sight. It feels uninhabited, more or less, and it looks roadless, and the mountains to the north, snow-capped very likely if it is winter, look like the inaccessible peaks of some other country altogether: yet nothing is far away really, every valley down there is snugly farmed, and almost nowhere in that whole wide wilderness would you be out of reach of a cup of tea.

Hallucinatory grandeur, romantic exoticism, Outback emptiness – and finally, away to the south we may find lowland landscapes of a Loire-like gentleness: where the Tywi river loiters among its dairy farms towards the sea, say, or the meadows shelter in the lee of the Epynt moors. These are hardly dramatic prospects, but rather wistful – landscapes for impressionist painters, and summer evening reveries, and picnics, and country race meetings, and market days.

There are castles about, in such a pastoral Welsh setting – probably not spectacular castles, but modest ones, crumbling on bluffs above rivers, protruding apologetically above car parks. There are thickets of beech or sessile oak, and neat fir plantations, and hedges meticulously layered. Gentlemanly streams sprawl through the countryside between shingly flats or wooded banks, small grey towns stand beside bridges, and the meadows all around are grazed by plump and genial Herefords. It is milk and salmon country, serene, constant: the heroines, monsters and fairy animals of Welsh lore frequent those river reaches, and are portrayed on jugs in road-side workshops by ecologically-minded potters.

7

STONE HOUSES OF THE COTSWOLDS
(1909)

Stewart Dick

In the woodlands and plains of the southern counties, the typical forms are the half-timbered house, and the still more humble mud-walled cottage. In these districts stone is only used, even when plentiful, for churches, noblemen's seats, and such other important buildings. The fact is, that the expense of working stone outweighed other considerations, even where its first cost was not great. The mason was not so common a figure in those days as he is now, and he might have to be fetched from a distance, while for the ordinary post and panel house, the village carpenter was architect and builder both, and was always on the spot. In the northern and barer parts of the country, the moors of Yorkshire and the mountains of Wales, the country was too poor to maintain other dwellings than the rugged castles of the nobles and the rude hovels of the peasantry; but in the Cotswold district we had quite another set of conditions.

Here we have a rolling upland district spreading over several counties where a great belt of limestone strikes across the country, forming a plateau of from eight hundred to twelve hundred feet high. Almost treeless, except in the valleys, yet this was a rich country, and not a poor one. For those Cotswold slopes, bare and uncultivated, were the richest pasturelands in England, and the wool-growing industry, which we have seen exercised so evil an effect on the prosperity of the agricultural districts, here had its headquarters. The fleeces of the Cotswold sheep were famous for their weight and fine quality, and were eagerly sought after, both at home and abroad.

When the price of wool rose, landowners in other parts hastened to put their lands under pasture, but the wool they produced could never equal that of the Cotswold hills which, with their short crisp turf, formed an ideal grazing ground. It was the overproduction of these inferior grades of wool that ultimately lowered the prices, but even when it ceased to be profitable elsewhere, the wool of the Cotswold district always found a ready market. . . .

The wool merchants of Campden, Burford, and the other little Cotswold towns were among the wealthy men of England, and when they came to build their houses, with a fine instinct they used the material that lay ready to their hand, the limestone hidden under the turf of the softly moulded hills. But not only did the prosperous merchants fill the little towns with beautiful buildings, so that the High Street of Campden has hardly its equal in England, but in the country districts the farmhouses and humble cottages were built of the same materials, and in the same style. This style was absolutely different from that of the half-timbered structures a few miles away in the Warwickshire valleys, for the hard limestone demanded quite a different treatment, but is full of the same sensitive feeling for proportion, the same simplicity and directness, and the same air of homely comfort.

It is a beautiful country, and though the railways cross it in several places, yet the bulk of it lies off the beaten track, and is little frequented by the tourist. There is something big and inspiring about the wide sweeps of unbroken pastureland, the shoulder of the hill right up against the white clouds and the blue sky beyond. The woodlands have their charm, their sense of mystery, but these windy uplands seem to have something of the boundless freedom of the sea. It is a place to go to breathe, to get one's lungs expanded.

It would be difficult to find a stone more suitable for building purposes than the Cotswold limestone. It lies only a few feet below the surface, and is soft and easily worked when newly quarried, but becomes hard by exposure – an excellent weathering stone. In colour yellowish at first, it bleaches after a time and then takes on all sorts of soft, rich hues, every variety of beautiful grey, especially when lighted up by sunshine. Such a material had more than a local reputation. Not only is the stately town of Bath built of this stone, but near Burford is the quarry which supplied the stone for St Paul's Cathedral. A strange contrast that the stone from the one quarry should blacken in London smoke in one of the greatest buildings in the land, while that from another but a short distance away has formed little cottages that nestle in the neighbouring valley. Christopher Kempster was the master-mason who superintended the work at St Paul's, and the quarries are still called by his name, Kit's Quarries. Every village once had its local quarry, but most of these are now disused, for when a new house is built now, no one thinks of using the home materials. It is cheaper to use imported bricks.

The chief difference that strikes one between the Cotswold houses and the half-timbered cottages of the plains, is that the former seem much more formal and precise. They are built in a more unyielding material. The oak timbers in the frames of the latter have a certain elasticity. They twist and bend like the timbers of a ship. In thatched roofs also there is a softness and fullness of outline, very far removed from the clean-cut, decided lines of the slate roofs of the limestone houses. There is not the happy-go-lucky, go-as-you please sort of feeling about the stone houses. They seemed to have stayed as they were built, while the others have changed and altered with the times.

Thrown out a wing here, added a lean-to there, until the original plan is half effaced. But in the eighteenth century the prosperity of the district died down, and since then there has been little cause to add to the stone houses, which to begin with were planned on a generous scale. Perhaps there is just a tinge of bleakness about them. Though much more elegant, they do not look so cosy as the half-timbered cottages. They have a colder air, as if they belonged to a severer and more northern clime, and remind one a good deal of the best class of old stone buildings in the lowlands of Scotland.

The plan is usually a parallelogram as in other old cottages. The house is just one room in depth, of a breadth of from sixteen to eighteen feet, and this the roof crosses in one span. If more accommodation is wanted, wings are added, the plan being L-shaped, E-shaped, or H-shaped, but in all cases the single span roof is retained. Where the cottage is small the roof has usually no lateral support, but just rests on the walls, which are often pushed outwards by the strain. But this system of building one room deep only, had its disadvantages. It left none of the little nooks and crannies which are so convenient. There were no store cupboards, no larders, nothing but the four bare walls. Often there were no corridors or passages, and one room opened into another. Frequently you had a series of bedrooms built in this way, all opening one out of the other. In a large farmhouse of the old style the master and mistress had their room in the centre at the top of the staircase. All the other bedrooms were only accessible through it. To the right was a door opening to rooms occupied by the sons of the house; through these were the quarters of the male servants. To the left was another door leading to the apartments of the daughters and the maid-servants. When the family retired, therefore, the head of the house had the whole household under lock and key. Nowadays, however, we find generally that a separate staircase has been added to the servants' quarters. The bedrooms in these houses had often another disadvantage. In the seventeenth century, when many of them were built, it was thought for some reason to be unhealthy to have the sun shining into a bedroom, and so they were built to face the north and east, and are apt to be chilly and cold.

In fact, despite their exquisite proportions and fine air of elegance, one can find many faults in these old houses. Their admirable simplicity was obtained by ignoring many things which to modern ideas are absolutely necessary. In the words of an enthusiastic admirer, 'the breadth of wall space was unbroken by the vertical lines of down pipes, which cut all modern buildings into strips, and such things as ventilation pipes and sanitary monstrosities were unknown.' In other words, there was practically no provision for sanitation, and all water had to be carried from the well in buckets. Also the houses are often built on a slope, and the lower rooms are so damp that most of them are now disused. The stone floors, indeed, were laid direct on the ground, damp courses were unknown, so no wonder that the houses were not dry. Many of them, too, had no foundations whatever, and in some cases the turf was not even removed, the walls being begun simply on the ground. Eaves, gutters, or downspouts are unknown, for lead is only used for glazing; the rain runs off the roofs on to the ground and soaks in at the base of the walls, which thus gets decayed and worn. The site was frequently very ill-chosen, often lying low and close to streams, while no attention was paid to aspect. It is just as well to remember these things, for we are apt to laud the old buildings as everything that is good, while we condemn the modern as everything that is bad, whereas it is just as indisputable that we have improved in matters of comfort and sanitation as that we have sadly deteriorated in matters of artistic excellence.

The walls, as a rule, are from eighteen inches to two feet thick. Sometimes the stone is used just as it comes from the quarry, sometimes it is roughly dressed. In any case the window openings are finished with dressed stone, as is also the doorway. At times the walls are very badly built, being a mere shell filled with rubble; on other occasions the building is excellent. Often the surrounding walls and even the outbuildings are built without any mortar, like the Scotch dry-stone dykes, but so well is this done that it is impossible to dislodge the smallest stone. Sometimes the chimneys are at the gable ends, and often the kitchen chimney is a separate stack built on outside the house. In that case we have a very large fireplace, often six feet or more in width, and from four to five feet high, crossed by a stone arch or a great oak beam. Wood was the usual fuel, and pots and kettles were not placed on the fire, but hung from an iron trivet hinged to the wall. Often an ingle-nook was formed on each side of the fire, a seat being hollowed out of the thickness of the wall just large enough for one person, and arched above his head. On each side a few inches up were hollows for the elbows or for a glass as the case might be. In village inns these corners, in spite of the pungent smoke from the fire, are reserved for prime favourites, or old customers. Sometimes the ingle-nook is lit by a little window. The flue is tall and tapering, and goes straight up, being open to the sky. As a rule, it smokes badly. The partitions between the rooms are generally not of stone but of oak frames filled in with lath and plaster, or with oak-panelling. The staircases are usually circular and of stone, built with a central newel like the stair in a church-tower.

The roofs are covered with stone slates not unlike the Horsham slabs, but much smaller in size. The roof is quite high in pitch, unlike the Surrey and Sussex roofs, where the heavy Horsham slabs necessitate a flatter roof. The slates are laid with great care, the thickest being placed at the eaves and the thinnest at the top, and are fastened down with oaken pegs. They are obtained from the local quarries, and are not split by hand but in a very curious manner. During the season (May till October) they are quarried and laid out on the ground in thick slabs. There they are allowed to remain all winter. They absorb a certain amount of moisture which works in between the layers of the stone. Then come the winter frosts, and the water freezes and expands. The result is that in the spring a few taps with the hammer suffices to divide the thick slab into a series of thin flakes. If, however, the winter is mild, the stones do not split, and there is nothing for it but to allow them to lie for another year. It is a leisurely way of working that sounds very attractive. These grey slates covered with lichen are very beautiful, and are almost imperishable. Roofs three hundred years old are as good as new. If the wood foundation is decayed, or the pegs have given way, the slates can be taken off and rehung. Like the old tiles, the old slates are much better than the modern ones. The mechanical precision with which the latter are turned out, all as smooth and thin as possible, and the edges exactly true, makes them have a hard and cold effect. There is no variety in a roof of such slates, but the old varied in size and thickness. Also the old oak-laths on which the original slates were hung were often not quite straight, and the result was a beautiful wavy line. The old slates too were more durable. Being rough, they did not lie absolutely close (perhaps, however, they leaked on this account), and thus the wet dried out of them easily, for there was free ventilation. The new fit so closely, that there is no circulation of air, and when moisture thus collects, there is more chance of the frost getting in and doing damage.

A very quaint and interesting feature in those cottages is the series of little name-plates on the walls, little chiselled tablets of stone giving the name or initials of the owner, and usually the date. It is the owner's name evidently, not the builder's, for in some cases there are several such inscriptions on the same cottage. Simple though these name-tablets are, they are executed with skill and freedom, and form a pleasant ornament.

8

WITHOUT THE ELMS
(1976)

Wilson Stephens

Creak and crash. Another elm tree staggers, leans, and hits the
turf. Its branches splinter under a vista of sky where no sky was.
Rooks wheel and caw. What fell was their ancestral home. Our
own homes, though not fallen, look different now. From the
surrounding downs the once plumed village lies bare, its lines
unsoftened by the crowns through which the chain-saws have
gnawed for weeks. Our elms have become memories.

While hopes remained that perhaps the disease was less real
than had been reported, or that it might somehow be cured or
contained, we had thought what has happened to be impossible.
Who could imagine England without elms? Now we need imagine
no longer. We can see. We do not enjoy the new scene. Stark
white houses are set in a hard composition of man-made lines and
angles. This year there will be no top shade from summer
greenery, nor the gold of autumn. The branches which held the
leaves are going up in smoke. Raw stumps are their memorials.

So we have decided to replace what we have lost. We shall plant
other trees, one for every man, woman and child in the village, all
249 of them. Everybody, from the oldest inhabitant to the baby
born just two hours before the list closed, on the last strokes of last
year's last midnight, will lend their names to our new trees. We
have planned where they shall grow. Each head of a household
was asked to help pay for them. There were no backsliders. Such
is the effect of trees. No other cause would have produced so
much ready cash, nor so little argument. All have had a chance to
name a preferred species. Mine is a beech, my wife opts for
maple, and our daughters, copper beech and cherry. So the
village will begin to see its post-elm age skyline, and a pattern of
colours it has never known before.

As years go by, and horizons shorten as Close of Play approaches, I shall look forward to the short walk to my beech tree, to
check its progress. By then, with luck, it will be well away. Perhaps
the first initials and entwined hearts will have been carved upon
its bark, as is the fate of beech trees. So much for prospects.

It will have cost us more than £600 to put in a tree per villager.
Foresters would plant for less, because planting more closely and

with seedlings. But not all that much more cheaply, and our effort opened my eyes to the funds needed to keep a woodland productive. Because trees are with us for longer than a human lifetime we take them for granted.

Some people create great fuss at their felling. But few, especially in government seemingly, consider how trees come to be present at all, or how and at whose expense they are cared for across centuries. But unless a tree is to be felled at a time when it is in good health it cannot become part of the useful product of the countryside. To leave it to the downward cycle of old age until, for safety reasons, it has to be thrown as our elms have been, wastes its whole existence. So it is difficult to find common cause with the amiable but distraught ladies who protest at nearly every felling.

Even so, apocalypse was in the air when I walked an oak wood after its timber had been tushed out, the cordwood carted, and the brash burned. Ruts the size of trenches criss-crossed acres of lifeless soil, stamped with black circles of ashes. It was the omega and the alpha of timber, the land's slowest crop. For the first time since the Napoleonic Wars, direct sunshine fell on the forest floor. It brings recovery, and at first the tempo will be fast.

Rosebay (fireweed on Severnside) will glow next autumn. Primroses will bloom next spring. The summer to follow will see bramble back, and pheasants to sunbathe in the low cover. If the owner can afford to put them in, a new generation of young trees should then be there. And if the owner cannot afford it, the result will be what the rest of us cannot afford, either, idle acres. Now, when the elms have gone because of a beetle, is the time to consider which trees will go next because of neglect. Go they will, for one reason or another. Even trees are not immortal. Unless authority makes their replacement justifiable in terms of cost, which is a measure of reality not cupidity, our village a century hence may have its first ever claim to fame – trees, the rarity of the future.

9

ON THE ROAD TO GLEN COE
(1803)

Dorothy Wordsworth

Saturday, September 3rd, 1803 – When we have arrived at an unknown place by moonlight, it is never a moment of indifference when I quit it again with the morning light, especially if the objects have appeared beautiful, or in any other way impressive or interesting. I have kept back, unwilling to go to the window, that I might not lose the picture taken to my pillow at night. So it was at Ballachulish and instantly I felt that the passing away of my own fancies was a loss. The place had appeared exceedingly wild by moonlight; I had mistaken cornfields for naked rocks, and the lake had appeared narrower and the hills more steep and lofty than they really were.

We rose at six o'clock, and took a basin of milk before we set forward on our journey to Glen Coe. It was a delightful morning, the road excellent, and we were in good spirits, happy that we had no more ferries to cross, and pleased with the thought that we were going among the grand mountains which we saw before us at the head of the loch [Leven]. We travelled close to the water's edge and were rolling along a smooth road when the horse suddenly backed, frightened by the upright shafts of a roller rising from behind the wall of a field adjoining the road. William pulled, whipped, and struggled in vain; we both leapt upon the ground, and the horse dragged the car after him, he going backwards down the bank of the loch, and it was turned over, half in the water, the horse lying on his back, struggling in the harness, a frightful sight! I gave up everything, thought that the horse would be lamed and the car broken to pieces. Luckily a man came up in the same moment and assisted William in extricating the horse, and, after an hour's delay, with the help of strings and pocket-handkerchiefs, we mended the harness and set forward again, William leading the poor animal all the way, for the regular beating of the waves frightened him, and any little gushing stream that crossed the road would have sent him off. The village where the blacksmith lived was before us – a few huts under the mountains and, as it seemed, at the head of the loch; but it runs further up to the left, being narrowed by a hill above the village, near which, at the edge of the water, was a slate quarry, and many large boats with masts on the water below, high mountains shutting in the prospect, which stood in single, distinguishable shapes, yet clustered together – simple and bold in their forms, and their surfaces of all characters and all colours – some that looked as if scarified by fire, others green; and there was one that might have been blasted by an eternal frost, its summit and sides for a considerable way down being as white as hoar-frost at eight o'clock on a winter's morning. No clouds were on the hills; the sun shone bright, but the wind blew fresh and cold.

When we reached the blacksmith's shop, I left William to help to take care of the horse and went into the house. The mistress, with a child in her arms and two or three running about, received me very kindly, making many apologies for the dirty house, which she partly attributed to its being Saturday; but I could plainly see that it was dirt of all days. I sat in the midst of it with great delight, for the woman's benevolent, happy countenance almost converted her slovenly and lazy way of leaving all things to take care of themselves into a comfort and a blessing.

It was not a Highland hut, but a slated house built by the master of the quarry for the accommodation of his blacksmith – the shell of an English cottage, as if left unfinished by the workmen, without plaster, and with floor of mud. Two beds, with not over-clean bedclothes, were in the room. Luckily for me there was a good fire and a boiling kettle. The woman was very sorry she had no butter; none was to be had in the village: she gave me oaten and barley bread. We talked over the fire; I answered her hundred questions, and in my turn put some to her. She asked me, as usual, if I was married, how many brothers I had, etc etc. I told her that William was married and had a fine boy; to which she replied 'And the man's a decent man too.' Her next-door neighbour came in with a baby on her arm, to request that I would accept of some fish, which I broiled in the ashes. She joined in our conversation, but with more shyness than her neighbour, being a very young woman. She happened to say that she was a stranger in that place, and had been bred and born a long way off. On my asking her where, she replied, 'At Leadhills'; and when I told her that I had been there, a joy lighted up her countenance which I shall never forget, and when she heard that it was only a fortnight before, her eyes filled with tears. I was exceedingly affected with the simplicity of her manners; her tongue was now let loose, and she would have talked for ever of Leadhills, of her mother, of the quietness of the people in general, and the goodness of Mrs Otto who, she told me, was a 'varra discreet woman.' She was sure we should be 'well put up' at Mrs Otto's, and praised her house and furniture; indeed, it seemed she thought all earthly comforts were gathered together under the bleak heights that surround the villages of Wanlockhead and Leadhills. And afterwards, when I said it was a wild country thereabouts, she even seemed surprised, and said it was not half so wild as where she lived now. One circumstance which she mentioned of Mrs Otto I must record, both in proof of her 'discretion' and the sobriety of the people at Leadhills, namely, that no liquor was ever drunk in her house after a certain hour of the night – I have forgotten what hour; but it was an early one, I am sure not later than ten.

The blacksmith, who had come in to his breakfast, was impatient to finish our job, that he might go out into the hayfield for, it being a fine day, every plot of hayground was scattered over with hay-makers. On my saying that I guessed much of their hay must be spoiled, he told me no, for that they had high winds, which dried it quickly – the people understood the climate, 'were clever at the work, and got it in with a blink.' He hastily swallowed his breakfast, dry bread and a basin of weak tea without sugar, and held his baby on his knee till he had done.

10

THE APPEARANCE OF IRELAND
(1185)

Giraldus Cambrensis

The land is fruitful and rich in its fertile soil and plentiful harvests. Crops abound in the fields, flocks on the mountains, and wild animals in the woods. The island is, however, richer in pastures than in crops, and in grass than in grain. The crops give great promise in the blade, even more in the straw, but less in the ear. For here the grains of wheat are shrivelled and small, and can scarcely be separated from the chaff by any winnowing fan. The plains are well clothed with grass, and the haggards are bursting with straw. Only the granaries are without their wealth. What is born and comes forth in the spring and is nourished in the summer and advanced, can scarcely be reaped in the harvest because of unceasing rain. For this country more than any other suffers from storms of wind and rain. A north-west wind, along with the west wind to its south, prevails here, and is more frequent and violent than any other. It bends in the opposite direction almost all the trees in the west that are placed in an elevated position, or uproots them.

The island is rich in pastures and meadows, honey and milk, and wine, but not vineyards. Bede, however, among his other praises of the island, says that it is not altogether without vineyards. On the other hand, Solinus says that it has no bees. But if I may be pardoned by both, it would have been more true if each of them had said the opposite: it has no vineyards, and it is not altogether without bees. For the island has not, and never had, vines and their cultivators. Imported wines, however, conveyed in the ordinary commercial way, are so abundant that you would scarcely notice that the vine was neither cultivated nor gave its fruit there. Poitou out of its own superabundance sends plenty of wine, and Ireland is pleased to send in return the hides of animals and the skins of flocks and wild beasts. Ireland, as other countries, has bees that produce honey; but the swarms would be much more plentiful if they were not frightened off by the yew trees that are poisonous and bitter, and with which the island woods are flourishing. It is possible, of course, that in Bede's time there were, perhaps, some vineyards in the island; and some people say that it was Saint Dominic of Ossory who brought bees into Ireland – and that was long after the time of Solinus.

This is the most temperate of all countries. Cancer does not here drive you to take shade from its burning heat; nor does the cold of Capricorn send you rushing to the fire. You will seldom see snow here, and then it lasts only for a short time. But cold weather does come with all the winds here, not only from the west-north-west and north but also equally from the east, the Favonius and the Zephyr. Nevertheless, they are all moderate winds and none of them is too strong. The grass is green in the fields in winter, just the same as in summer. Consequently the meadows are not cut for fodder, nor do they ever build stalls for their beasts. The country enjoys the freshness and mildness of spring almost all the year round.

The air is so healthy that there is no disease-bearing cloud, or pestilential vapour, or corrupting breeze. The island has little use for doctors. You will not find many sick men, except those that are actually at the point of death. There is here scarcely any mean between constant health and final death. Anyone born here, who has never left its healthy soil and air, if he be of the native people, never suffers from any of the three kinds of fevers. They suffer only from the ague and even that only very seldom. This indeed was the true course of nature; but as the world began to grow old and, as it were, began to slip into the decrepitude of old age, and to come to the end, the nature of almost all things became corrupted and changed for the worse. There is, however, such a plentiful supply of rain, such an ever-present overhanging of clouds and fog, that you will scarcely see even in the summer three consecutive days of really fine weather. Nevertheless, there is no disturbance of the air or inclemency of the weather such as inconveniences those that are in health and spirits, or distresses those that suffer from nervous disorders.

11

WILDLIFE ON RAASAY
(1773)

Samuel Johnson

Raasay has wild fowl in abundance, but neither deer, hares, nor rabbits. Why it has them not, might be asked, but that of such questions there is no end. Why does any nation want what it might have? Why are not spices transplanted to America? Why does tea continue to be brought from China? Life improves but by slow degrees, and much in every place is yet to do. Attempts have been made to raise roebucks in Raasay, but without effect. The young one is extremely difficult to rear, and the old can very seldom be taken alive. Hares and rabbits might be more easily obtained. That they have few or none of either in Skye, they impute to the ravage of the foxes, and have therefore set, for some years past, a price upon their heads, which, as the number was diminished, has been gradually raised from three shillings and sixpence to a guinea, a sum so great in this part of the world that, in a short time, Skye may be as free from foxes, as England from wolves. The fund for these rewards is a tax of sixpence in the pound, imposed by farmers on themselves, and said to be paid with great willingness.

The beasts of prey in the Islands are foxes, otters and weasels. The foxes are bigger than those of England; but the otters exceed ours in a far greater proportion. I saw one at Armidel, of a size much beyond that which I supposed them ever to attain; and Mr Maclean, the heir of Col, a man of middle stature, informed me that he once shot an otter, of which the tail reached the ground when he held up the head to a level with his own. I expected the otter to have a foot particularly formed for the art of swimming; but upon examination I did not find it differing much from that of a spaniel. As he preys in the sea, he does little visible mischief and is killed only for his fur. White otters are sometimes seen.

In Raasay they might have hares and rabbits, for they have no foxes. Some depradations, such as were never made before, have caused a suspicion that a fox has been lately landed in the island by spite or wantonness. This imaginary stranger has never yet been seen, and therefore, perhaps, the mischief was done by some other animal. It is not likely a creature so ungentle, whose head could have been sold in Skye for a guinea, should be kept alive

only to gratify the malice of sending him to prey upon a neighbour; and the passage from Skye is wider than a fox would
venture to swim, unless he were chased by dogs into the sea, and
perhaps then his strength would enable him to cross. How beasts
of prey came into any islands is not easy to guess. In cold countries they take advantage of hard winters, and travel over the ice:
but this is a very scanty solution; for they are found where they
have no discoverable means of coming.

12

FRUITS OF THE EARTH
(1917)

Mary Webb

On a bright, rook-haunted September morning, in the wide upland pastures where kestrels scream and the sheep cry across the
dew, it is good to be astir very early. Then the rabbits and
the young foxes are playing in the shadow at the wood's edge,
magpies in the tall trees are calling to one another in their
harsh voices, and the woodpecker's laughing note re-echoes.
Every grass-blade and hedge, and the long, purple-jewelled
blackberry vines are hung with white cobwebs sewn with
diamonds, like elfin awnings. Even in October, when the last bee
is gone and the fruits are sodden and frosted, the blackberry is
lovely with leaves that burn from yellow to crimson. Not many
scents are so rich, so racy of the soil, as the scent of blackberries
and wimberries.
  Of all wild fruits the wimberry, or cloud-berry, should rank
first. Its colour is the bloomy purple of distant hills. It tastes of
Faery. It will grow only in beautiful and mysterious places. High
on the airy hill, far from any sound of village or hamlet, voice or
bell – except the voice of the shepherd and the sheep-bell's silver
tinkle – is the chosen haunt of the wimberry. Countless acres are
covered with the neat, shining bushes, tall beside the streams,
lowly on the summits. In spring, the leaf green is splashed with
a beautiful red, like the colour of a ladybird; then come pink
flowers, honeyed and waxen, and above their sweet acres the
large, almost black bumble-bees of the hills coast to and fro with
their deep murmur, like far-off seas in a dream. At the end of

June, when young curlews run among the bushes, like yellow chickens pencilled with brown, the fruit begins to ripen, but it is not often ready for picking until after Saint Swithun's. From that date until late September a tide of life, gypsy and cottager and dweller in the plain, flows up into our hills. To the Stiperstones, to the Longmynd, to the wild, lonely stretches of Clun Forest, come the stooping, neutral-tinted figures – the lads with their little home-made trucks, the wise babies whose wimberry-picking is not yet, and whose task is simply to be good. Alone beside the family kettle amid the day's provisions he sits, the baby, smiling, gazing trustfully at the blue, arching sky, so deeply saturated with wimberry juice that one doubts if many Saturday tubs will clean him. He achieves the end and aim of his day: he is good. On every side of him stretch the purple plateaux, dotted with busy figures. Here and there, at a lost signpost or a mountain ash, is the trysting-place of the wimberry higgler. Twice a week he appears with his cart and his rough pony, and over the green, deeply rutted tracks, down valleys brimful of shadow and along precipitous roads, the wimberries go on their journey to the cities of England.

Cranberries grow on some of our hills, but sparsely, in crevices of the black rock and on bare summits. The polished leaves, the waxen-white blossoms, the large coral-tinted berries, glow on their sombre background like richly coloured statues of saints and Madonnas set up in sorrowful places. Under grieved autumn

skies, amid bitter juniper and withered heather and riven rock, they achieve the beauty which is at once delicate and hardy, and they bless the gaunt solitudes where only the anxious sheep lift amber eyes as the cranberry picker passes, and only the hovering kestrel and the peregrine falcon, dark upon the driving sky, look down.

In the plain, when the winter strips the hedges and the honeysuckle has not yet sent out her bright pairs of leaves, the fruited blackthorn reigns. She is a creature of dark weather. From her first adventure into a cold March world, with her gift of sweet, golden-anthered blossom, to her wintry ripening, she has no kinship with the luxurious daughters of summer. Not for her the slow-falling, scarlet fruit of August: but when the cherry and the apple have laid aside their beauty, she sets her black twigs with bloomy, purple fruit, austerely gorgeous. The berries give the impression of melting the frost by their rich warmth, and there is no fruit-gathering that brings more zest than the gathering of the sloe in the whistling hedges with a robin for company.

The fruit of the spindle-tree has a strangeness and an ancientry in its down-hanging, petalled cup of deep rose and orange. A tall, slender spindle set with shining pink lamps makes an exquisite, almost an exotic picture on a white-frost morning. No one plants the spindle now, but it must have been one of the October beauties of the countryside when in every home the busy hum of the spinning-wheels filled the fire-lit evening. It is to be found today in old woods and in hedges that have, with the lapse of time, ceased to be hedges and become groves of trees. Soon, perhaps, it will be gone, like the sweet faces, the little hands, that once watched and tended the whispering wheels.

Once a year the elder attains perfect beauty. She paints her leaves with pale rose, primrose and gold, crimson and violet, and sets forth her fruits like elfin grapes. Then every elder is full of little wings, and shrill with small, thankful bird-notes. If there come a rainy day, the elder hangs beneath every purple berry a silver berry. Then woods grow vague in the thickened atmosphere, the courses of the streams are marked in mist, and on the first morning of sharp frost the painted curtains of the elder fall upon the grass.

It was in clear October weather, in a green valley beneath a steep, dark mountain, that I found the long avenue of fruited rowans growing on either side of a half-obliterated road where once marched the Romans. The trunks were gnarled and riven, but the trees stood against the hill, beneath the egg-shell sky, in the vital colours of youth. And all about them, like angels in a picture, hovered creatures winged with bright black and pale silver, creatures too eerily fair to be only blackbirds and thrushes. They seemed like spirits bound to the trees by a charm; and indeed the whole valley was bewitched, far gone in spells.

And so we come to the yew – the yew, that sets beneath her brooding branches a fruit vivid and unearthly, startling the eye inured to darkness with sudden living red as if she lit, for comfort in the night, above the cold sleepers in her keeping, a galaxy of burning hearts.

13

THE VILLAGE GREEN
(1914)

Ernest C. Pulbrook

Many are the scenes which may be regarded as characteristic of rural England, but most typical of all is the village green, that epitome of the countryside and its requirements. Grouped round the greens of many villages are nearly all the features common to a country community, and some, more favoured, possess in addition simple emblems of good government and modest enjoyment. On one side, half hidden by surrounding trees, stands the church; close by is the entrance gateway of the manor house; here is the vicarage; there the home farm; the tinkle of iron upon iron draws attention to the forge; and in one corner, beside the road leading to the outer world, a swinging sign board indicates the inn standing back out of sight. Dotted round in picturesque irregularity are the cottages of the villagers, the gardens gay with flowers, while on the green itself may be found the well, the pond, and perhaps a pound.

Go almost where we will we shall find a village green, although in parts of the country they are comparatively rare, while some, alas! have been enclosed and cultivated or even built over. Maybe the green is a tiny triangular strip of well-kept turf in the centre of a village at cross-roads, its size determined by the highways on

either side, which have sadly curtailed its original area. On the other hand there may be an extensive piece of undulating common; to this, however, the name green is perhaps hardly applicable, for the village belongs to the common rather than the other way about. Such may be met with in country where sand and gravel come to the surface and the soil is too poor for cultivation; they are to be found in Essex and Buckingham among other counties. As a rule the green is in the centre of the village, but occasionally it will be seen on one side of the church or behind the houses, this being often the case where the houses fringe both sides of a road.

What the common was to the villager's material wants the green was to his leisure moments, and since the enclosures he has turned the smaller green to the same purposes as the common so far as present circumstances and latter-day requirements permit. In days gone by the cottager was more or less self-supporting; he cut his own fuel from the wood or the waste and he turned his cow and geese out on the common, but now, owing to altered circumstances, he buys nearly all he requires. However, the village green still enables us to understand something of olden cottage economy. Here a flock of geese promenades with noisy shriekings, offering opposition to timid children and presenting a hostile front to the strange passer-by, whom they seem to pick out by instinct, as they invariably retreat before the native; a donkey or a goat is tethered to a peg; and round the pond a number of ducks divide the day between slumber and sudden bursts of activity.

But above all the green provided a recreation-ground for the villagers. Here the fair was held and here the bonfire was lit on Guy Fawkes' night. Life in the past was not the dull uneventful existence that some might suppose. Long holidays were not the rule as now, but numerous rural festivals provided fun and amusement for all. Most of these had some connection with the Church, for times of fasting were preceded and followed by days of merrymaking. Some of these festivals were connected with rural occupations, and perhaps the most important was the day sacred to the saint to whom the village church was dedicated, the village revel, as it was often called and as it is to this day in some places. Although the day began with a religious service it ended with mirth and merrymaking. Many were the sports held on the village green; there were foot races and wrestling, the catching of a greased pig, and quarter-staff bouts. Archery might have its place, and the women would race for an embroidered smock or shift. When dusk had fallen the fiddlers would strike up and gaily would the lads and lasses dance the country measures.

On the village green the quintain was erected, and merry were the shouts when the tilter failed to hit the board in the middle and was hurled from his saddle by the swinging arm or enveloped in a shower of soot or flour. This has now passed into the category of obsolete sports, and the only quintain left in England still stands, though desolate and forlorn, upon the green at Offham in Kent. Before Puritan days every village possessed its maypole upon the green, but the opponents of rejoicing and dancing frowned upon the May Day revels, and since their time the maypole has almost completely disappeared. A few remain as reminders of 'Merrie England'; that really charming English village of the past, Fontmell Magna in Dorset, has one, as has Shillingstone, not far away, while Barwick-in-Elmet, in Yorkshire, is proud of one, and others also survive at Ickwell in Bedfordshire and Warcop in Westmorland. Here and there the rejoicings at the coming of May have been revived, but the dancing is confined to children, for we have grown more self-conscious than of yore. Clifton in Nottinghamshire is one of the places where dancing round the maypole and the crowning of the May Queen upon the green have been revived.

The village green was not only the scene of merrymaking but the place of punishment. Here the stocks were usually placed, and the delinquent in his undignified position was made the butt of the boys who mocked him regardless of the retaliation that would follow when he was free. Here, too, was the village pound in which stray animals were penned until their owners paid for their release. Pounds may still be seen, but they are falling into decay from want of use, or they have been utilized for other purposes. On occasion obstreperous roysterers have found a lodging in the pound, but not a few villages possess a proper 'lock-up,' such as that at Shenley in Hertfordshire, in the shape of a round house by the pond. On the green at Harrold, Bedfordshire, is a curious little 'round house,' in company with another but open circular building, probably of the eighteenth century.

The cross also stood upon the green; now, if it remains at all, there is but a stump, although it is far more frequent than the stocks, which, if preserved, are often merely mouldering relics in the church porch. However, there are exceptions to every rule, and at Gretton in Northamptonshire the stocks and whipping-post are still in place upon the green, while Lymm in Cheshire rejoices in the possession of both stocks and cross.

Another feature of village greens past and present is the pump, that once important institution which is now regarded as the symbol of local pettiness, for any gathering that is contemptible is referred to as a 'meeting about the parish pump.' Yet though the pump and the village meeting may be set at naught by the towns-man, they can be of vital concern to the immediate countryside. In days of drought the water gives out and there is tribulation in the village; if this is imminent the cottagers hoard the precious drops jealously lest any be wasted. In places the pump is enclosed in a picturesque little pent house, of which there is a somewhat modern example at Ickenham, Middlesex, one of the many vil-lages destined to be absorbed in the maw of London. Some wells are memorials to a popular resident, or have been presented by a benefactor of the village, such as that at Stoke Row, Oxfordshire, a reminder of the generosity of the Maharajah of Benares. Maybe the place of the pump is taken by an old-fashioned bucket and windlass well, frequently covered by a simple roof; to prevent accidents railings enclose it, and so the users must first unlock the gate. Pumps and wells are seemly and in keeping with a green, but what can be said of those villages which have so far forgotten fitness and tradition as to install a glorified standpipe? Convenient it may be, but its place is not upon the green, but rather up an alley between cottages.

The pond must not be forgotten, for it is either in the middle of the green or at its edge beside the road, so that horses passing through can stop to drink. It may form the realm of a swan who stalks about with dignity, now visiting the cottages for food, now asserting his authority by driving off a goose which has broken some law of the green. The ducks, as being of little importance, are left in peace to follow their inclinations, although on occasion one of them does presume on his position and is brought to book. In dry summers the pond often saves the situation for some hill-farmer; at intervals through the day his carts bring down barrels to replenish the drinking-troughs of his animals.

In rare instances the green testifies to past importance; on it stands some relic of the days when the place was the centre of its district. For instance, at Elstow in Bedfordshire, Bunyan's village, is a fine timbered building known as the Moot Hall, which dates from the fifteenth century. Modern erections usually compare unfavourably with the work of the villagers of the past – pillars and obelisks to commemorate the Jubilee of Queen Victoria, modern coronations, or memorials to those who fell in the South African War.

Greens vary according to the localities in which they are found. Here and there they are cut up by roads into a number of squares, triangles, or odd-shaped patterns; one of them half surrounds the pond, on another is a tree, its girth encircled by a seat; one long piece juts into the wood or the fields; on another is the well; the cottages are usually grouped in picturesque array round the out-skirts, but one or two stand alone beside one of the strips. Such a one is Finchingfield, one of many charming village greens that Essex has to show. In some counties greens pass insensibly into commons, crossed by many paths and dotted here and there with clumps of gorse and bushes, their margins shaded by wide-spreading trees; ponds there may be one or two, and in the centre a well-rolled cricket pitch roped off during the summer. Such may be found in Hampshire and Buckingham and Surrey, where there are also smaller greens, bits of commons like that at Cobham, or little strips of turf as smooth and well-kept as lawns. In the centre of Chalfont St Giles, a typical English village, is a small green, the playground of children, but, alas! its surround-ings are changing.

Sussex and Kent must not be forgotten, for both counties possess village characteristics of rural England in every way. On the border of the two counties are Groombridge and Frant with greens that will stand comparison with any. In the weald of Sussex are greens which often broaden into commons, as at Henley Hill, and on the Downs are hamlets with greens so small they hardly deserve the name. The name of almost any county recalls some pleasant green – Oxfordshire and Berkshire, Hertfordshire and Warwick, all have their claims. Gloucestershire and Worcester-shire share in the Cotswold greens; what a picture is Broadway, with its gabled stone houses set round the green! Cubberley and Frampton-on-Severn are other villages in these shires, the latter as charming as can be imagined; timbered cottages and stone, with little dormer windows and well-thatched roofs, cluster round the green, delightful both in itself and for the grouping of the village around.

Greens there are beside a river where it is pleasant to loiter on a summer's day, as all will say who have lingered beside the Ouse at Nun Monkton in Yorkshire, where the red roofs set off the colour of the turf. And Bosham green is beside the sea, not on the crumbling cliff like the lost green of Pakefield in East Anglia, but on the shores of Chichester Harbour. From the churchyard it slopes gently to the quay; along one side flows the tree-bordered mill-leat, and a gate in a corner gives a vista over meadow and water. In the West Country greens are few and far between, but this only adds to the charm of Selworthy. Grouped irregularly round are its cottages with eyebrowed windows and roofs of deep brown thatch; the tree-clad slopes of Selworthy Beacon shelter it from the rude sea blasts, and one looks across the valley to the heights of Exmoor.

But wherever situated and of whatever description, the village green remains at once the centre and the background of English village life; on it generation after generation have gathered in revelry or met in sober conclave to discuss affairs; and to it our forefathers came on their daily round of trivial errands and in the stress of great events.

14

THE COTTAGE GARDEN
(1909)

Stewart Dick

It is with a special pride that the cottager clings to his garden. In its small space it contains so much. Flowers in profusion everywhere. Roses tended with loving care, for the rose is the cottager's flower *par excellence*. Tall hollyhocks reaching almost to the thatched eaves, sweet-smelling wallflowers spreading their fragrance far out into the dusty road. Pansies – heart's-ease is the homelier name – and in their season, snowdrops, crocuses, primrose and violet. The more material part is not neglected, for away behind you will find a goodly store of vegetables. A row or two of peas and beans, turnips, carrots, lettuce, cabbage and cauliflower, and a patch of rhubarb, with its great spreading leaves, in the corner by the hedge.

You do not look for rarities in the cottager's garden, just the sweet, homely flowers, and the wholesome vegetables. Fruit trees, too, are there, fine old apple trees, pears, plums, and thick-set little bushes, with currants red and black and gooseberries galore. Sometimes there is a little bit of glass, a cucumber frame or two, where the valued pot plants are brought on till they can be displayed in the window.

The flower garden in front and the kitchen garden behind, that is the usual plan, and from the road the cottage seems embedded in a nosegay, while the presiding spirit, an old woman in a white cap, stands at the door. I remember years ago finding such a little cottage in Kent. Its soft red brick was half hidden with trailing wisteria, one mass of pale-purple blossoms. I stopped to sketch it, and the dear old lady came out and refreshed me with cowslip wine and little home-made cakes.

One of the characteristic features of these cottage gardens, especially the front part, is the style of their fences or other boundaries. The commonest, and perhaps the most beautiful, is the simple green hedge, but this is not always a sufficient protection, as it is apt to grow open at the foot. Sometimes wooden fences are used, and these are of various sorts. In Berkshire, and also in Wiltshire, you may still see wattled fences, in the Cotswolds dry-stone walls, and in Devonshire stone walls covered with white-wash, while in Cheshire stone slabs placed on end are sometimes used, as in the north of Scotland. The gate itself is often an ornamental feature. Fine wrought-iron examples of simple design are still to be met with in out-of-the-way places, but for the most part they are of wood. Sometimes a rose or other bush will be trained into an arch above the gate, and in Scotland two rowan trees are often so intertwined, for no witch or fairy can enter through the arch of rowan.

15

ALL THIS IS WALES
(1948)

Gwyn Jones

I have just come down from the hill fronting my home in mid-Cardiganshire. It is like half a hundred hills in this part of Wales, rounding out of a bramble-filled dingle on the southern side, a dingle blue-black with juiced fruit in autumn, with a sun-shot fringe of scrub oak and alder, and a noble ash tree rearing from

the bottom, its roots much exposed and straddling the course of a
fast-running brook. Beyond the dingle is gorse-striped rough
grazing for a couple of ponies, and in a cleft a hundred yards
away a pink-washed farm with squat outbuildings has been sited
to miss the prevailing south-wester. Then one skirts a ploughed
field much admired of herring gulls and crows, and a short ascent
brings one to the overswell of land and to sight of the sea.

In season the hillside is ablaze with gorse and alive with rabbits.
Blue and gold, the sea and land: gold and blue, the earth and sky.
To the north, over the first hump of ground, one sees the far side
of the Clarach valley, then a lovely patchwork hill, downpitched to
the sea in eighty-foot cliffs. Further away are the yellow bank
of the Dyfi and the dark hills of Meirionydd. Then these are
dwarfed by the huge whaleback of Cader Idris, and beyond
Cader, unseen, is the tide-washed estuary of the Mawddach. The
prospect ends with fitting splendour: the northern claw of
Cardigan Bay, the long peninsula of Lleyn, reaches out over

thirty miles to Bardsey, and from that western extremity the eye moves back from mountain to mountain, the two summits of Yr Eifl, round Moel Hebog, the spike of Cnicht, to the exquisite cone of Snowdon himself, and the confused masses that buttress his eastern and south-eastern approaches. Now turn the head. Confronting Leyn to the south, across seventy miles of heaped-up water, is the long rocky headland of Pembrokeshire, running to the claw-tip of St David's Head, with the magic mountains of Prescelly hanging inland like a haze. Turn again, for behind one the Plynlymon massif is displayed in a score of rosy lumps, divagated by green valleys, black woodlands, the silver ribbons of rivers, its fields brown, grey, pink, emerald, until the blunted tops of the five mountains are lost in purple distance half-way to the English border. All this is Wales, and this is half of Wales.

The view, necessarily and properly, is inconstant. Heat haze, cloud or rain turns the peninsulas to a smudge or to nothing at all. In sea mist one is content to see not the next county but the next hummock. Under a bruised sky the seaward horizon encroaches on the beaches, and Plynlymon, like the water, shows a dull-grained navy blue. Conversely, air washed by summer rain and then dried out by a warm breeze gives the coastline the brilliance of glass. Thus one has heard men on the cliffs near Pentrebont claim they can discern Bardsey like a thumb in the water. Maybe they can. Until they claim to see the lighthouse I am with them all the way. For one evening in late July of 1943, sober, solitary, and in my five senses, from the high point of ground this side of Clarach I beheld, fifteen minutes before the going down of the sun, the western mountain wall of north Wales swung forward and westward through thirty degrees of the compass. Every mountain was an island, the point of Lleyn was a finger's breadth from the sun. Between the mountains that were islands the sea poured pale smoky streams, and one saw the sea *behind* them, fluorescent as a fresh-caught mackerel. Each mountain top was gold, their lower slopes were mauve where they were drowned in sea. Never had the sun shown more evening splendour: it hung from long blackish bars of the oncoming dark, a polished copper cauldron. Inshore the water was a milky blue, then came a ten-mile band of salmon-rose, growing tawnier as it receded towards a charcoal horizon. Washes of yellow and red stained the sky behind the black cloud-bars. All along the coast folk must have been exclaiming at the glory of the sunset, but this other and ultimate glory, this dislocation in space, was pure magic and illusion. It lasted the brief third of an hour, but when I forget it wholly, the axe will be laid to the root of the tree.

16

ON HEARING THE FIRST CUCKOO
(1913)

The Times

From Mr Lydekker, FRS, Hertfordshire   *6 February 1913*

Sir,
   While gardening this afternoon I heard a faint note which led me to say to my under-gardener, who was working with me, 'Was that the cuckoo?' Almost immediately afterwards we both heard the full double note of a cuckoo repeated either two or three times – I am not quite sure which. The time was 3.40; and the bird, which was to the westward – that is to say, to windward – appeared to be about a quarter of a mile away. There is not the slightest doubt that the song was that of a cuckoo.
   The late Professor Newton, in the fourth edition of Yarrell's 'British Birds' (Vol II, p389, note), stated that although the arrival of the cuckoo has frequently been reported in March, or even earlier, such records must be treated with suspicion, if not with incredulity. And Mr J. E. Harting ('Handbook of British Birds,' p112) goes even further than this, stating that there is no authentic record of the arrival of the cuckoo in this country earlier than 6 April.

                                                R. Lydekker

12 February 1913

Sir,
   I regret to say that, in common with many other persons, I have been completely deceived in the matter of the supposed cuckoo of February 4. The note was uttered by a bricklayer's labourer at work on a house in the neighbourhood of the spot whence the note appeared to come. I interviewed the man, who tells me that he is able to draw cuckoos from considerable distances by the exactness of his imitation of their notes, which he produces without the aid of any instrument.

                                                R. Lydekker

17

THE HENS' DOMAIN
(1966)

Fred Archer

Around the farms in our village, in the rickyards, the cowsheds and granaries, the hens scratched around the cockerels and the long-spurred cocks strutted as if they had the right to enter every building, the right to sample any foodstuffs around. Yes, the barndoor hens had enjoyed this position for so many generations. They scratched the muck buries for worms, they obtained their grit from the village street, and on a bare patch in our rickyard where the grass has been killed by the scratching over the years of our hundred or so fowl, we fed them twice a day, broadcasting the mixture (half wheat and half kibbled maize) calling the stragglers from their hiding places – bid, bid, bid, bid and whistling, as near as I remember, fee-oo, fee-oo, fee-oo. In winter time Dad cooked potatoes and fed them hot mashed with Sussex grown oats and a little spice. This was their morning breakfast. Where did the fowl roost at night? Come with me on a winter's night with a lantern around the buildings. In our old stone barn with the blue lias threshing floor, the beams ran across the width of the roof and across those beams the fruit picking ladders were stored away for the winter. In fact, all the ladders were there except the strong thirty-rung one with the iron spiked feet which Tom Wheatcroft used to start a cut on the hay ricks. First of all the hens fled up into the tallet and from there it was a mere flutter for them to reach the ladders. The more agile Anconas – a breed which so easily becomes airborne – reached to the height of the barn while the stately Light Sussex cocks perched on the railings surrounding

the calf-pens. The sight on the hay loader which stood just inside
the barn with its rows and rows of lathes horizontal and joined
together with cords, looked as if it had been designed for one
purpose – a hen roost on wheels.

As we stood there on a winter's night, the calves licking our
hands and pulling our coats (they were just curious about the
lantern), it made one think of a portion of the terrace at Villa Park
just at the beginning of an International match. The hens looked
as if they had been placed, row by row, in such precision. They
craned their necks at the lantern and a few more droppings fell
between the rows of sleepers adding to the heap of the real stuff
which accumulated at the foot of the loader all the winter.

As we entered the empty stable, the odd rat bolted down his
hole from the wooden mangers where he had been cleaning up a
few odd bits of bait left by the horses when they were turned out
on to the fields soon after tea. The odd early broody hen ruffled
her feathers and squawked disapprovingly as we shone the light
on her as she was sitting tight on a few eggs. While we think of
eggs, egg collecting was an exciting business. No, the eggs didn't
roll down out of wire cages in an orderly fashion; these eggs had
to be won. Sometimes we lay on our sides and reached them from
an awkward spot under an old manger. This was fairly simple
providing a broody hadn't decided to be sitting there.

It was dark under these mangers and I have put my hand on a
hedgehog, but never mind, I was paid a penny a dozen for all

eggs which I found which were not laid in the usual places; for instance, the rows of pot hampers lined with hay in the dark corners under the tallet.

Some laid in the many clumps of stinging nettles in the spring time – no one had thought of using sodium chlorate to destroy the nettles in those days just after the First World War. But what a pleasant surprise when a hen hatched her brood of chicks in such places. Dad and I would move the brood after dark, away from the harm of rats, and there was always a possibility of a fox coming down off the hill and taking them. An old tea chest and a bit of wire and soon the mother hen was safe with her chicks and as we said 'she had stolen her nest' – what a picture!

18

PLEASANT WILTSHIRE
(1826)

William Cobbett

Wednesday, 30 August, 1826
My ride yesterday from Milton to this city of Salisbury was, without any exception, the most pleasant; it brought before me the greatest number of, to me, interesting objects, and it gave rise to more interesting reflections than I remember ever to have had brought before my eyes, or into my mind, in any one day of my life; and therefore this ride was, without any exception, the most pleasant that I ever had in my life, as far as my recollection serves me. I got a little wet in the middle of the day; but I got dry again and I arrived here in very good time, though I went over the Accursed Hill (Old Sarum) and went across to Laverstoke before I came to Salisbury.

Let us now, then, look back over this part of Wiltshire. . . . The farms are all large and, generally speaking, they were always large, I dare say; because sheep is one of the great things here; and sheep, in a country like this, must be kept in flocks to be of any profit. The sheep principally manure the land. This is to be done only by folding; and to fold, you must have a flock. Every farm has its portion of down, arable, and meadow; and in many places, the latter are watered meadows, which is a great resource where sheep are kept in flocks because these meadows furnish grass for the suckling ewes early in the spring; and indeed, because they have always food in them for sheep and cattle of all sorts. These meadows have had no part of the suffering from the drought this year. They fed the ewes and lambs in the spring, and they are now yielding a heavy crop of hay; for I saw men mowing in them in several places, particularly about Netheravon, though it was raining at the time.

The turnips look pretty well all the way down the valley; but I see very few, except swedish turnips. The early common turnips very nearly all failed, I believe. But the stubbles are beautifully bright; and the rickyards tell us that the crops are good, especially of wheat. This is not a country of peas and beans, nor of oats, except for home consumption. The crops are wheat, barley, wool and lambs, and these latter not to be sold to butchers, but to be sold, at the great fairs, to those who are going to keep them for some time, whether to breed from or finally to fat for the butcher. It is the pulse and the oats that appear to have failed most this year; and, therefore, this valley has not suffered. I do not perceive that they have many potatoes; but what they have of this base root seem to look well enough. It was one of the greatest villains upon earth, Sir Walter Raleigh, who (they say) first brought this root into England. He was hanged at last! What a pity, since he was to be hanged, the hanging did not take place before he became such a mischievous devil as he was in the latter two-thirds of his life!

The stackyards down this valley are beautiful to behold. They contain from five to fifteen banging wheat-ricks, besides barley-ricks and hay-ricks, and also besides the contents of the barns, many of which exceed a hundred, some two hundred, and I saw one at Pewsey and another at Fittleton, each of which exceeded two hundred and fifty feet in length. At a farm which, in the old maps, is called Chissenbury Priory, I think I counted twenty-seven ricks of one sort and another, and sixteen or eighteen of

them wheat-ricks. I could not conveniently get to the yard
without longer delay than I wished to make; but I could not be
much out in my counting. A very fine sight this was, and it could
not meet the eye without making one look round (and in vain) to
see the people who were to eat all this food; and without making
one reflect on the horrible, the unnatural, the base and infamous
state in which we must be, when projects are on foot and are
openly avowed, for transporting those who raise this food,
because they want to eat enough of it to keep them alive; and
when no project is on foot for transporting the idlers who live in
luxury upon this same food; when no project is on foot for
transporting pensioners, parsons, or dead-weight people!

A little while before I came to this farmyard I saw, in one piece,
about four hundred acres of wheat stubble, and I saw a sheep-
fold which, I thought, contained an acre of ground and had in it
about four thousand sheep and lambs. The fold was divided into
three separate flocks; but the piece of ground was one and the
same; and I thought it contained about an acre. At one farm,
between Pewsey and Upavon, I counted more than three
hundred hogs in one stubble. This is certainly the most delightful
farming in the world. No ditches, no water-furrows, no drains,
hardly any hedges, no dirt and mire, even in the wettest seasons
of the year: and though the downs are naked and cold, the valleys
are snugness itself. They are, as to the downs, what ah-ahs! are in
parks or lawns. When you are going over the downs you look *over*
the valleys, as in the case of the ah-ah; and if you be not
acquainted with the country, your surprise when you come to the
edge of the hill is very great. The shelter in these valleys, and
particularly where the downs are steep and lofty on the sides, is
very complete. Then the trees are everywhere lofty. They are
generally elms, with some ashes, which delight in the soil that they
find here. There are almost always two or three large clumps of
trees in every parish and a rookery or two (not rag-rookery) to
every parish. By the water's edge there are willows; and to almost
every farm there is a fine orchard, the trees being in general very
fine, and this year they are in general well loaded with fruit.
So that, all taken together, it seems impossible to find a more
beautiful and pleasant country than this, or to imagine any life
more easy and happy than men might here lead if they were
untormented by an accursed system that takes the food from
those that raise it, and gives it to those that do nothing that is
useful to man.

Here the farmer has always an abundance of straw. His farmyard is never without it. Cattle and horses are bedded up to their

eyes. The yards are put close under the shelter of a hill, or are protected by lofty and thick-set trees. Every animal seems comfortably situated; and in the dreariest days of winter these are, perhaps, the happiest scenes in the world; or, rather, they would be such if those whose labour makes it all, trees, corn, sheep and everything, had but their fair share of the produce of that labour. What share they really have of it one cannot exactly say; but I should suppose that every labouring man in this valley raises as much food as would suffice for fifty or a hundred persons, fed like himself!

19

CONCERNING GRASS
(1940)

Robert Gibbings

I suppose that in the whole pageant of river scenery there can be no item more recurrent to human eyes than grass, yet, in proportion to its constant reappearance, there can be no form of life which receives less attention from the passer-by. Just as to the great Dr Johnson one green field was like another green field, so to most people grass is just grass, something that cattle eat or something that man can turn into lawns. They do not realize the infinite variety of growth in every yard of turf or the infinite

63

beauty of the individual flowers: the crowded spike-like inflores-
cences of the foxtail, the trembling florets of the quake-grass, the
wild proud panicle of the oats. There is no greater competition
for existence anywhere than in a meadow. Even human footsteps
will encourage those grasses which prefer a firm tilth, to the
detriment of those who like a looser soil. Hence the clearly
marked line of a footpath, where the grasses which thrive happen
to be of a dark colour.

Until recently I was as ignorant on this subject as any one else.
I knew that hay from newly sown meadows was best for thoroughbred horses, and that hay from old pasture land was 'good
enough' for cattle, but I had no idea that cocksfoot, sweet vernal,
timothy, and other such pretty titles were anything more than
names in children's posies. But a colleague of mine, John Waldie,
BSc, devotes his whole life to grass. No quadruped could be a
greater connoisseur. He knows the flavour of every blade, the
amount of proteins, minerals, carbohydrates, and fats possessed
by each. He knows at what week in the year they start and finish
growing, and which of them need protection from their more
thrusting neighbours. From him I have learned that the science of
grazing is as important a matter for the farmer as rotation
of crops.

It seems that some of the nutritive species of grasses begin their
period of growth early in the year, and continue it late into
the autumn. Heavy grazing in early spring may therefore do
permanent harm to the pastures for, by long-continued cropping,
these early-growing species will be deprived of strength and will
be unable to compete in the struggle for existence when activity
sets in among the coarser and less desirable varieties later in the
year. Moreover, cattle and sheep are selective feeders and their
grazing needs careful supervision lest they exterminate the more
palatable components of a meadow.

Apart from this utilitarian side of the subject, there is an irresistible appeal, even to the most casual passer-by, in the rich
growth of a grass-field in spring and early summer. There seems
no breathing space left in the thick felt which covers the soil, and
yet the fields are powdered with the gold of buttercups and
trefoils, the purple of clovers and vetches, the red of sorrel and
the white of the ox-eye daisies, all of them holding their own in
the struggle. And as the days lengthen, the grasses continue their
growth, until in June we have all the wealth and fragrance of the
hayfield. Then is the time when labour becomes a pleasure, when
old-time stories pass, and legends are handed down from generation to generation. In the heat of the noonday sun the clank of

the mowing machine, the 'wheetly-harp-harp' of the sharpening stone on the scythe, and the cheery shout of the driver to his horses are sounds to gladden the heart of any man. In the evening, when the corncrake is heard calling to its straying youngsters, and when the white ghost-moth hovers over the few grasses still standing by the hedge, there is no sweeter site for lovers' dalliance than among the haycocks in the close-mown field.

Raising the rick is an event of the year, and proud the young labourer when first allowed to shape the corners. Nowadays most of the hay is conveyed on to the rick by elevators, but when I was a boy we forked it up from the horse-drawn cart, and each man emulated the other in throwing the largest forkfuls.

'Wanderful forks. Wanderful forks,' said old Boss Galvin, who was directing operations on the rick. 'Is it sweating ye are?'

'The river isn't flowing faster,' said Taedy Cronin, who was on the cart beside me.

'A provision of nature,' said Galvin.

'A what?' asked Taedy.

'It's my belief,' said the old man, 'that the rain that you soaks in the winter you sweats in the summer.'

Talking of hay reminds me of a man I once knew, named Macrae. He was from the south of Scotland, and one of his jobs was to buy hay for the firm that employed him in the north of Ireland. He was a very particular kind of man about details, especially such little matters as the exact weight of a hayrick. It was no good the farmer saying it was *about* five ton or *about* eight ton or *about* ten ton, for in the mind of this honest Presbyterian there was always a doubt.

Now doubt is no harm in itself, but when buying hay it should be tactfully expressed, and the man from over the water had just a shadow of bluntness in his speech. Mr Murphy from near Ballyclare did not like that.

'I tell you there's sixteen ton if there's a pound,' he said on one occasion.

'I'd like to see it weighed,' said Macrae.

'I wouldn't be surprised if it wasn't eighteen ton,' said Murphy, 'and sweeter hay doesn't grow in Ulster.'

'It has got to be weighed,' said Macrae.

'And where will I weigh it?' asked Murphy.

'At the public weighbridge in the town,' said Macrae.

'He'd skin a flea for the fat,' thought Murphy to himself. But he didn't say that; instead, he just asked: 'And how will you have it delivered?'

'Send me a load a week.'

So the bargain was made.

It was a wet year, and when the days were fine Murphy had much to do on his farm besides carting hay. For this reason he always chose wet weather for delivery of the goods. But, lest it should be said that the drop of rain might add weight to the hay, he took care always to cover the load with a large tarpaulin. So scrupulous indeed was he that he took along a spare tarpaulin of the same size to be weighed separately, so that the weight could be deducted from that registered on the scales. In this way the whole sixteen tons was delivered, one ton at a time.

Macrae was well pleased with the transaction, but he didn't know till many years afterwards that he had paid for an extra ton. The fact of the matter was that every time the cart went on the scales Mickey, the farmer's son, who weighed ten stone himself, was snuggled away under the waterproof covering, only to slip out later when a convenient moment arrived.

20

IRISH SKETCHES
(1868)

W. M. Thackeray

The beautiful Blackwater river suddenly opened before us, and driving along it for three miles through some of the most beautiful, rich country ever seen, we came to Lismore. Nothing can be certainly more magnificent than this drive. Parks and rocks covered with the grandest foliage; rich, handsome seats of gentlemen in the midst of fair lawns, and beautiful bright plantations and shrubberies; and at the end, the graceful spire of Lismore church, the prettiest I have seen in, or, I think, out of Ireland. Nor in any country that I have visited have I seen a view more noble – it is too rich and peaceful to be what is called romantic, but lofty, large, and *generous*, if the term may be used; the river and banks as fine as the Rhine; the castle not as large, but as noble and picturesque as Warwick. As you pass the bridge, the banks stretch away on either side in amazing verdure, and the castle-walks remind one somewhat of the dear old terrace of St Germains, with its groves, and long grave avenues of trees. . . .

Round the coach [at Dunmanway] came crowds of raggery, and

blackguards fawning for money. I wonder who gives them any? I have never seen any one give yet; and were they not even so numerous that it would be impossible to gratify them all, there is something in their cant and supplications to the Lord so disgusting to me, that I could not give a halfpenny.

In regard of pretty faces, male or female, this road is very unfavourable. I have not seen one for fifty miles; though as it was market day all along the road, we have had the opportunity to examine vast numbers of countenances. The women are, for the most part, stunted, short, with flat Tartar faces; and the men no handsomer. Every woman has bare legs, of course; and as the weather is fine, they are sitting outside their cabins, with the pig, and the geese, and the children sporting around. Before many doors we saw a little flock of these useful animals, and the family pig almost everywhere. You might see him browsing and poking along the hedges, his fore and hind leg attached with a wisp of hay, to check his propensity to roaming. Here and there were a small brood of turkeys; now and then a couple of sheep or a single one grazing upon a scanty field, of which the chief crop seemed to be thistles and stone; and, by the side of the cottage, the potato-field always.

The character of the landscape for the most part is bare and sad, except here and there in the neighbourhood of the towns, where people have taken a fancy to plant, and where nature has helped them, as it almost always will in this country. If we saw a field with a good hedge to it, we were sure to see a good crop

inside. Many a field was there that had neither crop nor hedge. We passed by and over many pretty streams, running bright through brilliant emerald meadows; and I saw a thousand charming pictures, which want as yet an Irish Berghem. A bright road winding up a hill; on it a country cart, with its load stretching a huge shadow; the before-mentioned emerald pastures and silver rivers in the foreground; a noble sweep of hills rising up from them, and contrasting their magnificent purple with the green; in the extreme distance the clear cold outline of some far-off mountains, and the white clouds tumbled about in the blue sky overhead. It has no doubt struck all persons who love to look at nature, how different the skies are in different countries. I fancy Irish or French clouds are as characteristic as Irish or French landscapes. It would be well to have a Daguerreotype and get a series of each. Some way beyond Dunmanna the road takes us through a noble savage country of rocks and heath. Nor must the painter forget long black tracts of bog here and there, and the water glistening brightly at the places where the turf has been cut away. Add to this, and chiefly by the banks of rivers, a ruined old castle or two: some were built by the Danes, it is said. The O'Connors, the O'Mahonys, the O'Driscolls, were lords of many others, and their ruined towers may be seen here and along the sea.

21

JOURNEY THROUGH WALES
(1191)

Giraldus Cambrensis

This country sufficiently abounds with grain, and if there is any deficiency it is amply supplied from the neighbouring parts of England; it is well stored with pastures, woods and wild and domestic animals. River fish are plentiful, supplied by the Usk on one side and by the Wye on the other; each of them produces salmon and trout; but the Wye abounds most with the former, the Usk with the latter. The salmon of the Wye are in season during the winter, those of the Usk in the summer; but the Wye alone produces the fish called umber, the praise of which is celebrated in the works of Ambrosius, as being found in great numbers in the rivers near Milan; 'What,' says he, 'is more beautiful to behold,

more agreeable to smell, or more pleasant to taste?' The famous lake of Brecheinoc [Llangorse] supplies the country with pike, perch, excellent trout, tench, and eels.

The lake also (according to the testimony of the inhabitants) is celebrated for its miracles; for, as we have before observed, it sometimes assumed a greenish hue, so in our days it has appeared to be tinged with red, not universally, but as if blood flowed partially through certain veins and small channels. Moreover it is sometimes seen by the inhabitants covered and adorned with buildings, pastures, gardens and orchards. In the winter, when it is frozen over, and the surface of the water is converted into a shell of ice, it emits a horrible sound resembling the moans of many animals collected together; but this, perhaps, may be occasioned by the sudden bursting of the shell, and the gradual ebullition of the air through imperceptible channels. This country is well sheltered on every side (except the northern) by high mountains; on the western by those of cantref Bychan; on the southern by that range of which the principal is Cadair Arthur [Bannan Brycheiniog], or the chair of Arthur, so called from two peaks rising up in the form of a chair, and which, from its lofty situation, is vulgarly ascribed to Arthur, the most distinguished king of the Britons. A spring of water rises on the summit of this mountain, deep, but of a square shape, like a well, and although no stream runs from it, trout are said to be sometimes found in it.

Being thus sheltered on the south by high mountains, the cooler breezes protect this district from the heat of the sun, and, by their natural salubrity, render the climate most temperate.

The castle called Maenor Pyrr [Manorbier], that is, the mansion of Pyrrus, who also possessed the island of Chaldey, which the Welsh call Inys Pyrr, or the island of Pyrrus, is distant about three miles from Penbroch. It is excellently well defended by turrets and bulwarks and is situated on the summit of a hill extending on the western side towards the sea port, having on the northern and southern sides a fine fish pond under its walls, as conspicuous for its grand appearance as for the depth of its waters, and a beautiful orchard on the same side, enclosed on one part by a vineyard and on the other by a wood, remarkable for the projection of its rocks and the height of its hazel trees. On the right hand of the promontory, between the castle and the church, near the site of a very large lake and mill, a rivulet of never-failing water flows through a valley, rendered sandy by the violence of the winds. Towards the west the Severn sea, bending its course to Ireland, enters a hollow bay at some distance from the castle; and the southern rocks, if extended a little further towards the north, would render it a most excellent harbour for shipping. From this point of sight, you will see almost all the ships from Great Britain, which the east wind drives upon the Irish coast, daringly brave the inconstant waves and raging sea. This country is well supplied with corn, sea fish and imported wines; and what is preferable to every other advantage, from its vicinity to Ireland, it is tempered by a salubrious air. Demetia, therefore, with its seven cantreds, is the most beautiful, as well as the most powerful district of Wales; Penbroch, the finest part of the province of Demetia; and the place I have just described, the most delightful part of Penbroch. It is evident, therefore, that Maenor Pyrr is the pleasantest spot in Wales; and the author may be pardoned for having thus extolled his native soil, his genial territory, with a profusion of praise and admiration.

22

WHITE OWLS
(1773)

Gilbert White

To the Hon Daines Barrington
Selborne, July 8, 1773

Dear Sir,

We have had, ever since I can remember, a pair of white owls that constantly breed under the eaves of this church. As I have paid good attention to the manner of life of these birds during their season of breeding, which lasts the summer through, the following remarks may not perhaps be unacceptable. About an hour before sunset (for then the mice begin to run) they sally forth in quest of prey, and hunt all round the hedges of meadows and small enclosures for them, which seem to be their only food. In this irregular country we can stand on an eminence and see them beat the fields over like a setting-dog, and often drop down in the grass or corn. I have minuted these birds with my watch for an hour together, and have found that they return to their nests, the one or the other of them, about once in five minutes; reflecting at the same time on the adroitness that every animal is possessed of as far as regards the wellbeing of itself and offspring. But a piece of address, which they show when they return loaded, should not, I think, be passed over in silence. As they take their prey with their claws, so they carry it in their claws to their nest: but, as the feet are necessary in their ascent under the tiles, they constantly perch first on the roof of the chancel, and shift the mouse from their claws to their bill, that the feet may be at liberty to take hold of the plate on the wall as they are rising under the eaves.

White owls seem not (but in this I am not positive) to hoot at all: all that clamorous hooting appears to me to come from the wood kinds. The white owl does indeed snore and hiss in a tremendous manner; and these menaces well answer the intention of intimidating for I have known a whole village up in arms on such an occasion, imagining the churchyard to be full of goblins and spectres. White owls also often scream horribly as they fly along; from this screaming probably arose the common people's imaginary species of screech-owl, which they superstitiously think attends the windows of dying persons. The plumage of the remiges of the wings of every species of owl that I have yet examined is remarkably soft and pliant. Perhaps it may be necessary that the wings of these birds should not make much resistance or rushing, that they may be enabled to steal through the air unheard upon a nimble and watchful quarry.

While I am talking of owls, it may not be improper to mention what I was told by a gentleman of the county of Wilts. As they were grubbing a vast hollow pollard-ash that had been the mansion of owls for centuries, he discovered at the bottom a mass of matter that at first he could not account for. After some examination he found that it was a congeries of the bones of mice (and perhaps of birds and bats) that had been heaping together for ages, being cast up in pellets out of the crops of many generations of inhabitants. For owls cast up the bones, fur, and feathers of what they devour, after the manner of hawks.

When brown owls hoot their throats swell as big as an hen's egg. I have known an owl of this species live a full year without any water. Perhaps the case may be the same with all birds of prey. When owls fly they stretch out their legs behind them as a balance to their large heavy heads for as most noctural birds have large eyes and ears they must have large heads to contain them.

23

NATURE'S DEFECTS
(1891)

Oscar Wilde

Cyril (*coming in through the open window from the terrace*) My dear
Vivian, don't coop yourself up all day in the library. It is a
perfectly lovely afternoon. The air is exquisite. There is
a mist upon the woods, like the purple bloom upon a
plum. Let us go and lie on the grass and smoke cigarettes
and enjoy Nature.

Vivian Enjoy Nature! I am glad to say that I have entirely lost
that faculty. People tell us that Art makes us love Nature
more than we loved her before; that it reveals her secrets
to us; and that after a careful study of Corot and
Constable we see things in her that had escaped our
observation. My own experience is that the more we study
Art, the less we care for Nature. What Art really reveals to
us is Nature's lack of design, her curious crudities, her
extraordinary monotony, her absolutely unfinished condition. Nature has good intentions, of course, but, as
Aristotle once said, she cannot carry them out. When I
look at a landscape I cannot help seeing all its defects. It is
fortunate for us, however, that Nature is so imperfect, as
otherwise we should have had no art at all. Art is our
spirited protest, our gallant attempt to teach Nature her
proper place. As for the infinite variety of Nature, that is
a pure myth. It is not to be found in Nature herself. It
resides in the imagination, or fancy, or cultivated blind-
ness of the man who looks at her.

Cyril Well, you need not look at the landscape. You can lie on
the grass and smoke and talk.

Vivian But Nature is so uncomfortable. Grass is hard and lumpy
and damp, and full of dreadful black insects. Why, even
Morris's poorest workman could make you a more comfortable seat than the whole of Nature can. Nature pales
before the furniture of 'the street which from Oxford has
borrowed its name,' as the poet you love so much once

vilely phrased it. I don't complain. If Nature had been comfortable, mankind would never have invented architecture, and I prefer houses to the open air. In a house we all feel of the proper proportions. Everything is subordinated to us, fashioned for our use and our pleasure. Egotism itself, which is so necessary to a proper sense of human dignity, is entirely the result of indoor life. Out of doors one becomes abstract and impersonal. One's individuality absolutely leaves one. And then Nature is so indifferent, so unappreciative. Whenever I am walking in the park here, I always feel that I am no more to her than the cattle that browse on the slope, or the burdock that blooms in the ditch.

24

THE WYLYE VALLEY
(1910)

W. H. Hudson

There are other chalk streams in Wiltshire and Hampshire and Dorset – swift crystal currents that play all summer long with the floating poa grass fast held in their pebbly beds, flowing through smooth downs, with small ancient churches in their green villages, and pretty thatched cottages smothered in flowers – which yet do not produce the same effect as the Wylye. Not Avon for all its beauty, nor Itchen, nor Test. Wherein, then, does the 'Wylye bourne' differ from these others, and what is its special attraction? It was only when I set myself to think about it, to analyse the feeling in my own mind, that I discovered the secret – that is, in my own case, for of its effects on others I cannot say anything.

What I discovered was that the various elements of interest, all of which may be found in other chalk-stream valleys, are here concentrated, or comprised in a limited space, and seen together produce a combined effect on the mind. It is the narrowness of the valley and the nearness of the high downs standing over it on either side with, at some points, the memorials of antiquity carved on their smooth surfaces, the barrows and lynchets or terraces, and the vast green earthworks crowning their summit. Up here on the turf, even with the lark singing his shrill music in the blue heavens, you are with the prehistoric dead, yourself for the time one of that innumerable, unsubstantial multitude, invisible in the sun, so that the sheep travelling as they graze, and the shepherd following them, pass through their ranks without suspecting their presence. And from that elevation you look down upon the life of today – the visible life, so brief in the individual, which like the swift silver stream beneath, yet flows on continuously from age to age and for ever. And even as you look down you hear, at that distance, the bell of the little hidden church tower telling the hour of noon, and quickly following, a shout of freedom and joy from many shrill voices of children just released from school. Woke to life by these sounds, and drawn down by them, you may sit to rest or sun yourself on the stone table of a tomb overgrown on its sides with moss, the two-century-old inscription well-nigh obliterated, in the little grass-grown, flowery churchyard which serves as village green and playground in that small centre of life, where the living and the dead exist in a neighbourly way together. For it is not here as in towns, where the dead are away and out of mind and the past cut off. And if after basking too long in the sun in that tree-sheltered spot you go into the little church to cool your-self, you will probably find in a dim corner not far from the altar a stone effigy of one of an older time; a knight in armour, perhaps a crusader with legs crossed, lying on his back, dimly seen in the dim light, with perhaps a coloured sunbeam on his upturned face. For this little church where the villagers worship is very old; Norman on Saxon foundations; and before they were ever laid there may have been a temple to some ancient god at that spot, or a Roman villa perhaps. For older than Saxon foundations are found in the vale, and mosaic floors, still beautiful after lying buried so long.

All this – the far-renowned events and periods in time – are not in the conscious mind when we are in the vale or when we are looking down on it from above: the mind is occupied with nothing but visible nature. Thus, when I am sitting on the tomb, listening to the various sounds of life about me, attentive to the flowers and bees and butterflies, to man or woman or child taking a short cut through the churchyard, exchanging a few words with them; or when I am by the water close by, watching a little company of graylings, their delicately-shaded, silver-grey scales distinctly seen as they lie in the crystal current watching for flies; or when I listen to the perpetual musical talk and song combined of a family of greenfinches in the alders or willows, my mind is engaged with these things. But if one is familiar with the vale; if one has looked with interest and been deeply impressed with the signs and memorials of past life and of antiquity everywhere present and forming part of the scene, something of it and of all that it represents remains in the subconscious mind to give a significance and feeling to the scene, which affects us here more than in most places; and that, I take it, is the special charm of this little valley.

25

NOTES ON THE LAKE DISTRICT
(1855)

Nathaniel Hawthorne

[*July 13th, 1855*] There are a good many trees on the hills and round about, and pleasant roads loitering along by the gentle riverside, and it has been so sunny and warm since we came here [to Newby Bridge] that we shall have quite a genial recollection of the place if we leave it before the skies have time to frown. The day after we came, we climbed a high and pretty steep hill, through a path shadowed with trees and shrubbery, up to a tower, from the summit of which we had a wide view of mountain scenery and the greater part of Windermere. The lake is a lovely little pool among the hills, long and narrow, beautifully indented with tiny bays and headlands; and when we saw it, it was one smile (as broad a smile as its narrowness allowed) with really brilliant sunshine. All the scenery we have yet met with is in excellent taste, and keeps itself within very proper bounds – never getting too wild and rugged to shock the sensibilities of cultivated people, as American scenery is apt to do. On the rudest surface of English earth, there is seen the effect of centuries of civilization, so that you do not quite get at naked Nature anywhere.

July 16th – On Saturday we left Newby Bridge and came by steamboat up Windermere lake to Lowwood Hotel, where we now are. The foot of the lake is just above Newby Bridge and it widens from that point, but never to such a breadth that objects are not pretty distinctly visible from shore to shore. The steamer stops at two or three places in the course of its voyage, the principal one being Bowness, which has a little bustle and air of business about it proper to the principal port of the lake. There are several small yachts, and many skiffs rowing about. The banks are everywhere beautiful, and the water, in one portion, is strewn with islands, few of which are large enough to be inhabitable, but they all seem to be appropriated, and kept in the neatest order. As yet, I have seen no wildness; everything is perfectly subdued and polished and imbued with human taste. . . .

There is a very pretty vicinity, and a fine view of mountains to the north-west, sitting together in a family group, sometimes in full sunshine, sometimes with only a golden gleam on one or two of them, sometimes all in a veil of cloud, from which here and there a great, dusky head raises itself, while you are looking at a dim obscurity. Nearer, there are high, green slopes, well wooded, but with such decent and well-behaved wood as you perceive has grown up under the care of man; still no wildness, no ruggedness – as how should there be, when, every half mile or so, a porter's lodge or a gentleman's gateway indicates that the whole region is used up for villas. On the opposite shore of the lake there is a mimic castle, which I suppose I might have mistaken for a real one two years ago. It is a great, foolish toy of grey stone.

A steamboat comes to the pier as many as six times a day, and stage-coaches and omnibuses stop at the door still oftener, com- municating with Ambleside and the town of Windermere, and with the railway, which opens London and all the world to us. We get no knowledge of our fellow-guests, all of whom, like ourselves, live in their own circles, and are just as remote from us as if the lake lay between.

Yesterday forenoon J. and I walked to Ambleside, distant barely two miles. It is a little town, chiefly of modern aspect, built on a very uneven hillside, and with very irregular streets and lanes, which bewilder the stranger as much as those of a larger city. Many of the houses look old, and are probably the cottages and farmhouses which composed the rude village a century ago; but there are stuccoed shops and dwellings, such as may have been built within a year or two; and three hotels, one of which has the look of a good old village inn; and the others are fashionable or commercial establishments. Through the midst of the village comes tumbling and rumbling a mountain streamlet, rushing through a deep, rocky dell, gliding under an old stone arch, and turning, when occasion calls, the great block of a watermill. This is

the only very striking feature of the village – the stream taking its rough pathway to the lake as it used to do before the poets had made this region fashionable.

In the evening, just before eight o'clock, I took a walk alone, by a road which goes up the hill, back of our hotel, and which I supposed might be the road to the town of Windermere. But it went up higher and higher, and for the mile or two that it led me along, winding up, I saw no traces of a town; but at last it turned into a valley between two high ridges, leading quite away from the lake, within view of which the town of Windermere is situated. It was a very lonely road, though as smooth, hard, and as well kept as any thoroughfare in the suburbs of a city; hardly a dwelling on either side, except one, half barn, half farmhouse, and one gentleman's gateway, near the beginning of the road, and another more than a mile above. At two or three points there were stone barns, which are here built with great solidity. At one place there was a painted board, announcing that a field of five acres was to be sold, and referring those desirous of purchasing to a solicitor in London. The lake country is but a London suburb. Nevertheless, the walk was lonely and lovely; the copses and the broad hillside, the glimpses of the lake, the great misty company of pikes and fells, beguiled me into a sense of something like solitude; and the bleating of the sheep, remote and near, had a like tendency. Gaining the summit of the hill, I had the best view of Windermere which I have yet attained – the best, I should think, that can be had, though, being towards the south, it brings the softer instead of the more striking features of the landscape into view. But it shows nearly the whole extent of the lake, all the way from Lowwood, beyond Newby Bridge, and I think there can hardly be anything more beautiful in the world. The water was like a strip and gleam of sky, fitly set among lovely slopes of earth. It was no broader than many a river, and yet you saw at once that it could be no river, its outline being so different from that of a running stream, not straight nor winding, but stretching to one side or the other, as the shores made room for it. . . .

[*July 21st*] The gardener took leave of us at the front entrance of the grounds, and, returning to the King's Arms [Keswick], we ordered a one-horse fly for the fall of Lodore. Our drive thither was along the banks of Derwentwater, and it is as beautiful a road, I imagine, as can be found in England or anywhere else. I like Derwentwater the best of all the lakes, so far as I have yet seen them. Skiddaw lies at the head of a long even ridge of mountains, rising into several peaks, and one higher than the rest. On the eastern side there are many noble eminences, and on the west, along which we drove, there is a part of the way a lovely wood, and nearly the whole distance a precipitous range of lofty cliffs, descending sheer down without any slope, except what has been formed in the lapse of ages by the fall of fragments, and the washing down of smaller stones. The declivity thus formed along the base of the cliffs is in some places covered with trees or shrubs; elsewhere it is quite bare and barren. The precipitous parts of the cliffs are very grand; the whole scene, indeed, might be characterized as one of stern grandeur with an embroidery of rich beauty, without lauding it too much. All the sternness of it is softened by vegetative beauty wherever it can possibly be thrown in; and there is not here, so strongly as along Windermere, evidence that human art has been helping out Nature.

I wish it were possible to give any idea of the shapes of the hills; with these, at least, man has nothing to do, nor ever will have anything to do. As we approached the bottom of the lake, and of the beautiful valley in which it lies, we saw one hill that seemed to crouch down like a Titanic watchdog, with its rear towards the spectator, guarding the entrance to the valley. The great superiority of these mountains over those of New England is their variety and definiteness of shape, besides the abundance everywhere of water prospects, which are wanting among our own hills. They rise up decidedly, and each is a hill by itself, while ours mingle into one another, and, besides, have such large bases that you can tell neither where they begin nor where they end. Many of these Cumberland mountains have a marked vertebral shape, so that they often look like a group of huge lions, lying down with their backs turned towards each other. They slope down steeply from narrow ridges; hence their picturesque seclusions of valleys and dales, which subdivide the lake region into so many communities. Our hills, like apple-dumplings in the dish, have no such valleys as these.

There is a good inn at Lodore – a small, primitive country inn, which has latterly been enlarged and otherwise adapted to meet the convenience of the guests brought thither by the fame of the cascade; but it is still a country inn, though it takes upon itself the title of hotel. We found pleasant rooms here, and established ourselves for the night. From this point we have a view of the beautiful lake, and of Skiddaw at the head of it. The cascade is within three or four minutes' walk, through the garden gate, towards the cliff, at the base of which the inn stands. The visitor would need no other guide than its own voice, which is said to be audible sometimes at the distance of four miles. As we were coming from Keswick, we caught glimpses of its white foam high up the precipice; and it is only glimpses that can be caught any-where, because there is no regular sheet of falling water. Once, I think, it must have fallen abruptly over the edge of the long line of precipice that here extends along parallel with the shore of the lake; but in the course of time, it has gnawed and sawed its way into the heart of the cliff, this persistent little stream, so that now it has formed a rude gorge, down which it hurries and tumbles in the wildest way, over the roughest imaginable staircase. Standing at the bottom of the fall, you have a far vista sloping upward to the sky, with the water everywhere as white as snow, pouring and pouring down, now on one side of the gorge, now on the other, among immense boulders which try to choke its passage. It does not attempt to leap over these huge rocks, but finds its way in and out among them, and finally gets to the bottom after a hundred tumbles. It cannot be better described than in Southey's verses, though it is worthy of better poetry than that.

26

AS CUNNING AS A FOX
(1891)

Charles St John

I stopped for an hour or two about Loch Laighal, one of the most beautiful of the lakes in Sutherland. Ben Laighal is a fine and picturesque mountain, and of great extent. We learned at a shepherd's house that the fox-hunter of that district had been up on the mountain since three o'clock in pursuit of some foxes who had established themselves in the rocky corries near the summit, and had commenced killing the old sheep. It is not the general custom of foxes to destroy the old and full-grown sheep where lambs are plentiful; but a colony or pair of foxes having once commenced this habit, the mischief and havoc which they commit are beyond calculation, more particularly as they seldom tear or eat much of so large an animal, but feed on the blood. According to the accounts of the shepherds, the foxes of Ben Laighal are very prone to this kind of prey and kill the old sheep in preference to lambs or game.

The foxes in the Highland districts must frequently be put to many shifts for their living, and no doubt become proportionately cunning. To keep himself in the fine and sleek condition in which a fox always is, many a trick and *ruse de guerre* of surpassing cleverness must be practised. The stories of their manoeuvres to catch animals are endless; and though many of them would be amusing enough, I do not like quoting as facts incidents of this kind, the authenticity of which I cannot vouch for, however much I may believe them to be true, and I must confess to being very credulous on this point.

I have been assured by a person not given at all to exaggerate nor easily deceived, that he once witnessed the following trick. Very early one morning he saw a fox eyeing most wistfully a number of wild ducks feeding in the rushy end of a Highland lake. After due consideration the fox, going to windward of the ducks, put afloat in the loch several bunches of dead rushes or grass, which floated down amongst the ducks without causing the least alarm. After watching the effects of his preliminary fleet for a short time, the fox, taking a good-sized mouthful of grass in his jaws, launched himself into the water as quietly as possible, having nothing but the tips of his ears and nose above water. In this way he drifted down amongst the ducks, and made booty of a fine mallard.

Though this story seems extraordinary, it must be remembered that the fox manages to capture wild ducks, wood-pigeons, hares, and numberless other animals, sufficient to keep himself and family; and it is self-evident that in doing so he must practise many a trick and manoeuvre that would seem most improbable if related, and quite beyond the instinct of animals. I have seen one in confinement lay out a part of his food just within reach of his chain, in order to attract the tame ducks and chickens about the yard, and then, having concealed himself in his kennel, wait in an attitude ready to spring out till some duck or fowl came to his bait, which he immediately pounced upon. Those, too, who have trapped foxes can tell of the extreme cunning and sagacity displayed by them in avoiding danger. In fact, altogether a fox in a

state of nature is as interesting an animal as he is beautiful, and nothing can exceed the grace and agility of his movements when he is hunting, or playing unobserved, as he fancies, by his enemy man. It has happened to me frequently to have opportunities of watching a fox, and I have always been unwilling to put a stop to my amusement by shooting him, which, in a country where hounds cannot be kept, one feels bound to do, as a punishment for the endless mischief which he commits.

27

FROM PENZANCE TO TRURO
(1698)

Celia Fiennes

I continued my return from Pensands [Penzance] to Hailing [Hayle] and now the tide was down and so much land appeared which lay under water before, and I might have forded quite across; many that know the country do, but I took the safer way round by the bridge. Here is abundance of very good fish though they are so ill supplied at Pensands because they carry it all up the country, east and southward. This is an arm of the north sea which runs in a great way into the land. It's a large bay when the sea comes in, and upon the next hill I ascended from it could discover it more plain to be a deep water and the supply of the main ocean. Just by here lay some ships and I perceived as I went, there being a storm, it seemed very tempestuous and is a hazardous place in the high tides; so I came to Redruth.

I perceive they are very bleak in these countries, especially to this north ocean, and the winds so troublesome they are forced to spin straw and so make a caul or net work to lay over their thatch on their ricks and outhouses, with weights of stones round to defend the thatch from being blown away by the great winds, not but they have a better way of thatching their houses with reeds and so close that when it's well done will last twenty years; but what I mention of braces or bands of straw is on their ricks which only is to hold a year. These places as in some other parts, indeed all over Cornwall and Devonshire, they have their carriages on horses' backs, this being the time of harvest, though later in the year than usual, being the middle of September, but I had the advantage of seeing their harvest bringing in, which is on a horse's back with sort of crooks of wood like yokes on either side – two or three on a side stand up in which they stow the corn and so tie it with cords, but they cannot so equally poise it but the going of the horse is like to cast it down sometimes on the one side and sometimes on the other, for they load them from the neck to the tail and pretty high, and are forced to support it with their hands. So to a horse they have two people, and the women lead and support them as well as the men and go through thick and thin – sometimes I have met with half a score horses thus loaded. They are indeed but little horses, their canelles as they call them, and so may not be able to draw a cart, otherwise I am sure 3 or 4 horses might draw 3 times as much as 4 horses do carry. And where it is open ground and roads broad, which in some places here it was, I wondered at their labour in this kind, for the men and the women themselves toiled like their horses, but the common observation of custom being as a second nature, people are very hardly convinced or brought off from, though never so inconvenient.

From Redruth I went to Truro 8 mile, which is a pretty little town and seaport and formerly was esteemed the best town in Cornwall, now is the second next Lanstone [Launceston]. It's just by the copper and tin mines and lies down in a bottom, pretty steep ascent as most of the towns in these countries, that you would be afraid of tumbling with nose and head foremost. The town is built of stone – a good pretty church built all stone and carved on the outside, it stands in the middle of the town, and just by there is a market house on stone pillars and hall on the top; there is also a pretty good key. This was formerly a great trading town and flourished in all things, but now as there is in all places their rise and period so this, which is become a ruinated disregarded place.

85

28

MOORS OF A THOUSAND MOODS
(1933)

John Prioleau

A friendly reader of some notes I wrote last year on two ways to Scotland avoiding the Great North Road, asked me for a detour through the north country so planned that he could take it from either the western or the eastern of the two roads I sketched out. He was fired with the ambition to climb as high as possible on to the moors between Leeds and the Wall, and, presumably owning an active car, positively demanded steep hills.

He had a glorious prospect before him. Only when they are drowned in snow or blotted out in fog are the moors of Durham, Yorkshire, Cumberland, and Westmorland anything but places of real peace and beauty of a very specially English kind. It may be blisteringly hot or as cold as you please (and it can be both at the proper time to a degree incredible to a southron); it may blow a hurricane, and for days on end there may not be enough stir in the air to blow out a candle; the sun may blaze down on the heather as if it were growing a couple of thousand miles farther south, as resplendently in the silver light of winter as in high summer; whole days may pass under a sky of grey. The moors have a thousand moods.

They have the Yorkshire quality of vigour at all seasons, though in September, towards the end of the perfect month, you will sometimes catch them in reflective mood. Anywhere else you would say, confronted with those wide expanses of heathery hill and dale and those far horizons, that the September softness had fallen upon them, but as you stare into those distances and fore-grounds that fill you with so satisfying a sense of space, you see that softness is not the word. The outlines of the fells may not seem so sharp-cut as they were when you saw them in June or March. There may be, as there is over the hills of the south, a little haze about their bold heads and flanks, but it is not of the sort that softens. It is translucid, and through it you still see the forthright architecture of the wildest hills in England.

Yet I believe the moors are at their best in autumn – though I have little doubt I should deny it in May. Certainly their colouring is unsurpassed, glowing with deeper fire day after day, until the inevitable change and storm, when winter begins to stretch her pale fingers over the North Sea and everything is frozen into the colours of a shadow. Go in early autumn, before the east winds and the slanting rain make the pilgrimage too dubious. If you find only a couple of proper September days, copper and silver over the heather and the little becks and the bigger rivers, you will have seen something worth while. Look on your map for the Swale and the Esk, the Tees and the Wear, for the Cleveland Hills, and for the fells that stand sentry on the border, and let your car find her way without thought of time or season.

29

CORNISH WILDS
(1924)

H. J. Massingham

'Character,' spoke the oracle, 'character is a more valuable element than culture in the life of a nation like the British.' For days, even weeks, I had been dreaming, half thinking about Cornwall, and this importunate fly-imp of a sentence kept buzzing round me, settling on my nose, crawling up my sleeve, striding along the bridle-path of my hair, until I thirsted for its blood. Many times I flattened it out, but it always returned, so that in time I had elaborated enough argument in my head not merely to hew that fly limb from limb, but, granted publication, to carry me to the toe of Cornwall and back with the proceeds. Is it that you and bishops don't hit it off, I asked myself, or is it that you cannot let pass so gross an insult upon the worth of your countrymen?

Indeed, the episcopal utterance is really too hard on us, even as a modern industrial nation, when we consider that the 'character' of every civilization known to us in the past – Egyptian, Pacific, Minoan, Mycenaean, Hellenic, Mesopotamian, Chinese – is expressed through their culture. The superior culture of Egypt created the whole of civilization and gave it to the whole world. For centuries Egypt was the world by virtue of her arts and crafts alone. By their works of art in their growth and flowering and decay shall ye know the nations, and our own perhaps will be known to posterity because, though in its latest phase it has belittled the arts and narrowed their range, yet almost as much against its will as its knowledge it is in process of making an art of science. To say that character is a more valuable element than culture in a nation's life is equivalent to saying that bricks are a more valuable element than houses in a street, or that coal is a more valuable element than fires in the winter.

I was staying in September on the Penwith uplands which, with the Bodmin moors in the north and the Goonhilly Downs in the south, are one of the three great regions of Cornish moorland, and I had climbed Zennor Tor, which rises some seven hundred and fifty feet above the sea about a quarter of the way out from St Ives to the Land's End, with a missionary purpose. It was with three friends of W. H. Hudson's, to one of whom he owed much happiness, and once his life from illness, and our object was to find a suitable stone among the granite boulders of the Tor on which to have inscribed, 'W. H. Hudson often came here.' He came here many times while he was living at Zennor, whose church tower from the Tor looks no bigger than a stepping-stone between the moors and the stone-hedged fields, and yet whose geometric relation with heath and headland and sea is so true that it is the node to them all. And he came here to travel, rather than travelled to come here. From a pearly cloud to the north, which is Trevose Head, past headland and cove and cove and headland, and out to sea beyond the Pendeen lighthouse to the Scillies, which are not a school of whales, you can travel a matter of seventy miles on a turn of the head, and behind you again over the purple-brown shoulders of the moor, laced with the old gold of the furze, to the other sea, and the Atlantic still. But that's nothing, for the sun is ahead of you, and sailing among its own islands and headlands with the golden moors behind them, which you can reach simply by opening your eyes. Open them well and take them in, for the golden isles are, alas, a good deal further off than can be reckoned by their mileage.

No book has ever been any use to me in trying to understand this unique peninsula, except Hudson's own, *The Land's End*, partly because Hudson's spirit is, a portion of it, Cornwall's, as a portion is Wiltshire's. One might, indeed, have inscribed the stone, 'W. H. Hudson often comes here.' But ultimately there is no knowing Cornwall out of books. Being unwell, I spent the whole of one day simply in looking out of the window at the slope leading up to Zennor Tor, and feeling at the end of it as I did when I left school – that I had spent six years in learning that I had learned nothing.

There is no green anywhere on the moors, except that darkest green of the furze, which is a shade, almost a bloom, that shifts to glaucous in the autumn, and there are no trees which would be as out of place there as Cleopatra's needle is on the Embankment. Even the bushes do not break up the lines and contours of the moor to anything like the same extent as do the cairns and granite piles and Egyptian-Neolithic monuments. They look, one and all, as though they had been reared by some monstrous semi-human brood of nature, so mythically human-like are the piling of the slabs of granite, one upon another, on the summits of the slopes, and the castles on the headlands, so savagely natural seem the quoits, kistvaens, and cromlechs that abound upon these once populous solitudes. On the tops of many of the natural cairns, there are often little hollows scooped out of the rocks and filled with water to serve as bathing pools for the small birds. Surely they must have been made with hands, but they were not, unless it was Nature herself in her personified form who delved them for that purpose.

But, unlike the granite, the bramble, furze and blackthorn do not stand up to the elements nor bide the pelting of the wind, but, huddling, twisting, creeping close to the hollow soil, become its very garment. The shuffling badger that lives among the cairns, the little pennywort or navelwort that swings its bells in their safe niches are not in their way more reticent than is the gorse. Even so, the Atlantic gales have nibbled off their tops and mounded them into tiny ranges, through which the ling forces its purple spires, so that the flowers of each plant grow intermingled, in pressed clusters and on the same level. This blending is very beautiful, for the September gorse (*Ulex nanus*), which is a sub-species or variety of *Ulex europæus* that sets the moors in points of smokeless flame in spring, is of the deep but subdued colouring of old gold. In wide patches grow the bents or white moor-grass, all silver and silk, and of a texture so fine that when the wind ripples their surface it is as though its wavelets had suddenly become visible. The same wind grips the waters and crunches the ships to tatters, and pounds and crumbles the granite into the mazy sculpture of the coves and shatters even the iron-stone.

One day, as I sat on Zennor Head, I saw Cornwall rise out of nothingness, as it once rose out of the sea and has remained, a barbarian Anadyomene, for ever unchanged. All day the Atlantic mist had covered it in a grey night, until all of a sudden it broke and trailed in thin scud off the armoured hide and warted snout of the Gurnard's Head. In a few moments the whole grim land came to itself. Again the suggestion was that contending races of semi-human giants had fought their last battle and annihilated each other the day before you came. The heaped boulders washed by the 'still-vexed' Atlantic three hundred feet below hid the body of one of them, and the broken tower on the edge of the abyss that the pressure of a butterfly might surely topple over into it was what he did against his enemy before he died. And inland the far more wonderful megaliths of human workmanship, built up by a little people with Egyptian or Phoenician overlords, a giant race indeed! So this was the peninsula of Cornwall. But it wasn't; it was its rudiments, a passing glimpse of its 'character' and original design.

Very different is its expression of that 'character,' its 'culture,' if I may fall back upon the bishop. The subtle delicacy and variations of the moorland colouring are really a match for those of the sea and the light of setting suns, that sea of Madonna blue which inshore becomes the emerald shade of the shags' eyes, and breaks into an embroidery of dazzling white round the isolated grey stacks where they stand like green idols. The moorland is worthy of sea and sky, not so much in brilliance, except when the gorse is flaming in the spring, as in depth. The colour, that is to say, does not appear as painted over the earth, as one often feels it to be in Devonshire for instance, but its natural complexion. The moors blush their colouring, and distil it from their strength, so that the words 'a sense of something far more deeply interfused' become really living and dramatic.

In many other ways, too, the Cornish wilderness is a stage for a kind of pageant of evolution. It presents the steepest contrasts between the beginnings and the prime of things, the primitive and the complex, the mighty and the fragile, the bare and the luxuriant, the material rude and raw and perfection. Yet there is no discord between them all. The appearance of the north coast between St Ives and 'dark Bolerium, seat of storms' is grandly symmetrical, in spite of its ruggedness, the often fantastic shapes of the cliff castles and the headlands with their vaguely beastlike and humanlike effigies, and the rock-litter in the coves. It is along the flanks of these coves where the tiny troutleted streams go bounding and twisting among the boulders that the brute force of nature runs headlong into luxury. The furze quite loses its moorland habit here, and becomes almost tree-like in its excess of growth, while the bramble and ivy and blackthorn form thickets so dense that there is no forcing a way through them. 'To live rightly,' says Havelock Ellis in a study of St Francis, 'we must imitate both the luxury of Nature and her austerity.' Then it would be well to live in Cornwall, only there is much more in it than these two bits of contrasting mosaic to fit into the general pattern.

30

THE FARMHOUSE
(1879)

Richard Jefferies

The stream, after leaving the village and the washpool, rushes swiftly down the descending slope, and then entering the meadows, quickly loses its original impetuous character. Not much more than a mile from the village it flows placidly through meads and pastures, a broad, deep brook, thickly fringed with green flags bearing here and there large yellow flowers. By some old thatched cattlesheds and rickyards, overshadowed with elm trees, a strong bay or dam crosses it, forcing the water into a pond for the cattle, and answering the occasional purpose of a ford; for the labourers in their heavy boots walk over the bay, though the current rises to the instep. They call these sheds, some few hundred yards from the farmhouse, the 'Lower Pen.' Wick Farm – almost every village has its outlying 'wick' – stands alone in the fields. It is an ancient rambling building, the present form of which is the result of successive additions at different dates, and in various styles.

When a homestead, like this, has been owned and occupied by the same family for six or seven generations, it seems to possess a distinct personality of its own. A history grows up round about it; memories of the past accumulate and are handed down fresh and green, linking today and seventy years ago as if hardly any lapse of time had intervened. The inmates talk familiarly of the 'comet year,' as if it were but just over; of the days when a load of wheat was worth a little fortune; of the great snows and floods of the previous century. They date events from the year when the Foremeads were purchased and added to the patrimony, as if that transaction, which took place ninety years before, was of such importance that it must necessarily be still known to all the world.

The house has somehow shaped and fitted itself to the character of the dwellers within it: hidden and retired among trees, fresh and green with cherry and pear against the wall, yet the brown thatch and the old bricks subdued in tone by the weather. This individuality extends to the furniture; it is a little stiff and angular, but solid, and there are nooks and corners – as the window-seat – suggestive of placid repose: a strange opposite mixture throughout of flowery peace and silence, with an almost total lack of modern conveniences and appliances of comfort – as though the sinewy vigour of the residents disdained artificial ease.

In the oaken cupboards – not black, but a deep tawny colour with age and frequent polishing – may be found a few pieces of old china, and on the table at tea-time, perhaps, other pieces, which a connoisseur would tremble to see in use, lest a clumsy arm should shatter their fragile antiquity. Though apparently so little valued, you shall not be able to buy these things for money – not so much because their artistic beauty is appreciated, but because of the instinctive clinging to everything old, characteristic of the place and people. These have been there of old time: they shall remain still. Somewhere in the cupboards, too, is a curiously carved piece of iron, to fit into the hand, with a front of steel before the fingers, like a skeleton rapier guard; it is the ancient steel with which, and a flint, the tinder and the sulphur match were ignited.

Up in the lumber-room are carved oaken bedsteads of unknown age; linen presses of black oak with carved panels, and a drawer at the side for the lavender-bags; a rusty rapier, the point broken off; a flintlock pistol, the barrel of portentous length, and the butt weighted with a mace-like knob of metal, wherewith to knock the enemy on the head. An old yeomanry sabre lies about somewhere, which the good man of the time wore when he rode in the troop against the rioters in the days of machine-burning – which was like a civil war in the country, and is yet recollected and talked of. The present farmer, who is getting just a trifle heavy in the saddle himself, can tell you the names of labourers living in the village whose forefathers rose in that insurrection. It is a memory of the house how one of the family paid £40 for a substitute to serve in the wars against the French.

The mistress of the household still bakes a batch of bread at home in the oven once now and then, priding herself that it is never 'dunch' or heavy. She makes all kinds of preserves, and wines too – cowslip, elderberry, ginger – and used to prepare a specially delicate biscuit, the paste being dropped on paper and baked by exposure to the sun's rays only. She has a bitter memory of some money having been lost to the family sixty years ago through roguery, harping upon it as a most direful misfortune: the old folk, even those having a stocking or a teapot well filled with guineas, thought a great deal of small sums. After listening to a tirade of this kind, in the belief that the family were at least half-ruined, it turns out to be all about £100. Her grandmother after marriage travelled home on horseback behind her husband; there had been a sudden flood, and the newly-married couple had to wait for several hours till the waters went down before they could pass. Times are altered now.

Since this family dwelt here, and well within what may be called the household memory, the very races of animals have changed or been supplanted. The cows in the field used to be longhorns, much more hardy, and remaining in the meadows all the winter, with no better shelter than the hedges and bushes afforded. Now the shorthorns have come, and the cattle are housed carefully. The sheep were horned – up in the lumber room two or three horns are still to be found. The pigs were of a different kind, and the dogs and poultry. If the race of men have not changed they have altered their costume; the smock-frock lingered longest, but even that is going.

Some of the old superstitions hung on till quite recently. The value of horses made the arrival of foals an important occasion, and then it was the custom to call in the assistance of an aged man of wisdom – not exactly a wizard, but something approaching it nearly in reputation. Even within the last fifteen years the aid of an ancient like this used to be regularly invoked in this neighbourhood; in some mysterious way his simple presence and goodwill – gained by plentiful liquor – was supposed to be efficacious against accident and loss. The strangeness of the business was in the fact that his patrons were not altogether ignorant or even uneducated – they merely carried on the old custom, not from faith in it, but just because it was the custom. When the wizard at last died nothing more was thought about it. Another ancient used to come round once or twice in the year, with a couple of long ashen staves, and the ceremony performed by him consisted in dancing these two sticks together in a fantastic manner to some old rhyme or story.

The parlour is always full of flowers – the mantel piece and grate in spring quite hidden by fresh green boughs of horse-chestnut in bloom, or with lilac, bluebells, or wild hyacinths; in summer nodding grasses from the meadows, roses, sweet-briar; in the autumn two or three great apples, the finest of the year, put as ornaments among the china, and the corners of the looking-glass decorated with bunches of ripe wheat. A badger's skin lies across the back of the armchair; a fox's head, the sharp white tusks showing, snarls over the doorway; and in glass cases are a couple of stuffed kingfishers, a polecat, a white blackbird, and a diver – rare here – shot in the mere hard by.

On the walls are a couple of old hunting pictures, dusky with age, but the crudity of the colours by no means toned down or their rude contrast moderated: bright scarlet coats, bright white horses, harsh green grass, prim dogs, stiff trees, human figures immovable in tight buckskins; running water hard as glass, the sky fixed, the ground all too small for the grouping, perspective painfully emphasized, so as to be itself made visible; the surface everywhere 'painty' – in brief, most of the possible faults compressed together, and proudly fathered by the artist's name in full.

PART II

COUNTRY
PEOPLE

1

BEGINNING THE DAY
(1976)

Wilson Stephens

From my window in Scotland four human figures meet the eye when, at about seven each morning, I draw the curtain to see what like of a day it is. Two of them are scarecrows. Only after checking their bearings can I be wholly sure which of the four are the neighbouring crofters. Their blocky figures, clad in faded blue boiler suits, may be anywhere about their fields. What is unthinkable is that they will be moving. This is the hour of stillness. Obviously they must move to have left their steadings, and to return again. But to see them doing so is one of Nature's rarest sights.

Willie stands immobilized for a timed twenty minutes after letting out his hens. In that time I bath, shave and dress. He contemplates his flock. His great bronzed hand has not shifted its grip on the feed bucket handle. His brown bald head still lines up with the haycock behind him. Doubtless he moves an inch or so in some direction; but not more. Jamie props his elbows on a dry-stone wall to look his beasts. His ample posterior adds to the landscape a feature best described as rock solid. There he stays while the odours of breakfast coffee waft upwards, and I can look no longer.

Not that I am fool enough to suppose that they waste their time. Each head will be far from empty. Having turned all relevant factors over in his mind, Willie must ken fine which bird is next destined for the pot. Jamie's brain will be full of arithmetic, of which steers are due for mart, and what the margins may be. Both shall surely be right in terms of maximum advantage and minimum disadvantage. Morning is the time to make decisions, and they are best reached in tranquillity. The rest of the day is available for the lesser matter of carrying them out.

Of course the Highlands offer opportunities for tranquillity unexcelled elsewhere. Perhaps this is why the larger world ticked better when statesmen and politicians spent a month or two each year in these parts. A mind made up in the morning calm may well be better so than one bustled about in airports, and limousines to and from No. 10. Mankind in general prefers a slow start to the day and in this differs from womankind. From the moment when women step crisply laundered into public view they perform at full operational efficiency. Not so us men. In me, and apparently in most of us, is a strong element of Willie and Jamie, but with seldom the chance of indulging it to their extreme lengths. Under my own roof far south in Wessex I ask but one thing on waking. It is that nobody, not even my nearest and dearest, shall speak to me for the first hour. Small chance indeed that this should happen. My family have a capacity for sleep (especially after daybreak) which makes a dormouse seem insomniac.

Perhaps there are supermen who in that fresh prime stride purposefully about, getting things done, telephoning people, and in general behaving like women. Not I. With my early tea at hand I sit in peace and cultivate that valuable thing, a complete mental vacuum. In the space thus created constructive thoughts may form. After twenty minutes or so (the Willie and Jamie time-scale) I shower and shave. What more significant moment than that in which the soap is sloshed on in great hot dollops and the day ahead, until now a confused miasma, begins to assume shape, proportion and priorities?

If a day is worth living, or a thing worth doing, it is worth starting slowly so that the best may come of it. That unrivalled occasion for the measurement of self against the everlasting, a day's stalking, exemplifies this. However far the march, no man strides out in the first mile. So give to me, indeed give us all, peace at the start. In worldly terms Willie and Jamie may not have much. But they have this. The great, hot dollops being now dispersed, it is time to check their progress.

Both are now in different places. I bet nobody saw them move. To see a crofter change position before the dew is up is like

waiting for a gecko to cross an Indian ceiling. One becomes aware of it only after it happens. Jamie has come to rest amid his barley stooks. One hand is on a sheaf-top, perhaps crumbling away the awns to judge how many days before they stack. Willie is frozen like Lot's wife, scrutinizing a calf. For his sake, I hope it proves golden.

2

THE PLOUGHMAN
(1969)

Derek Warren

I have been ploughing continuously since last June. All the time. Now it is February and I haven't stopped. I have ploughed every day, Sundays too, for eight months. But it is nearly finished now. There will be a break until after the harvest, then, as soon as a field is cleared, I'll be on it. There are about 400 acres of corn-land and I plough it all. All the fields are different. They have their names and they feel to be different places. It is how it should be. I wouldn't like the village to become a Tannington where the hedges have gone and the ploughman doesn't know where he is. A well-kept hedge is a good sight and tells you where you are. The hedges belong to the village. You get so used to seeing them standing there – they are like buildings and you miss them when they are knocked down. Some hedges are important and when they go you feel as bad as if a wood had been taken away. I think that there are certain hedges which the farmers shouldn't touch without asking the people – although I can't see this happening.

I'm contented here. I haven't got the education for a farm manager's job and I wouldn't like it even if I had. All the same, as things are today you really do want some education whatever you do. But if you haven't got it you must learn contentment. Without education you can pick up plenty of practical experience on the farm, but you'll never grasp the new theory or understand the money. If I had gone to the agricultural college it would all have been different, no doubt. I started off working with the cows when I first left school. I didn't like this. I hoped I was going to be a keeper but it never happened. 'You won't like it,' they said. 'It is seven days a week and a young lad likes his week-ends off.' I don't know why they said this. They knew I had no Sundays, so to speak. I was in working clothes and round the woods of a Sunday, just as of an ordinary day, so I might just as well have been paid for it. You see, keeping is *the* job for a man who has an eye to nature. There will be something different to look at every day and you'll have never seen it all. But there is no keeper in the village now. The last keeper had the double job of forester and keeper. He had to plant trees when he wasn't feeding pheasants. Whether you can really do both these jobs together, I don't know. There wouldn't be much time to think if you did. You'd have to be two men, which one man can't be if he's to stay honest. But there you are, that's modern demands for you! All the same, keeping would have suited me wonderfully.

I started ploughing, with a reversible plough, when I was eighteen. Somebody took me up to Scarlett Hill and said, 'This handle turns this over, this does something else – and away you go!' I kept straight as I could but I don't trouble so much these days. I don't know why. Because of the plough I suppose. With the old plough you had to have everything marked out and the furrows had to be kept straight if you wanted to finish up anywhere at all. The old men criticize. 'That wouldn't have done,' they say. 'You'd have had to have made a better job of it than that when I was a boy – God's truth, you would!' But they forget that they had the labour to do these fine things. There is double the arable in the village and few men wanting to stay and work it, so fancy fine ways aren't needed. The old men will tell you what an interest they took in their tasks – you could call this their main argument. They were brought up on quality work. Now it is quantity work –

you've got to cover the ground. I can plough up two acres of the clay land in a day, and more on a light field.

I am a man on my own. I am not interfered with much. I am on the plough and that is where I keep. I am alone nearly all my work time but I can't say that I feel lonely. Not ever, not at all. People say, 'There's Derek, by himself up on that great old field, turning round, going back . . . he's lonely. He must be lonely!' Not at all – and what is 'lonely'? I am watching the whole time, you see. I might have more than a hundred birds in my wake. It is surprisingly interesting. The gulls are with me. But now and then it's nice to see a face and have a chat. Somebody will come past and speak, and that is good. It makes a break. After all, I'm a man and not a bird! But, honestly, if I knew that I was lonely, I'd pack it up tomorrow.

I think my wife feels she misses something by being in a remote village like this. She used to live in Leiston before we were married and she still misses being able to shut the front door and walk along to the shops and such-like. She says that going to the village shop isn't shopping. She didn't know anybody when she came here and she still misses her friends. But she is settling down. We have a car so she isn't stranded. I hope she is happy here. I like my work and I like the open air. I couldn't be put to work inside. Although I knew a man from this village who went to work in an Ipswich factory after being a gardener here until he was forty-five. He settled down easily. He put his mind to it, you see. I couldn't put my mind to it.

There was a junior branch of the Suffolk Naturalists when I was at the school – this is how I began to take an interest in birds. About fifteen boys joined but the club is disbanded now. They learned a few things but probably the only thing they still keep up is a spot of fishing – if you can call that natural history. As for wild birds, they might pick you out a sparrow or a swallow, but other than this they won't know much. I may be wrong. It is difficult for me to explain to you what all these living creatures mean to me. I can't really say that I study them although I write down anything unusual that I happen to see. It is just that I seem to know where they all live and what they do. The pesticides are having a nasty effect. I mean a bird can adapt itself to most things but it can't adapt itself to poison. Dressed corn is poisoned corn. It must kill. The kestrels are getting scarce. There were always several pairs in the air here when I was a boy. You could always look up and see them hovering about on the wind then. Now you'll be lucky if you see as many as three pairs on the entire estate. Linnets, too, used to be a common sight but I don't recall seeing a linnet for many a year. It is a seed-eater, so you can imagine what has happened to it. The wrens got very scarce after the hard winter [1962–63] but they're recovering. And the hard winter took the kingfishers off the pond, where I'd seen them for six years. They had a nest where the old boathouse used to be – where the stream runs away from the pond and down towards the bottom pasture. I saw one flash there last summer while I was fishing pike. There are new birds up on the old aerodrome – waders and redshanks. They feed in the shallows where they have pulled the concrete runways up. We have had a flock of waxwings on the big cotoneaster up at the Big House, and there are always the martins. Each house seems to have so many people in it and so many martins. You must never bang their mud nests down or make them unwelcome, it is very unlucky. It is thought poor manners to destroy a martin's nest while he is abroad.

A lot of my friends have left the village. Most of the old gang. I am about the only one still here. They've all got jobs away. They got married and their wives took them away. Kelsale, Leiston, Ipswich, they've all gone away.

I don't go to the pub. I haven't been inside the door for six years. It is something you've got to like doing – to go in two or three times a week – I'd have no interest in that. But the young chaps who work with me would sooner go there than anywhere else. I watch television with my wife. I like travellers' tales abroad. The tribes of people faraway.

3

THE VILLAGE BARD
(1890)

Reverend Sabine Baring-Gould

How completely the itinerant singer of ballads and teller of folk tales has disappeared – driven from the houses of the gentle, because the young people have books now, and amuse themselves with them, and he lingers on only in the ale-houses; such men are few and far between, feeble old men, who can now hardly obtain a hearing for their quaint stories, and whose minor melodies are voted intolerable by young ears, disciplined only to appreciate music-hall inanities. There are still a few of these men about, and as I have taken a good deal of pains to get into their confidence, and collect from them the remains – there exist only remains – of their stories, musical and poetical, I am able to give an account of them which ought to interest, for the old village bard or song-man is rapidly becoming as extinct as the dodo and the great auk.

The village bard or song-man is the descendant of the minstrel. Now the minstrels were put down by Act of Parliament in 1597, and were to be dealt with by the magistrates with severity as rogues and vagabonds. That sealed the doom of the old ballad. All such as were produced later are tame and flat in comparison with the genuine songs of the old times, and can at best be regarded only as modern imitations. The press has preserved in broadsides a good number of ballads, and *The Complete Dancing Master* and other collections have saved a good number of the old tunes from being irrevocably lost. But by no means all were thus preserved; a great many more continued to be sung by our peasantry, and I quite believe the old men when they say that at one time they knew some one hundred and fifty to two hundred distinct songs and melodies; their memories were really extra-ordinary. But then they could neither read nor write, and the faculty of remembering was developed in them to a remarkable extent. I have heard of two of these men meeting to sing against each other for a wager. They began at sunset; one started a ballad, sang it through, then his opponent sang one, and so on. The object was to ascertain which knew most. The sun rose on them, and neither had come to an end of his store, so the stakes were drawn.

Very few of the songs of the Restoration have lingered on in the memory of our minstrels, if ever they were taken into their store. Many of the songs of that period were set to tunes that have passed on from generation to generation, up to the present age, when they are all being neglected, for wretched, vulgar songs, without fun and without melody. The ballad especially is death-smitten. Folks nowadays lack patience, and will not endure a song that is not finished in three minutes. The old ballad was a folk tale run into jingling rhyme, and sung to a traditional air; it is often very long. One I have recovered, 'The Gipsy Countess,' runs through over twenty verses. The very popular 'Saddle to Rags' runs through some twenty-two, 'Lord Bateman' has about fifty and 'Arthur of Bradley' has hardly any end to it. A ballad cannot be pared down greatly, as that destroys the story, which is set to verse to be told leisurely, with great variety of expression.

When I was a boy I was wont to ride about my native county, putting up at little village inns for the night, and there I often came in for gatherings where the local song-man entertained the company. Unfortunately I did not make any collection at the time, though snatches of the songs and wafts of the strains lingered in my head. I dare say that there are still singers of ballads in other parts of England, but my researches have been confined to the West. Somerset had its own type of songs with peculiar cadences, and Devon and Cornwall were rich to overflow in melodies. Wherever I go in quest of a song-man, I hear the same story. 'Ah! there was old So-and-so, eighty years of age, died last winter of bronchitis, he was a singer and no mistake.' They have been struck down, those old men, and therefore we must prize the more those that are left.

Anciently – well, not so very anciently either, for it was within my memory – almost every parish had its bard, a man generally the descendant of a still more famous father, who was himself but the legatee of a race of song-men. This village bard had his memory stored with traditional melodies and songs and ballads, committed to him as a valuable deposit by his father, wedded to well-known ancient airs, and the country singer not only turned from the affectation of the new melodies, but with jealous tenacity clung to the familiar words. Words became so wedded to airs that the minstrels, and their hearers and imitators, could not endure to have them dissociated.

I had an instance of this three winters ago, when, at a village concert, I sang an old ballad, 'The Sun was Set behind the Hill,' set by a friend to a melody he had composed for it. A very old labourer who was present began to grumble. 'He's gotten the words right, but he's not got the right tune. He should zing 'un right or not at all,' and he got up and left the room in disdain.

The village minstrel did certainly compose some of the

melodies he sang, generally to a new ballad, or song that was acquired from a broadside, or to one he had himself made. This the old men have distinctly assured me of. They did not all, or a large number of them did not, pretend to the faculty of musical composition, but they have named to me men so gifted, and have told me of melodies they composed. There was, and is, a black-smith in a remote village in Devon who is reported to be able to play any musical instrument put into his hands, at all events after a little trial of its peculiarities. He is said to be able to set any copy of verses offered him to original melodies.

Davey, the writer of 'Will Watch' and other pleasant songs of the Dibdin period and character, was a Devonshire blacksmith. But, as already hinted, these men also composed verses. There was such a one, a village poet in the parish in which I lived as a child. His story was curious. He had bought his wife in Okehampton market for half-a-crown. Her husband, weary of her temper and tongue, brought her to the 'Gigglet' fair with a rope round her neck, and the minstrel had the hardihood to buy her. I know that it has often been charged by foreigners on English people that they sell their wives thus, but this was a fact. The woman was so sold, and so bought; the buyer and seller quite believed that the transaction was legal. She lived with the purchaser till her death, and a very clean, decent, hard-working woman she was. She had, indeed, a tongue; but when she began to let it wag, then the minstrel clapped his hands to his ears, ran out of the house, and betook himself to the ale-house, where he was always welcome, and from which he did not himself return, but was conveyed home – in a wheelbarrow. This man regarded himself as the poet of the place, and nothing of import-ance took place in my grandfather's family without his coming to the house to sing a copy of verses he had composed on the occasion. Many a good laugh was had over Jim's verses, which, like those of Orlando, 'had in them more feet than the verses would bear; and the feet were lame, and could not bear them-selves without the verse.'

One very odd feature, by the way, of these singers is the manner in which they manufacture syllables where the verse halts. Thus when 'gold-en' comes in place of two trochees, they convert it into 'guddle-old-en'; even, when the line is still more halting, into 'guddle-uddle-old-en.' In like manner 'soul' or 'tree' is turned into 'suddle-ole' or 'tur-rur-ree.'

There was another village poet who flourished in the same epoch as the Jim cited above. His name was Rab Downe. He had a remarkable facility for running off impromptu verses. On one occasion at a wrestling match, he began swinging himself from foot to foot, and to a chant – these fellows always sing their verses – described the match as it went on before him, versifying all the turns and incidents of the struggle, throwing in words relative to the onlookers, their names and complementary expletives. No doubt that much of the compositions of these men was mere doggerel, but it was not always so. In their songs gleam out here and there a poetic or, at all events, a fresh and quaint thought. What is always difficult to ascertain is what is original and what traditional, for when they do pretend to originality they often import into their verses whole passages from ancient ballads.

4

THE THATCHER
(1969)

Ernie Bowers

I started thatching along with my dad at the age of fourteen. This would be round about 1929. My dad had been a thatcher ever since his boyhood. He left school when he was eleven and went along with the local thatcher and he picked the trade up off him. There was a great lot of thatching in those days, you can be sure. And there was plenty of straw to do it with, although straw is rare stuff now.

A thatcher then would have two boys to help through the summer-time but after October he'd just have the one. The other was stood off and had to fend for himself until the summer came round again. That is how it was. In those days it was seasonal work for some. There would be plenty of rick-thatching then, of course. The farmer would come along and say, 'We've got a couple of ricks want doing. You be along early.' And we were along early, I can tell you – five o'clock most likely. And we'd have done two ricks by midday. Then we would go back to our building job.

I was nineteen when I started on my own. My dad said, 'Well, son, it's up to you now.' It was our parting. That was all he said. I had two boys like the others and I was out on my own. That is how we worked it. The farmers didn't let the farm labourers do the thatching, they always came to us. It was different in Norfolk,

where they'd let anybody do a stack. But in East Suffolk it was a special job and my father and myself, working apart with our two boys each, would thatch anything up to 600 ricks a year. We charged according to the size of the rick. Some ricks would be 9 yards long by 5 yards wide, some would be 10 by 11, some 12 by 6 and some 13 by 7. When the rick thatching season was on you would go round and measure your work up and make out your accounts.

Every parish had its own thatcher in the 1920s. But in the 1930s things changed. Most of the good thatchers were getting on the old side and beginning to drop out. I can remember five or six thatchers of the old school dying then. Nobody replaced them. They were men of the old time – of the old life. They didn't teach their craft to apprentices, they would just pick up the odd man who was walking around on the dole and ask him to give them

a hand. They wouldn't teach this man anything. It was a bad
time and people were losing heart, I suppose. There wasn't the
money about and everything was terrible. Those who didn't see it
couldn't believe it. I would be cycling more than fifteen miles to
do a job, and in all weathers. There was skimping on the food.
We didn't have anything and we couldn't get anything. It was
impossible. People have quite forgotten what it was like not to be
able to get things. I spent 1s 6d a week on my pleasures and gave
everything else to Mother. But I got to know the things about the
thatching trade which only the old men knew. I can remember
the first house I thatched on my own and the first rick. I did the
rick alone because my dad fell ill. I was seventeen and it was a
stack of reeds at the Church Farm, Campsey Ash. The reeds had
been cut and brought up from Alde river at Snape. Thatching
reeds is a painful job and plays merry hell with your hands. They
were thatched at Campsey to keep them dry until they could be
used to mend the barn roof. Reeds are like everything else, you
just can't cut them and lay them in a heap and leave them. They
have to be cared for. We like reeds which grow in brackish water
best. We like them to grow in the brack caused by the salt tides
meeting the river waters every twelve hours. They're pickled a bit,
I suppose.

I never worked on a farm and was glad of it. I was my own man.
The farmers round here treated their men shameful before the
war and none of us forgets this. I've seen a lad only two minutes
late who'd be told to 'take the rest of the day off and come back
in the morning.' They had to be so careful. There was always
somebody waiting at the gate to take their place. I wasn't on the
farm but I saw it all. And now it's, 'Oh dear, oh dear, the poor old
farmer! He can't afford nothing but he has a new car every year.
Oh dear, oh dear!'

Thatching was very cheap when I was young. Labour was
cheap, everything was cheap. My father would re-lay a 10-foot
square of roof for £1 and think that he was earning money!
Today, a job like that would cost £30 and to thatch the roof of an
ordinary cottage will cost between £400 and £500. But you must
remember that you are getting a sixty-year roof – a marvellous,
beautiful roof, warm in winter, cool in summer – for this price.
There is nothing like it. A thatch is windproof, frost-proof and
good to look at. I cock my eye up at thatches I did twenty years
past and watch them getting better and better. I strip right down
to the rafters before I start – although some won't. They'll pile on
and pile on. Eventually, like too much sewing of a pair of shoes
which brings a pulling away from the welt, that thatch begins to

slip off. We did a job at Bacton last year where so much straw had been piled on to the roof over the years that it just fell into the house and the owner had to put a complete new roof on. Most of the old houses still have their original rafters. All of oak, they are and very, very old.

I make a roof thatch 14 inches thick, whether it is straw or reed. The reeds are driven into position with a legget, which is a flat piece of board covered with horseshoe nails and set on a handle at an angle. Cruel work, it is. You start at the bottom of the roof and move upwards till you reach the crown, driving the bundles of reeds into position and fastening them to hazel rods which you cut in the woods during the winter. We use hazel because it is the best splitting wood there is and the best to get a point on. Then comes the pattern. We all have our own pattern; it is our signature, you might say. A thatcher can look at a roof and tell you who thatched it by the pattern.

There used to be special patterns and decorations for the stacks years ago, particularly the round stacks. There were three kinds of stacks, the round, the boat-shaped and the gable-end, and the stack-yard was a nice place, I can tell you – very handsome. They were a way of decorating the village when the harvest was over and great pride went into putting them up. They were set where they could be seen from the farmhouse and from the road, so that they could be looked at and enjoyed. My dad always set a great sheaf of fine ears at the top of his round stacks and very nice they looked.

I work as we used to work. I stop thatching about the middle of December and spend the winter bushing-up. These are the four months when I'm not earning a halfpenny. Just collecting material. I have to search for wheat and rye straw from farms where they aren't using a combine. Thatching straw must be drum-thrashed and barley and oat straw is no use at all. I have to search the woods for hazel branches and cut them into lengths and cut the reeds from the marshes. This is the only cut you make on the reed, the one cut when you take it from the river. Thatching is very popular now and I am teaching the craft to my brother's son, who is eighteen. He'll carry on. I shall have to teach one of my boys too.

I get up at half past five of a morning. I work many hours. I get tired, but I will be all right, I suppose. There are all these great boys in the house – they keep you lively. But you can't get into conversation with a young person as you could years ago. They just haven't got the interest. They don't want our kind of talk. They're all strangers – all strangers.

5

THE SHEPHERD
(1879)

Richard Jefferies

The shepherd has a distinct individuality, and is generally a much more observant man in his own sphere than the ordinary labourer. He knows every single field in the whole parish, what kind of weather best suits its soil, and can tell you without going within sight of a given farm pretty much what condition it will be found in. Knowledge of this character may seem trivial to those whose days are passed indoors; yet it is something to recollect all the endless fields in several square miles of country. As a student remembers for years the type and paper, the breadth of the margin – can see, as it were, before his eyes the bevel of the binding and hear again the rustle of the stiff leaves of some tall volume which he found in a forgotten corner of a library, and bent over with such delight, heedless of dust and 'silver-fish' and the gathered odour of years – so the shepherd recalls *his* books, the fields; for he, in the nature of things, has to linger over them

and study every letter: sheep are slow. When the hedges are
grubbed and the grass grows where the hawthorn flowered, still
the shepherd can point out to you where the trees stood – here
an oak and here an ash. On the hills he has often little to do but
ponder deeply sitting on the turf of the slope, while the sheep
graze in the hollow, waiting for hours as they eat their way.
Therefore by degrees a habit of observation grows upon him –
always in reference to his charge; and if he walks across the parish
off duty he still cannot choose but notice how the crops are
coming on, and where there is most 'keep.' The shepherd has
been the last of all to abandon the old custom of long service.
While the labourers are restless, there may still be found not a few
instances of shepherds whose whole lives have been spent upon
one farm. Thus, from the habit of observation and the lapse of
years, they often become local authorities; and when a dispute
of boundaries or water rights or right of way arises, the question is
frequently finally decided by the evidence of such a man.

6

THE UMBRELLA MAN
(1909)

Edward Thomas

A beggar is a rich man on some of these August days, especially
one I know, whom I first met some Augusts ago now. A fine
Sunday afternoon had sprinkled the quiet and thinly-peopled
land with black-dressed men and white-dressed women, the older
married couples and their trains of children keeping chiefly to the
roads and most straightforward paths, the younger, with one
child or none, choosing rather the green lanes, while the lovers
and the boys found out tall hedge-sides and the footpaths across
which more than one year's growth of hazel had spread, so that
the shortest of the maids must stoop. Many showers following a
dry season made miles of the country as clean and fragrant as a
garden. Honeysuckle and privet were in every hedge with flowers
that bring a thrill of summer bridals on their scent. The brisk
wind was thymy from the Downs. The ragwort was in its glory; it
rose tall as a man in one straight leap of dark-foliaged stem, and
then crowned itself in the boldest and most splendid yellows

derived from a dark golden disc and almost lemon rays; it was as if Apollo had come down to keep the flocks of a farmer on these chalk hills and his pomp had followed him out of the sky. A few birds still sang; one lark now and then, a cirl-bunting among the topmost haws of a thorn, chiffchaffs in the bittersweet and hazel of the little copses.

There was apparently comfort, abundance and quiet every-where. They were seen in the rickyards where grand haystacks, newly thatched, stood around ancient walnut trees. Even the beeches had a decorous look in their smooth boles and perfect lavish foliage. The little patches of flowery turf by the roadside and at corners were brighter and warmer than ever, as the black bees and the tawny skipper butterflies flew from bloom to bloom of the crimson knapweed. Amplest and most unctuous of all in their expression of the ceremonious leisure of the day and the maturity of the season were the cart-horses. They leaned their large heads benignly over the rails or gates; their roan or chestnut flanks were firm and polished; manes, tails and fetlocks spotless; now and then they lifted up their feet and pressed their toes into the ground, showing their enormous shoes that shone and were of girth sufficient to make a girdle for the lightest of the maids passing by.

Sunday with not too strict a rod of black and white ruled the land and made it all but tedious except in the longest of the green lanes, which dipped steeply under oaks to a brook muffled in leaves and rose steeply again, a track so wet in spring – and full of the modest golden green of saxifrage flowers – that only the hottest Sunday ever saw it disturbed except by carter and horses. In a hundred yards the oak-hidden windings gave the traveller a feeling of reclusion as if he were coiled in a spool; very soon a feeling of possession ripened into one of armed tyranny if another's steps clattered on the stones above. Sometimes in a goodly garden a straight alley of shadows leads away from the bright frequented borders to – we know not quite whither, and perhaps, too much delighted with half-sad reverie, never learn, smother even the guesses of fancy, lest they should bring some old unpleasant truth in their train; but if fancy will thread the alley and pass the last of the shadows it is into some such lane as this that it would gladly emerge, to come at last upon the pure wild. It seemed that I had come upon the pure wild in this lane, for in a bay of turf alongside the track, just large enough for a hut and thickly sheltered by an oak, though the south-west sun crept in, was a camp. Under the oak and at the edge of the tangled bramble and brier and bracken was a low purple light from those

111

woodside flowers, self-heal and wood-betony. A perambulator with a cabbage in it stood at one corner; leaning against it was an ebony-handled umbrella and two or three umbrella-frames; underneath it an old postman's bag containing a hammer and other tools. Close by stood half a loaf on a newspaper, several bottles of bright water, a black pot of potatoes ready for boiling, a tin of water steaming against a small fire of hazel twigs. Out on the sunny grass two shirts were drying. In the midst was the proprietor, his name revealed in fresh chalk on the side of his perambulator: 'John Clark, Hampshire.'

He had spent his last pence on potatoes and had been given the cabbage. No one would give him work on a Sunday. He had no home, no relations. Being deaf, he did not look for company. So he stood up, to get dry and to think, think, think, his hands on his hips, while he puffed at an empty pipe. During his meditation a snail had crawled half-way up his trousers, and was now all but down again. He was of middle height and build, the crookedest of men, yet upright, like a branch of oak which comes straight with all its twistings. His head was small and round, almost covered by bristly grey hair like lichen, through which peered quiet blue eyes; the face was irregular, almost shapeless, like dough being kneaded, worn by travel, passion, pain, and not a few blows; where the skin was visible at all through the hair it was like red sandstone; his teeth were white and strong and short like a dog's. His rough neck descended into a striped half-open shirt, to which was added a loose black waistcoat divided into thin perpendicular stripes by ribs of faded gold; his trousers, loose and patched and short, approached the colour of a hen pheasant; his bare feet were partly hidden by old black boots. His voice was hoarse and, for one of his enduring look, surprisingly small, and produced with an effort and a slight jerk of the head.

He was a Sussex man, born in the year 1831, on June the twenty-first (it seemed a foppery in him to remember the day, and it was impossible to imagine with what ceremony he had remembered it year by year, during half a century or near it, on the roads of Sussex, Kent, Surrey and Hampshire). His mother was a Wild – there were several of them buried not far away under the carved double-headed tombstones by the old church with the lancet windows and the four yews. He was a labourer's son, and he had already had a long life of hoeing and reaping and fagging when he enlisted at Chatham. He had kept his musket bright, slept hard and wet, and starved on 13d a day, moving from camp to camp every two years. He had lost his youth in battle, for a bullet went through his knee; he lay four months in hospital, and they took eighteen pieces of bone out of his wound – he was still indignant because he was described as only 'slightly wounded' when he was discharged after a 'short service' of thirteen years. He showed his gnarled knee to explain his crookedness. Little he could tell of the battle except the sobbing of the soldier next to him – 'a London chap from Haggerston way. Lord! he called for his mother and his God and me to save him, and the noise he made was worse than the firing and the groaning of the horses, and I was just thinking how I could stop his mouth for him when a bullet hits me, and down I goes like a baby.'

He had been on the road forty years. For a short time after his discharge he worked on the land and lived in a cottage with his wife and one child. The church bells were beginning to ring, and I asked him if he was going to church. At first he said nothing, but looked down at his striped waistcoat and patched trousers; then, with a quick violent gesture of scorn, he lifted up his head and even threw it back before he spoke. 'Besides,' he said, 'I remember how it was my little girl died. My little girl, says I, but she would have been a big handsome woman now, forty-eight years old on the first of May that is gone. She was lying in bed with a little bit of a cough, and she was gone as white as a lily, and I went in to her when I came home from reaping. I saw she looked bad and quiet-like – like a fish in a hedge – and something came over me, and I caught hold of both her hands in both of mine and held them tight, and put my head close up to hers and said, "Now look here, Polly, you've got to get well. Your mother and me can't stand losing you. And you aren't meant to die; such a one as you be for a lark." And I squeezed her little hands, and all my nature seemed to rise up and try to make her get well. Polly she looked whiter than ever and afraid; I suppose I was a bit rough and dirty and sunburnt, for 'twas a hot harvest and 'twas the end of the second week of it, and I was that fierce I felt I ought to have had my way. All that night I thought I had done a wrong thing trying to keep her from dying that way, and I tell you I cried in case I had done any harm by it. That very night she died without our knowing it. She was a bonny maid, that fond of flowers. The night she was taken ill she was coming home with me from the Thirteen Acre, where I'd been hoeing the mangolds, and she had picked a rose for her mother. All of a sudden she looks at it and says, "It's gone, it's broke, it's gone, it's gone, gone, gone," and she kept on, "It's broke, it's gone, it's gone," and when she got home she ran up to her mother, crying, "The wild rose is broke, mother; broke, gone, gone," she says, just like that,' said the old man, in a high finical voice more like that of a bird than a child.

'Then my old woman – well, she was only a bit of a wench too; seventeen when we were married – she took ill and died within a week after. There was a purpose in it. It was then the end of harvest. I spent all my wages down at the Fighting Cocks, and then I set out to walk to Mildenhall in Wiltshire, where my wife came from. On the way I met a chap I had quarrelled with in Egypt, and he says to me. "Hullo, Scrammy-handed Jack," with a sort of look, and I, not thinking what I did, I set about him, and before I knew it he was lying there as might be dead, and I went and gave myself up, and I don't mind saying that I wished I might be hanged for it. However, I did six months. That was how I came to be in the umbrella line. I took up with a chap who did a bit of tinkering and umbrella-mending and grinding in the roving way, and a job of hoeing or mowing now and then. He died not so very long after in the year of the siege of Paris, and I have been alone ever since. Nor I haven't been to church since, any more than a blackbird would go and perch on the shoulder of one of those ladies with feathers and wings and a bit of fox in their hats.'

Labourer, soldier, labourer, tinker, umbrella man, he had always wandered, and knew the South Country between Fording-bridge and Dover as a man knows his garden. Every village, almost every farmhouse, especially if there were hops on the land, he knew, and could see with his blue eyes as he remembered them and spoke their names. I never met a man who knew England as he did. As he talked of places his eyes were alight and turned in their direction, and his arm stretched out to point, moving as he went through his itinerary, so that verily, wherever he was, he seemed to carry in his head the relative positions of all the other places where he had laboured and drunk and lit his solitary fire.

'Was you ever at H——?' he said, pointing to the Downs, through which he seemed to see H—— itself. 'General ——, that commanded us, lived there. He died there three years ago at the age of eighty-eight, and till he died I was always sure of a half-crown if I called there on a Christmas Eve, as I generally managed to do.' Of any place mentioned he could presently remember something significant – the words of a farmer, a song, a sign-board, a wonderful crop, the good ale, the fact that forty-nine years ago the squire used to go to church in a smock frock.

All the time his face was moved with free and broad expressions as he thought and remembered, like an animal's face. Living alone and never having to fit himself into human society, he had not learned to keep his face in a vice. He was returning – if the grave was not too near at the age of seventy-seven – to a primeval wildness and simplicity. It was a pleasure to see him smoke – to note how it eased his chest – to see him spit and be the better for it. The outdoor life had brought him rheumatism, but a clear brain also and a wild purity, a physical cleanliness too, and it was like being with a well-kept horse to stand beside him; and this his house was full of the scent of the bracken growing under the oaks. Earth had not been a kind but a stern mother, like some brawny full-bosomed housewife with many children, who spends all her long days baking and washing, and making clothes, and tending the sick one, and cutting bread and pouring out tea, and cuffing one and cuddling another and listening to one's tale, and hushing their unanimous chatter with a shout or a bang of her enormous elbow on the table. The blows of such a one are shrewd, but they are not as the sweetness of her nursing voice for enduring in the memory of bearded men and many-childed women.

Once or twice again I met him in later summers near the same place. The last time he had been in the infirmary, and was much older. His fire was under the dense shelf of a spruce bough in a green deserted road worn deep in the chalk, blocked at both ends, and trodden by few mortal feet. Only a few yards away, under another spruce, lay a most ancient sheep who had apparently been turned into the lane to browse at peace. She was lame in one leg, and often fed as she knelt. Her head was dark grey and wise, her eyes pearly green and iridescent with an oblong pupil of blackish-blue, quiet, yet full of fear; her wool was dense but short and of a cinder grey; her dark horny feet were overgrown from lack of use. She would not budge even when a dog sniffed at her, but only bowed her head and threatened vainly to butt. She was huge and heavy and content, though always all alone. As she lay there, her wool glistening with rain, I had often wondered what those eyes were aware of, what part she played in the summer harmonies of night and day, the full night heavens and cloudless noon, storm and dawn, and the long moist heat of dewy morn-ings. She was now shorn, and the old man watched her as he drank the liquor in which a cabbage and a piece of bacon had been boiled. 'I often thinks,' he said, 'that I be something like that sheep ... "slightly wounded" ... but not "short service" now ... haha! left alone in this here lane to browse a bit while the weather's fine and folks are kind. But I don't know but what she is better off. Look there,' he said, pointing to a wound which the shearer had made in one of her nipples, where flies clustered like a hideous flower of crape, 'I have been spending this hour and more flicking the flies off her. Nobody won't do that for me – unless I come in for five shillings a week old age pension. But I reckon that won't be for a roving body like me without a letter-box.' In the neighbouring field a cart-horse shook herself with a noise of far-off thunder and laughed shrilly and threw up her heels and raced along the hedge. A bee could be seen going in and out of the transparent white flowers of convolvulus. The horse had her youth and strength and a workless day before her; the bee its business, in which was its life, among sunbeams and flowers; and they were glad. The old man smacked his lips as he drained the salty broth, tried three times to light his empty pipe and then knocked out the ashes and spat vigorously, and took a turn up the lane alone in the scent of the bracken.

7

THE HERBALIST
(1910)

Dion Clayton Calthrop

'About this garden of yours, Mr Noakes?' I asked.

He tapped his wooden box and said, 'If you want to know, I'm a herbalist. You can scarcely call me a civilized being, except on occasions when I do go among my fellow men to winter.' He pulled a cap and a pair of gloves out of his pocket. 'My titles to respectability,' he said.

'And in the Spring?'

'I take to the road with the coltsfoot and the butterburrs. I come out with the first violet, and the pussy cat willow. I wander, all through the year, up and down the length and breadth of England, with my box of herbs. I get my bread and cheese that way, while you draw for pleasure.'

'Partly.'

'It must be for pleasure, or you wouldn't take so much pains. I suppose you think I'm a very disgraceful person, a bad citizen, a worse patriot. But I know the news of the world better than those who read newspapers. Although I trade on superstitions, I do no harm.'

'Do you sell your herbs?'

'Colchicum for gout – autumn crocus, you know it,' he replied. 'Willow-bark quinine; violet distilled, for coughs. Not a bad trade – besides, it keeps me free.'

I hazarded a question. 'Tell me – you must observe these things – do swifts drink as they fly? It has often puzzled me.'

'I don't know,' said he. 'Ask Mother Nature. Some of these things are the province of professors. I'm not a learned man; just a herbalist.'

At that moment a thrush began to sing in a tree overhead. My friend cocked his head, just like an animal.

'There's the wise thrush,' he quoted softly. 'He sings his song twice over.'

'So you read Browning,' I said.

'I have a garret and a library,' he said. 'Winter quarters. We shall meet one day, and you'll be surprised. I actually possess two dress suits. It's a mad world.' He stopped abruptly to listen to the thrush. 'This is better than the Carlton or Delmonico's, anyhow!'

'What do you do?' I asked. 'Go from village to village selling herbs?'

'That's about it. Lord! Listen to that bird. I heard and saw a nightingale sing once in a shaw near Ewelme. I think a thrush is the better musician, though. Yes, I sell my herbs, all sorts and kinds. Drugs and ointments, very simple I assure you. Hemlock and poppy to cure the toothache. Wood sorrel – full of oxalic acid,

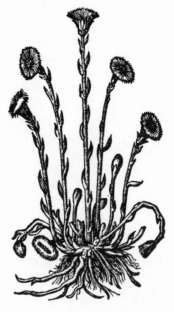

you know, like rhubarb – for fevers. Aconite for rheumatics – very popular medicine I make of that, sells like hot cakes in water meadow land, so does agrimony for fen ague. Tansy and camomile for liver – excellent. Hellebore for blisters, and cowslip pips for measles – I'm a regular quack, you see.'

'And it's worth doing, is it?'

He leaned back, his pipe between his lips, a very contented man. 'Worth doing!' he said. 'Worth owning England, with all the wonderful mornings, and the clean air; worth waking up to the scent of violets; worth lying on your back near a bean field on a summer day; worth seeing the bracken fronds uncurl; watching kingfishers; worth having the fields and hedgerows for a garden, full of flowers always – I should think so. I earn my bread, and I'm happy, far happier than most men.'

8

THE GAMEKEEPER
(1907)

Walter Raymond

A tall, upright man, and as tough as the ground-ash stick he carries in his hand. The light activity of early manhood he has lost. He no longer vaults the gate into the wood, but no youth of twenty could walk down the ride with a springier step. I have never seen him indoors. I picture him only in the open air, with the sky above his head and the turf on the mossy woodland glade beneath his feet. Even within the walls of his thatched cottage, close by the larch plantation, he would seem like a bird in a cage. And to be sure, from sunrise to evening he is rarely there, and sometimes not at night. He is a head-keeper, but not on one of the great estates. He was born in that cottage, and played in infancy on the plot where the spaniels and the great wavy-coated retriever are chained and set up such a chorus of barking when a stranger comes to the door. His father lived there and was keeper before him; and Jack, the youngest of a long family of sons, stayed at home, and in the end took his place. So from boyhood every nook of every field and spinney of the domain has been familiar to him. He knows them all by heart, and the ways of every living thing that inhabits them. Like them also, he has grown into harmony

118

with his environment; and as, in his grey-green jacket with the dull metal buttons, he passes along the hedgerows or through the wood, whether the hazel be in leaf or bare, he imperceptibly melts into the landscape.

I have been many a walk with John Beale. I have strolled with him in summer where the coops, on some heathy slope beside the wood, stand together yet apart, like villa residences at a health resort; and tramped around the boundary late in fall, when pheasants steal away after the ripe blackberries and falling acorns; and along the winter gutters of an early morning when snipe are in the meadows. I have heard him marshalling his beaters into line with a peremptory 'Hold back here,' 'Keep up there on the left,' amongst the rabbit-bitten dogwood and foot-ensnaring briers of the coppice. My heart has gladdened at his shout away over the broad stubble: 'Mark!' before the driven coveys came like a whirlwind over the hedge. But best of all I like to go upon his beat about nesting time, when full-blown primroses are fading and bluebells grow in strips and patches under the trees; when but for the stoat, the egg-stealing hedge-hog and rat, with now and then a jay or a sparrow-hawk, young life is to be fostered and slaughter has ceased.

John Beale, either by habit or nature, is reserved; but then he will talk. Then it is easy to recognize that, if born at the Hall instead of the cottage, he might have been as brave a soldier or as subtle a diplomatist as any squire's son. He speaks in a low voice, and all his utterances sound confidential. But, indeed, some of them are not to be repeated with time and place. The keynote of his character is a respect for 'rights' and a determination to defend them. As he talks of trespassers or other lawbreakers and offenders, his brows contract into a frown, begotten partly from habit of constant observation in the open air. When he has had his say, his mouth shuts like a steel trap, with an air of 'That's my opinion and I hold to it.'

Of one thing he is quite certain. He is not an arbitrary man. 'No,' said he one day, 'I see no need to tell all. 'Tis wiser much to use your judgment and sometimes to keep a still tongue. You see the little homestead away there on the hill. I stood on this very spot one afternoon, and the farmer's son, a sort of hobbledehoy fellar, took a pop over the hedge and knocked down two birds. He picked 'em up, clapped 'em in his pocket, and was back out o' sight again in half a minute. He could get home before I could meet with him. But I had a glass in my pocket. So I stopped where I was and watched the house. My gentleman went through the gate, climbed up on the wagon-shaft, and hid the birds on the rafter of the shed. Then I knew all about it.'

He stood in the ride and smiled.

'You knew he would leave them there until evening?' I asked.

'I knew he was acting on his own. If the old people had known his game he would have gone straight indoors as proud as a turkey-cock. So I walked straight down. He and his father stood there talking together, jus' by the poundhouse door. So I taxed the boy with the shooting, straight out. He swore I must ha' made a mistake, and his father took his part, too. But he didn't know how much I had seen, till I catched un hold by the elbow an' led un round an' pulled the birds off o' the beam. His father was in a terrible way. I said, "What right have you got to kill birds?" I said, "What right would you have anywhere without a certificate?" That lad turned so white as a ghost. He saw himself. There, his father was really a'most in tears. Now I'm paid to catch poachers. What did I ought to ha' done?'

He asked the question with deep seriousness, and a perception that he was propounding a very difficult ethical problem. I also perceived the whole matter as between Justice and Mercy to be involved in it.

'Well, now, I don't mind telling you, I held my tongue. Many a man would have told to prove his sharpness. But the lad got rid o' the gun and promised, and I let it pass. He's grown up now, and got the farm, and a very hard-working man. You see that was no real poacher. You don't want ill-will on a place. I tell you a wise keeper doesn't quarrel with good tenants. Give a young chap o' that class one chance, I say. I'm not a arbitrary man. I never was. But if a man won't heed, drop on him stiff. Drop on him all you can. That's what I say.'

We strolled onwards down the slope and through the cover. Sometimes he turned to glance at a vermin trap. Now and again, where the coppice had been cut, we looked at a pheasant's nest beneath the sprawling brambles or under the shelter of a fallen limb and counted the olive-brown eggs. . . .

We came to the edge of the wood, and he stood back out of sight and looked across the landscape.

'A man to be a keeper must have it in him to observe. Did you see that pigeon come out of the clump of firs beyond the lake? She came out in a hurry off her nest. 'Tis near a road, and the children creep in to pick flowers or to search for nests. The man that side must look round an' hunt 'em out. No; they can't do much harm, but they've got no right in there. In winter the pigeons drop in to roost in those trees. They come in twos and threes and circle round and then settle in. I was standing here last

December, and I saw one after another take a couple of turns and then make off. Somehow or other I guessed what was up. I nipped down, and came upon a couple of fellars a-ferreting. They bunked off. But I knew who they were. Cost 'em £2 a-piece. But la! they'll be here again next winter. There's no cure for a drunkard or a poacher – that's my opinion. And I'm not an arbitrary man.'

'I suppose if they know a place to be well watched they go elsewhere.'

'I'll tell you a tale about being frightened,' laughed John Beale. 'A funny thing happened down to that lake, years ago. I caught a young carter putting down a rat-gin for an eel. I had my doubts about that chap before. I could scarce keep a sober face, but I did. He had got the trap under water, tilled with a dead gudgeon, and made fast with a bit o' cord. I put on a fiercish look and I said, "What right have you got at this?" I said. "You'll hear more o' this matter." That was true enough, though I only meant a lesson, and no harm to the chap. For, though I say it myself, I'm not a arbitrary man. But he served seven years for that.'

'Seven years! For putting down a rat-trap to catch an eel? Why he ought to have had a medal for the originality of the idea.'

'Well, I suppose I did speak a bit sharp. But it frightened him and no mistake. In the night he ran off and enlisted. So I always said he served seven year for that. However, no harm was done. He stayed on, and he's a full sergeant now on the road for a pension.'

'And what about these thorough incurable poachers? They're a crafty lot, are they not?' said I.

John Beale tucked the ground-ash stick firmly under his arm and looked up at the sky. 'What I do know about poachers and their tricks and ways I tell no man,' replied he with a laugh. 'But least of all one who might set it down in print.'

9

THE FARM LAD
(c1830)

William Cobbett

WANTED

I want a young man from 16 to 18 years of age, as a sort of *farming* and *gardening* and *nursery-work* APPRENTICE. The case is this: my farm is taken care of by my only surviving brother, who has been either gardener or farmer all his life time, and who, though he is only thirteen months older than I am, is not able to move about so quickly, from place to place, as is necessary in a concern like mine; nor is it proper that he should be exposed to wet and cold so much as is absolutely necessary to the due looking after of ten or a dozen men. He has, from the fruit of his own labour, raised a family of ten able and good children, who have already brought him about a score of grand-children. I know that he began to work *hard* more than *fifty* years ago; and verily I believe him to have done more hard work than any man now living in

England. While his limbs feel the consequences of this, his experience and skill remain; and I want a young man, or lad, of the age above mentioned, to supply *legs*, which my brother cannot move so nimbly as the case requires.

He is not wanted to *work much*; but, if he learn to do every thing on a farm, it will do him no harm. He is wanted to see the orders of myself, or of my brother, obeyed. I do not want a *Bailiff*; for bailiffs do not think that they earn their wages, unless they furnish you with *science*, or, at least, with *advice*, as well as with care; and I want neither science nor advice. I want *legs* that will move nimbly and willingly, and a young head capable of *learning*. The lad ought to be *stout*, and not stunted; he ought to be able to read and write a little; but, two things are indispensable; namely, that his father be a *farmer*, and that the son has lived on a farm in *England*, all his life, and at a distance of not less than forty miles from London; and not less than twenty miles from Portsmouth, Plymouth, Bath, Bristol, Cheltenham, Liverpool, Manchester, Leeds, or Norwich. He is to sit at table with my brother and my niece (who is the housekeeper), and when I am at the farm, with me also; and is to be treated in every respect as *the young farmer of the house*. He is never to quit the farm; except on my business, and to go to the parish church on the Sunday, and is to be under the control of my brother as completely as if he were his son. He will here learn all about cultivation of Indian Corn, Mangel Wurzle, and of several things not very common. He will learn to sow and rear trees, and to plant and prune them. He will learn how to raise seeds of various sorts. He will learn how to grind and dress wheat and Indian Corn, and will see how the flour is applied. He will learn how to make beer; to see butter and cheese made before breakfast time; and he will have constantly before his eyes examples of early rising, activity, punctual attention to business, *content with plain living*, and *perfect sobriety*.

Now, if any farmer, who is of *my political principles, full up to the mark*, have such a son, nephew, or grandson, to dispose of in this way, I shall be glad to hear from him on the subject. If the lad stay a year out, I will make him *a present* of not less than ten or twelve guineas. It is, I hope, unnecessary to add, that this is a farm-house without a *tea-kettle* or a *coffee-pot*, and without any of the *sweets* that come from the *sweats* of African slaves. Please to observe, that I do not want a *young gentleman*; but a good, sturdy lad, whose hands do not instinctively recoil from a frozen chain, or from the dirty heels of an ox or a horse. I hope that the lad, or young man, that I am to have, will never have been at an *establishment*, vulgarly called a *boarding-school*: if he unfortunately have, and should suit in all

other respects, I must sweat the boarding-school nonsense out of him; that is all. If he have a mind to improve himself in study, here are books, and all the other means of well employing his leisure hours. – Letters to me on the subject to be *postage paid*.
Wᴍ COBBETT
183 Fleet Street, London

P.S. The *great qualities* are, a fitness to *give orders*, and *spirit to enforce obedience*; and, above all things, never to *connive* at the misconduct of the men; but invariably to make a true report of their behaviour, whether good or bad. It will be quite useless to engage a soft, milky thing, that has not the courage to make a lazy fellow stir, or to reprove a perverse one. Fathers will know what stuff their sons are made of, and will, of course, not recommend them to me, unless fit for my purpose. *They* know well *what I want*, and I beg them not to offer me what will not suit me. The lad will, of course, be boarded, lodged, and have his clothes washed in the house.

N.B. I will have no one who has any near relation that is a *tax-eater* of any sort.

10

YESTERDAY'S MEN
(1987)

Jack Hargreaves

During the age of the Shorthorn – after the Longhorns crossed the Atlantic and before the Black-and White cattle crossed the Channel – the people were very skilful. The evidence of the tasks they performed is to be seen hanging on the walls of pubs all over England. These artefacts were first exchanged for half-pints by the old men of the period during their last days when they hobbled around the village on two sticks. They had become redundant in an industrial change that got rid of a quarter-of-a-million farm hands without anyone seeming to notice. Had they been miners or social-workers we would have heard about it.

The evidence of the tools that are now displayed is often misinterpreted. Most of them are quite local and many of them very specialized, so that it is a bold man who sets up to be an expert on them. Even the yokel's tool-of-all-work, the billhook, exists in dozens of different shapes and sizes.

An old friend of ours who ran the threshing engine went to the blacksmith when he was a young man and got him to make a little sickle-hook – hardly bigger than a cut-throat razor – which he used all his life to cut the bond on the sheaves as he opened them up and slid them onto the canvases of the thresher. It was perfect for this task for which, generally, people favoured a lino knife. When the threshing-machine finally packed up we made a film to record how it did its job and showed the little hook. An expert wrote to tell me that I was quite wrong about the use of it. 'Such hooks,' he said, 'were invariably made for the harvesting of tick beans.' This one wasn't. We never saw any tick beans. An uncle of mine used to grow a few but he lived over where he could sell them to the pigeon-fanciers.

Some of these tools are so specialized that they may never be identified. There were quite a few in my collection when I gave it to the local museum that no one could put a purpose to. As a matter of fact, we have just discovered the truth about one after five years of trying. It is a very large combined mattock and drag with a hole that takes a thick, and therefore probably rather short handle. The blade on one side is broad and heavy. The two tines are sharp and 14 inches long. The most popular suggestion was that it was for planting and subsequently earthing up potatoes. I've grown enough potatoes to know that it would be hopeless for that. At last I found an old man who knew it, in fact thought that it once might have been his. There never were many about, he said. In the chalk country the old houses were built of the great flints which, year by year, rise up through the chalk. Under the influence of the plough, perhaps, they come up to show at the surface but don't break free. At the time of the stubble, and when the sheep were in hurdles on the chalkland, this old fellow went out with a horse and cart to collect the flints for building. As soon as he demonstrated how he dug away round the flint and then levered it out of its seat the clumsy thing could be seen to be perfect for the task. Now the label says 'Flint Pick.'

Even if the purpose is obvious you would be unwise to make even a rough guess at the age. I have a shepherd's crook that was found when ditching on a property called Shapwick, which is what a sheep farm was called in Saxon times. It is an elegant piece of smith's work but almost exactly like the one made in the forge for the father of our local shepherd. How far apart were they made? Five hundred years? Only a metallurgist could tell.

The village blacksmiths made the pikes for the Peasants' Revolt and some of them even made them again in 1940 for Dad's Army. In between they made everything that anybody did anything with, and so the forge had always been the centre of the village. It was the place where news was exchanged and where small boys kept warm on a winter's day and learned something about everything. A man would come in with a curly ashpole cut from the hedge a year earlier because it would just make a sned for his scythe. Now they had to be fitted together and it was a long job to satisfy him. Ten times the blade would go back to the fire for the heel of it to be turned or twisted a fraction. Each time you heard the rurping breath of the bellows. Then the hiss of steam as the iron was quenched and refitted for another try. 'Turn her heel up a bit, John. Point's low.' 'Have to go over a mite, John. Edge is looking down.' In the end as the old fellow swayed it across the floor the blade would travel flat and parallel a quarter-inch off the ground – ready to take a long, slicing cut of the grass instead of chopping at it.

That done, the blacksmith would turn to the next of a thousand jobs. He was endlessly patient and always good-natured. I think that blacksmiths, with their strength and social importance, never had anything to prove, like heavyweight boxers who never get into a fight outside the ring – except of course if they've had a losing run. If the next job was with heavy iron then soon we could hear the famous rhythmic ring of his sledge bouncing between the work and the anvil – the sound that could be heard further across the landscape than the church bells. 'Kerlanker! Kerlanker!' A traveller out of sight of houses could tell that a village was ahead of him. As the sound travelled further it lost its lower frequencies more and more and rose in pitch until it became just a tinkling version of itself. If you listen to the call of the Great Tit you will know why we knew it as the Anvil Bird. 'Klinker! Klinker!' it goes – a tiny anvil far away.

On the other side of the street Harry Brandon would have been glad to see the mower go on his way and hear the heavy hammer start to ring. He was waiting for John to weld up the heavy iron lock-rings for a waggon that was coming to completion. Harry was the wheelwright. It might have been truer to call him a wainwright since in the village his trade was heavy waggons and carts for the farmers. The traps and gigs and floats and ladies' chaises were made by the bigger firms in the market towns, drawing their trade from all around. But since the wheel was first invented the men who built vehicles have been named for it, because it was the wheel that made them possible. Given the wheels, any reasonable woodworker could make some sort of job

of the rest. And, no doubt, did. In one district close by a cart
was called a 'pair of trucks.' 'Truck' is just an old word for wheel.
A truckle bed is a bed with wheels made to be pushed under
another one.

So Harry was a wheelwright. He built the first waggon the Old
Man ever had, just about when the Old Queen died. They
ordered it after one harvest to be delivered in time for the next.
Mother told me that they paid half in advance and saved all year
to have the balance ready. It was £40 altogether. Harry would
build a waggon only as he thought it should be. Nobody argued
because there were several in the district still in work that had been

built by the Brandons a hundred years before. You could recognize them; but then once you knew the area you could recognize where each waggon or cart came from. In each place where they were made there was a family of wheelwrights who long ago had agreed with the local farmers what waggon was needed for the slopes and the soil and the roads and the crops of that district. Thus in the museums now you will see Sussex waggons, Berkshire waggons, Hereford, Dorset and Norfolk waggons.

For generations it had been a point of pride with the Brandons that none of them ever used any timber he had bought himself. That was put down to season for his son while he drew on the stocks that came from his father. In the big open hovel behind the shop Harry had a marvellous stock to draw upon, such timber as has not been seen since the two wars. Harry maintained the tradition. He bought ash for shafts and elm for body planks, bent oak boughs selected on site that would cut exactly to make the knees; and, strictest of Brandon rules, apple for the naves, which is what he called hubs. Most aficionados of rural tradition will tell you that the naves were made of elm, but whenever a big apple was being cut down in the district Harry had to be told. He cut it up into nave-blocks and put it away for his son, never knowing then that his boy would be welding up steel tractor-trailers.

When I was little there was no single power-tool in the shop. I used to go there to watch the men working in the sawpit. At the end of the shop, flanked by a shutter window each side that could direct the wind for blowing the sawdust, was a pit just about the size of a human grave. Above a big trestle with a top made of two planks with a gap between, through which the saw could pass. Between them were beams on which the wood could be laid. The top man stood on the trestle and pulled up. The pitman stood in the hole and pulled down. (Now you see why engineers call the bearing at the bottom of a crankshaft the 'pitman bearing.') Between them they worked the long two-man saw. The pitman's job was the one to avoid. He couldn't look up to see how things were going without getting his eyes full of sawdust. The top man holds the line.

Sometimes we can see an old pit-saw in a sale, and usually hear somebody say, 'Look, there's an old cross-cut.' That is exactly what it is not. A cross-cut saw works across the grain. A rip-saw works along the length of the wood. The teeth are filed quite differently. Pit-saws are always rippers. The saw-pit fell into disuse because Harry lashed out and bought a barn-engine, just about the same time that the Old Man got one. A great piece of modernization. It's hard to think of them that way now when those little thumpers are the joy of collectors. One of the clubs had them plonking away in the garden of our local only a week ago last Sunday.

At our place it was the best thing that happened to the boys. Up till then we used to be sent to turn handles on rainy days. One lad each side of the handle we turned the big cast-iron fly wheels – hours with the chaff-cutter, the kibbler, the cake-cracker and the mangold slicer. Now we just listened to the engine and watched the wide, slapping belts. If only the Old Man had managed to mechanize the hay-knife.

Down at the wheelwright's shop Harry got a circular saw, a band-saw and a pillar-drill. And – slicing across history with one blow – he got a lathe. This meant he would never again go down to the water mill. From time immemorial – or perhaps just from time medieval – the wheelwright had kept a primitive wooden lathe at the water mill. When the big apple wood naves had to be turned the blocks would be carted down to the mill, an extra belt slipped on the lathe, and the Brandons borrowed a share of the river-power for nave-turning. The old wooden lathe rotted away unused and so did the saw-pit trestle. And in the village street to the ring of the anvil was added the first throb of industry.

Meanwhile the quietest craftsman of all continued to work next door – the tailor. It's hard to believe that when I was little there was no such thing as reach-me-down clothes in the countryside. But it was so even for poor people. The poorest, of course, dressed in clothes handed on from other people and, in consequence, some of their outfits were quite bizarre. I've seen a hedge-cutter dressed in a swallow-tailed coat and army puttees. An old billy-cock hat was considered to require a bandana handkerchief knotted at the throat and the ends tucked under the braces. The ordinary respectable countryman wore the clothes the tailor made for him, for many years as 'best'; then when they were clearly too old for some special occasion – say the marriage of a daughter to a returning soldier – they were demoted to be working clothes and he returned to the tailor for new ones. But not for a suit. In those earliest days suits were not worn. Certainly the Gentry didn't wear them. In fact we heard that in London they each had both a tailor and a trouser-maker, so that the two halves of their attire were separately chosen and made by different people.

In the circumstances it was better for a man to stick to the traditional style of broadcloth coat, cord waistcoat and moleskin trousers. These the tailor made for him on average perhaps three times in a lifetime and equipped them with 'bone' buttons that never came off. Actually, they were cowhorn and made by a man

129

who worked in a shed alongside the slaughterhouse.

He also worked in Derby Twist and Cavalry Twill, since the best of his living came from outfitting the estate servants – grooms, gamekeepers, huntsmen; even the parson was allowed a suit a year with his living. The odds and ends he made into caps for small boys whose clothes were otherwise made at home by Mother. I used to go and watch him sometimes. He sat cross-legged on a low bench – just like the tailor in the book of Grimm's *Fairy Tales* – and I remember he sewed with a very short thread. The economy of that was interesting. He could re-thread a needle so fast – a second and a half I should think – that it was quicker to do that constantly than suffer the inconvenience of sewing with a long thread.

He was a cripple. Many tailors were, and so were saddlers. Village people knew that every boy-child must somehow be given a trade so if a boy was unmistakably crippled they would plan to get him apprenticed to a tailor. So our tailor was a cripple and so, for the same reasons, was the Snob.

There was always a Snob, even in the smallest village. He was the shoemaker and he, similarly, concentrated most of the time on one kind of footware – the hobnail boot. They were made of the best cow-hide with soles an inch thick and half an inch of welt, handsewn throughout and armoured with rows of hobnails and half-moon irons at toe and heel. We wore them first when we went to school and thenceforward for most of our waking hours. Women wore them when they went out to help in the fields and little girls even when they had summer pinnies and ribbons in their hair wore them with black woollen stockings for scampering over the countryside. You cannot convince people now how comfortable they were. They ironed out the flints on the roads. They took you through deep puddles without getting wet and they were perfect for making a slide across the playground in wintertime. The weight of them actually helped with walking. They seemed to swing your feet forward and eased you over the miles.

Old boots were old friends. Nobody liked starting on a new pair. But there was a secret to it that in later years we were able to impart to friends in the Army. You put the new boots in a tin bath and then filled it up with hot water. After topping them up hot for a couple of days they were as soft as pulp. Then you put them on wet over new thick socks and went for a ten mile walk. By the time you came back they were the same shape as your feet, and after that they were dried out at a safe distance from the stove and thereafter kept soaked with neatsfoot oil. I have a twenty-three-year-old pair of handsome shooting boots that still bear witness to the virtue of the method.

There was one tiny old man in the village whose craft quite often brought the gentry to his door. He made carriage whips, and they were very beautiful. The forester allowed him to stool certain holly trees up in the woods and thus he grew the holly saplings that at two or three years old were his raw material. He tended them like a gardener. At the time the wild swans were moulting he would wander the river bank collecting their big white quills, the same that in earlier years were cut into pens. He used them to make a splint joint between holly and whalebone just below where the bow-top of the whip turned over. Every good carriage whip has a swan-quill in it.

Long years before, Paddy had come over from Ireland, where his father was a whip-maker, to look for work with horses. We knew that in his prime he had been head nagsman at a distinguished private stable. When he retired he reverted to his father's trade. He also specialized in perfecting the manners of Ladies' hunters and hacks. This was the nearest thing to modern dressage training that we knew in our day and Paddy was the patient master of it. One evening just as dusk was falling I came upon him sitting on a horse that had stopped at the ford where the stream ran over the road. He was lighting his clay pipe with an air of perfect peace. 'What's the matter?' I said. 'Won't she go over?' 'She'll go over,' he said in his squeaky little voice, 'even if we're both late for breakfast.'

Over the years he squeaked a lot of things to me that taught me about horses. One winter's day I rode Quicksilver out shepherding as a change from Tony, and getting a sniff of the frost in her nostrils she went off bucking all round the Road Field. I just survived it and, as I got her under control, Paddy came through the gate riding one and leading another. 'Did you see, Paddy?' I cried. 'She bucked all round the field but I didn't come off.' 'Why did you let her buck?' he squeaked.

We never learned the secret of Paddy until after he died. Then the schoolmistress returned in a state of excitement from her weekly reading of *The Times* in the library on market day. She had found an obituary notice to Paddy. We all assembled at the school steps for her to read it. Long ago in Zululand as a corporal of the Household Cavalry he had won the VC.

And then there were the gypsies, who when I was young seemed to prefer to be called 'Travellers.' Mr Hughes, the head of one of the local Romany families, used to say 'You know Billy Elms, he's a travelling man.' Yet this last year at Appleby fair a man introduced himself to me and said 'I'm a gypsy.' I heard the word again several times more and then, listening to other conversations, I got an idea why. In the last few years there has been a growing mob of layabouts and ne'er-do-wells who have moved across the land in old lorries and buses. As they camped on farmers' land and seethed across Salisbury Plain they gathered large numbers of police and even more journalists. They call themselves the Travellers, so certainly the word should not be used for Romany people.

The gypsies of our district were well-known and well-liked – as they were in most country districts. We had the Hughes and the Penfolds and it was first names all round. It is a false idea to think of them as people always on their way to the far horizon. In fact, it was the same elsewhere as with us. Each gypsy family had a comparatively small home area – a territory – and they moved within it in a known way. They would be at the right place for the pea-picking and down along the woods when hazel was needed to split for basket-making. Yet, at the boundaries between one territory and another there was contact and information flowed. 'We can find you where any travelling man is in the country,' they would say. 'Just leave it ten days for the word to pass.'

Then three or four times a year the Romany people took to the road for the great meeting-places – Epsom Downs, Stow-on-the-Wold, Gallows Hill at Appleby. Here they speak with the voices of their own home district – gypsies with Welsh voices, with a touch of Warwickshire or Yorkshire or the Border. The Essex gypsies have a strong tang of London. Here they settle their affairs, arrange the marriages. Their daughters build the alliance and their many sons give support and protection. They are the old age pensions and the force of the law. All confrontations must be carried through – rather than lose face – and it may be better for tourists to stay off Gallows Hill as darkness falls.

Their culture is older than ours and many of their customs were brought from far away – like the burning that goes with death. The old lady of one of our families had become too frail to move around. She parked her van in one place and lived alone there with others coming by to call. All she seemed to ask was a can of milk every day and the can stood clean on the step each morning with a clean washed napkin over it. The lad who brought it from a nearby holding was frightened of her and tried to avoid a sight of her wizened face framed in lace and earrings. But he wondered at the cut-glass windows with the shelves of Crown Derby arranged inside, and the carving and gold-leaf on the Reading Van. One day when he came down the track it was all gone – nothing left but a pile of warm ashes. It's a tremendous votation to the earth gods and a most unselfish tribute to the dead.

Mrs Penfold used to like to teach me Romany words. What she really liked was to point out how many Romany words we already used. Did I know that pal is the Romany for brother? And the koochy which then cropped up in American popular songs is the Romany for pretty? And that kosh is their word for a stick?

'And what is a sign-post?'

I knew that one – 'A sign-post is a pukkering kosh.'

'It is! It is!' she would chuckle. 'It's a talking-stick that tells you where you're going! And a pukkerer is a talker, like Mrs Kent!' Mrs Kent was certainly the top pukkerer in our village. She would spend two hours of the morning on the door-step with anyone who would let her.

There was a woman who was a relative of the Penfolds who came through now and again to visit them. She drove a painted gypsy pot-cart and wore very fine clothes. She was a dukkerer, a fortune-teller, or literally, 'a weaver of spells.' She used to call on Mrs Kent and showed infinite patience in indulging her failing. In the following days she would knock on the doors of the district and offer her magic readings. She said to one young wife, 'I have a beautiful surprise for you. You're going to have a baby at last.' The girl was greatly excited. 'Are you sure?' she said. 'The doctor said Monday that he couldn't say for certain!' So, you see, every dukkerer needs a pukkerer.

Of course, the people of property didn't like them and urged their strappers against them. The police were against them, having at that time the primary purpose of protecting property and resenting the fact that the Romany kept their troubles to themselves. 'We got on well with the Dear Sirs,' said a woman in the forest to me. They called the gypsies by that name on account of the mode of address they used. 'We were all friends. Then after the war the well-to-do came and bought houses and got on the council. They wouldn't have them. Sent the keepers at night to tip them out of their beds.'

One sort of gypsy very well understood the well-to-do. That is the horse-dealers. The biggest of them that we knew was Ted Wing. Biggest, that is, in his operations. In person he was a tiny little man with his cap on straight and his gaiters polished and his whip held in a beautiful pair of dogskin gloves like the coach-men used to use. He turned up one Saturday morning just after the hunters were coming up from grass at the yard of a house belonging to a millionaire brewer – a name now known on many bottles.

It was his custom at a weekend to inspect his string and try them out, giving his authoritative orders to a file of cap-touching stable staff. Ted rode into the yard on a fine chestnut.

'What's that you've got there, Wing?'

'It's the horse for you if ever I saw it.'

'Oh, indeed – how much money?'

'I wouldn't come to money, Sir, not till I was sure of it. Anyone else and I'd say it was sound. But I wouldn't try to fool you, Sir. A while ago I thought I might have heard just a whisper in its wind.'

The brewer had it galloped on and listened to the wind. He put it in the stable and gave its wind time to settle and listened again.

'That horse is sound in wind, Wing.'

'I'd want nobody else's word for it, Sir. The price is four hundred pounds.' A lot of money then. The horse was led for a week and then the new owner decided to try it over jumps. It knocked a gate off its latches and galloped straight through an oxer fence. Blind in one eye and nearly blind in the other. So never let a conjurer catch your attention with his other hand.

Ted Wing is gone now, and so are nearly all the old men who limped about the village. A back that never recovered from loading corn. A thumb that was lost in the woods. A neck that acquired a poking thrust from being put into turnip fields with a hoe and left there for ten days. A hip that broke when a cow tipped a man over a gate as he walked between her and a hidden calf. As you played dominoes in the snug you could tell when the ploughman was coming. Plink – Plonk. Plink – Plonk. After years of one foot on the land and the other in the furrow he couldn't walk any other way.

They never knew the difference between work and leisure. They lived by the now disgraced work ethic and derived their manhood from it. The corn was put in canvas West of England sacks and each weighed two and a quarter hundredweight.'Just lift that one up in the waggon, Sonny.' A grown man could do it if his muscles were hardened and if he had the timing. It was – hup on the feet – hup on the knees – hup on the shoulder – hup up on the tailboard! We used to start trying it at fourteen. At the village fête they tossed double-size corn sheafs up over a sort of rugger goal post set at the full height of a load. The pitching-fork handle was 14 feet long and, when the weight had reached 45 degrees, you could follow the strain down the bending handle and the same curve of the man's spine. Never again, I think, will men do so much work, with such great skill for so little money and such an absence of self-pity.

PART III

COUNTRY
WAYS

1

ASSISTANCE AT LAMBING
(1948)

J. H. B. Peel

She lay on her side, heaving and evidently in trouble. The lamb's black forepaws were already showing, but, after a few moments' struggle, the ewe staggered to her feet, lurched forward a dozen paces and fell down once more, still heaving. The other ewes, alarmed by my approach, were scattering to a far corner of the meadow, and as this ewe seemed inclined to follow them I stood quite still lest she joined the stampede, and killed both herself and her lamb.

Neither the farmer nor any of his assistants was in sight, and I wondered whether it were wise to try to help the ewe (she was in great trouble by now, and the lamb's black paws came and went, came and went, in piteous rhythm). The ewe breathed with difficulty. From time to time she stretched herself and drew up her legs in an alarming way. She was a Cheviot. The rest of the flock was getting wild. I knew that she would run away if she saw me approach. Therefore I waited until she was grappling with another spasm, when I crept up behind her, as quickly as I could. By this means I managed to come upon her and press her neck and shoulders to the ground before she had time to escape.

With difficulty – for she tried to arise when I held her – I began to work the lamb's paws gently and in time to the ewe's heaving. Unfortunately (as I had learned from a wise farmer down in Warwickshire) the appearance of paws, and indeed of even the entire head, is no guarantee of safe birth, for sometimes the shoulders get in the way. This is what had happened with the lamb. Its shoulders, as I could feel, needed to be pressed inward if the creature were to emerge whole and alive.

I quickly understood that for this task I should need both of my hands, and that someone else must hold down the mother's head, for she was growing more restless every moment. Fortunately an Italian war-prisoner happened just then to bicycle along the lane, whistling snatches from *Il Trovatore*, with a clay pipe between his thick lips, and the backs of his brown hands arched negligently against his hips, like a defiant kitchen-maid. I made a sign to him to come over, and – as though in peacetime he were on the music halls – he put about in his own length, still with hand-less handlebars, and sped across the ridged meadow, whistling as he came, until he drew abreast of a gate, where he stopped, lowered his hands from his hips, and lifted the machine over the fifth bar.

'You speak English?' I asked.

'Sure thing, baby,' he replied.

'Good. Hold her head, please, and lean on the neck if she tries to get away. I don't think she will.'

Then, with both of my hands freed, I reached for those sooty legs, and began to ease them into the world, feeling so carefully as I could for the protruding shoulders. The ewe was panting now, but seemed easier, and she made no other sound. Still, I could not help wondering what pain each of the spasms must be causing her. At first I feared that this would be a long task, but just when I had decided that, after all, it had been rash of me to play midwife to another man's ewe, I felt the awkward shoulders slide smoothly toward me, and the lamb came out in his misty shroud – steaming, warm, and very still.

I uncovered him and breathed into his nostrils. He gave five jerks, then lay very still. While he was making his début to life, I felt the ewe again, to make sure that a double were not in transit. She was breathing more steadily now, but all the fight had gone out of her, and she lay listless, never stirring, oblivious of her son. The Italian, meanwhile, perceiving all this, released her neck, and stood beside me, gazing down at the lamb, with raised eyebrows, as much as to say, 'A tidy lamb.' Then the lamb began to jerk again, and actually leaped to his feet. He was evidently ready for a first meal. I laid him against his mother's nose, but she, poor soul, was too weak to make any sign of recognition or joy or even

of relief. I inserted a finger-tip into the little chap's mouth, to encourage him to suck. For perhaps twenty seconds he seemed puzzled, but very soon I was learning once more that sense of wonderment which not even time and frequent repetition have yet stilled in me. I wondered at the power that had taught the lamb to suck at birth, while its mother's entrails were still wrapped about it, and the heavy darkness of the womb upon its nostrils. I pressed the lamb's nose against a teat now heavy with the milk, and after a few prods into the smoking fleece, the lamb found its mark, and began to drink so fast and deeply that after a few seconds I pulled him away lest he choked himself to death of the very food that was binding him to life. When he had taken a bellyful, I pushed him for a third time under his mother's face, and at last she did recognize him, for she licked his eyes, and struggled to her feet, and began to wash him all over.

I do not know whether my assistant had been present at a birth before, nor am I likely to know, for he soon afterwards mounted his bicycle, and rode off. For myself, as I walked away, glancing back at the lamb shaky on his feet, and at the ewe now regarding me with anger and distrust, I marvelled at the intricacies of birth and at its pain. I marvelled also at the instinct to suck and to suckle, and at the power which, having effected all these wonders, could yet allow one old ewe to mistake friend for foe.

2

THE POINT-TO-POINT
(1932)

The Times

Those hills on the north-western edge of Wessex must have made, in ancient wars, superb places from which a sentinel might have watched the country for movements of an enemy force, as they must also well have served a rearguard covering the retirement of an army stricken on the plains and seeking shelter behind the ridge. How the pursuing soldiery, their ranks now broken by a tumbling boulder, now checked by a flight of arrows, must have cursed the steep sides of the hills, slippery with grass, barren of cover from sling or bow.

Deep, indeed, is the stillness that hangs about them now, but there is one hill among the rest upon the forward slope of which, on one day in the year, a multitude yet gathers. For this is still a place of vantage from which to study every movement in the valley below. And thus the judgment of the long-vanished sentry is unconsciously endorsed by every one of those who, on a Saturday in the spring of the year, climb to the top of the green grandstand the better to follow the fortunes of riders and horses in the point-to-point through the vale below.

It is an astonishing crowd that comes to see this event. It is utterly unlike most racecourse crowds, in the important particular that most of those who compose it really know what they are talking about – the character and qualities of horses. The mass is actually more interested in horses than in odds and the paddock gossip is a thing informed. And the point-to-point is a picnic that has been prepared for and talked about for weeks in advance. You may go to it in a gig or a motorcar or a lorry. Enthusiasm sufficiently high will even bear one there on one's feet – if they are really well shod and the weather is kindly. The walk then is entirely worth while.

On the gentler slope of the green hill there are tents in a meadow where they sell cakes and ale. There is a great array of parked motorcars, and half the space in every one of them seems to be filled with lunch. There are flags, red and white, that mark out the course down below, and there is no railway station within miles and miles. The bookmakers are on the crest of the hill; but they are only incidental and slightly more important than the 'Crown and Anchor' men.

Racing begins in the afternoon, when the sandwiches are nearly gone and the flasks are empty. Then opinion, in a burr that renders speech almost incomprehensible to the stranger, is voiced upon the merits of a string of good-looking horses that move presently, with careful and unhurried stride, down the easier slope of the hill, through a spinney flanking a near meadow, and so out to the starting point. So far as this, the first race, is concerned, the last venturesome half-crown has been hazarded; the race itself is the thing; it will provide real riding and a fine call on nerves and knees.

The cluster of riders in pink or black shows half a mile away through the bare trees, forms itself into a line, moves forward, moves backward, hesitates, and starts away. Your neighbour will name the owner of the first half-dozen meadows through which the bay or the chestnut is leading the rest; he may even know the height of the hedge that separates the dun field from the green

139

one, and so adroitly judges the possibility of the roan mare clearing it without a spill. He probably knows, too, the depth of the
brook at this time of the year – as at all times – the brook that
provides the water jump. And, while he has been talking, horses
and men have gone away into the blue of the afternoon, have
swung round the corner of a wood and reappeared.

Hedges, fences, and ditches have sorted out the bunch and
made a string of it. Hard going, where the soil is soggy, has
knocked yards off the pace. Pink and black and brown through
the trees, the flickering movement a mile away grows more
defined as the flying hoofs throw up great clods of earth, and
horses, that a moment since appeared to crawl, come flinging
down the valley, over the thorns, and straight for the water jump
that is so near to home, and, for those who refuse, so far away.
Here the leader thrusts a pair of obstinate feet into the crumbling
bank, flings back with a pettish gesture, and tries again. Here the
lean-flanked chestnut, mud-splashed and sweating, gathers every
sinew to a harp-string tautness, and is over and heading for the
ancient farm-cart where at the winning post the judges sit.

And behind are the downs, blue and grey and green, blotched
with yellow, rolling away into the sky; older than anything that
can be imagined and, by sheer attraction of shape and colour,
lifting the consciousness of whoever looks on them above and
beyond the passing fretfulness in the valley and his imagination
to the things that lie beyond. But the inconstant mind comes
hurtling back to the last hedge and the hundred yards of clean
turf where the black is gathering three inches in every stride from
the brown. Back on the hill-crest a man with a hoarse voice may be
handing somebody a five-pound note, albeit with no very good
grace.

3

PORTRAIT OF A VILLAGE
(1835)

Edward Jesse

There is something very pleasing in rural sounds and rural objects. The noise of village boys playing at cricket, the cawing of rooks in a still evening, the distant tread of a horse, the sheep bells, even the village clock, are all pleasant. I like to see cows going to be milked, and inhale with satisfaction the fresh and fragrant perfume which one perceives as they pass by. Those that have calves are always in advance, and show their impatience to reach their young by an occasional bellow and a short run, and then a sudden stop to listen whether they can hear the call of their calves. If they do, how eagerly do they advance to the gate of the farmyard, and show the utmost anxiety to have admittance. The clean, well-scoured milk-pails and churns are no unsightly objects; and while the process of milking is going on in a well-littered farmyard, the cows quietly chew the cud, and appear contented and happy. Those, however, which have been recently deprived of their young ones, show a reluctance to give down their milk, and many retain some of it, from a maternal feeling that their offspring may require it.

In the spring one hears the wild whirl of a number of sparrows as they rapidly pass by, and then settle in some neighbouring bush, or hedge, chirping and scolding one another, till some

culprit who has been pursued again takes flight and is again followed with the same clamorous noise. This is succeeded by the song of the thrush on the top of some high elm tree, and later in the evening the nightingale makes himself heard.

On a fine summer's day we hear the tinkling of pans and shovels, to persuade a hive of bees to settle in some cottage garden, and are pleased even with the whetting of scythes in a neighbouring field. The gobbling of a turkey-cock, the peevish call of a guinea-fowl, and the cry of pigs for their evening food, are far from being unpleasant sounds to those who delight, as I do, in the country.

I like also a village church. The peasant enters in his clean smock-frock, smooths down his hair, says, or appears to say, a word in his hat, which he carefully and deliberately hangs up, and then leans with crossed arms over the door of the pew till the service begins. Both before and after church he may be seen standing with his back against the low wall of the churchyard, with perhaps the hand of a favourite child in his, talking over some village news. As the squire or the clergyman pass by, he touches his hat to them with respect and affection, and in the evening he may be seen with his cottage door open, drinking tea with his wife and children, and then sauntering about with them either in his garden or some village lane.

The good old squire hobbles out of church, leaning on the arm of his daughter, and kindly inquires after the welfare of all about him. He sends food and money to the sick and needy, makes up quarrels as a magistrate, maintains a well-ordered Sunday school, and promotes the happiness of his villagers by every means in his power. If on returning from church he meets a smoking dinner going to a cottage from the village bakehouse, he generally slips a shilling into the hand of the bearer, for the purpose, as he says, of washing the dinner down with a little good ale. I must, however, add that the old gentleman sometimes slyly takes a good-looking potato out of the dish, which he eats with evident satisfaction.

But how shall I describe our curate? His sunny, good-humoured face is never seen without delight by young and old, rich and poor. He joins in the village sports, and is a famous hand at cricket, and even condescends sometimes to play at trap-ball with the boys, who hail his arrival with great glee. He visits and assists all who want relief, and is never wearied in doing good. He always considers it a bad sign if one of his poor parishioners passes him without his hat, or seems to avoid meeting him. He then with great tact and kindness takes him to task. I have heard him say that he is sure to find that the man has been either foolishly spending his money in the ale-house, or his mind has been tainted by listening to the speeches of some radical demagogue in the neighbouring town. In either case he mildly endeavours to convince the culprit of the folly of his conduct, and generally succeeds in setting him right.

To all this good feeling, our curate has a mind stored with learning, and a taste for the fine arts. He, moreover, dabbles a little in antiquities, and takes great delight in his naturalist's calendar, in which he makes observations equally agreeable and instructive.

Such was our village a few years ago, but, alas! alas! how it has been changed since! A travelling politician has been lecturing in one of our barns, and has made our poor labourers discontented, and consequently idle. All the influence of the good curate has not been able to stem the torrent, and he is about to quit the village in despair of doing any further good. The poor old squire has already left it, after having lowered his rents so much that he could no longer afford to live with his usual kindness and hospitality. He has therefore abandoned his estates, his tenants, and his labourers to the care of a mercenary bailiff, and is gone to reside in an over-grown town on the sea coast, upon the residue of a once ample income.

I consider the aspect of this town as one of the most melancholy features of the present times. It is now resorted to by many under the same circumstances with our squire, by those who ought to have made every sacrifice to stem the torrent of disaffection, who should have given up their horses, their carriages, their hospitalities, sooner than quit their villages and country houses, and sever the tie which connected them with their tenants and

THE COUNTRYSIDE COMPANION

labourers. They may hope to return in better times, and to replace things on their former footing. But that tie once broken cannot be restored, and it is melancholy to reflect on the consequences.

4

FOOD AND SHELTER IN SCOTLAND
(1773)

Samuel Johnson

Near the way, by the waterside [of Loch Ness], we espied a cottage. This was the first Highland hut that I had seen; and as our business was with life and manners, we were willing to visit it. To enter a habitation without leave seems to be not considered here as rudeness or intrusion. The old laws of hospitality still give this licence to a stranger. A hut is constructed with loose stones, ranged for the most part with some tendency to circularity. It must be placed where the wind cannot act upon it with violence, because it has no cement; and where the water will run easily away, because it has no floor but the naked ground. The wall, which is commonly about six feet high, declines from the perpendicular a little inward. Such rafters as can be procured are then raised for a roof, and covered with heath, which makes a strong and warm thatch, kept from flying off by ropes of twisted heath, of which the ends, reaching from the centre of the thatch to the top of the wall, are held firm by the weight of a large stone. No light is admitted but at the entrance, and through a hole in the thatch, which gives vent to the smoke. This hole is not directly over the fire, lest the rain should extinguish it; and the smoke therefore naturally fills the place before it escapes. Such is the general structure of the houses in which one of the nations of this opulent and powerful island has been hitherto content to live. Huts however are not more uniform than palaces; and this which we were inspecting was very far from one of the meanest, for it was divided into several apartments; and its inhabitants possessed such property as a pastoral poet might exalt into riches.

When we entered, we found an old woman boiling goats-flesh in a kettle. She spoke little English, but we had interpreters at hand; and she was willing enough to display her whole system of economy. She has five children, of which none are yet gone from her. The eldest, a boy of thirteen, and her husband, who is eighty years old, were at work in the wood. Her two next sons were gone to Inverness to buy meal, by which oatmeal is always meant. Meal she considered an expensive food, and told us that in spring when the goats gave milk, the children could live without it. She is mistress of sixty goats, and I saw many kids in an enclosure at the end of her house. She had also some poultry. By the lake we saw a potato-garden, and a small spot of ground on which stood four shucks, containing each twelve sheaves of barley. She has all this from the labour of their own hands, and for what is necessary to be bought, her kids and her chickens are sent to market. With the true pastoral hospitality, she asked us to sit down and drink whisky. She is religious and though the kirk is four miles off, probably eight English miles, she goes thither every Sunday. We gave her a shilling, and she begged snuff; for snuff is the luxury of a Highland cottage. . . .

[At Coriatachan on Skye] At the tables where a stranger is received, neither plenty nor delicacy is wanting. A tract of land so thinly inhabited must have much wild-fowl; and I scarcely remember to have seen a dinner without them. The moorgame is everywhere to be had. That the sea abounds with fish, needs not be told, for it supplies a great part of Europe. The isle of Skye has stags and roebucks, but no hares. They sell very numerous droves of oxen yearly to England, and therefore cannot be supposed to want beef at home. Sheep and goats are in great numbers and they have the common domestic fowls. But as here is nothing to be bought, every family must kill its own meat, and roast part of it somewhat sooner than Apicius would prescribe. Every kind of flesh is undoubtedly excelled by the variety and emulation of English markets; but that which is not best may be yet free from bad, and he that shall complain of his fare in the Hebrides has improved his delicacy more than his manhood. Their fowls are not like those plumped for sale by the poulterers of London, but they are as good as other places commonly afford, except that the geese, by feeding in the sea, have universally a fishy rankness. These geese seem to be of a middle race, between wild and domestic kinds. They are so tame as to own a home, and so wild as sometimes to fly quite away.

Their native bread is made of oats or barley. Of oatmeal they spread very thin cakes, coarse and hard, to which unaccustomed palates are not easily reconciled. The barley cakes are thicker and softer; I began to eat them without unwillingness; the blackness of their colour raises some dislike, but the taste is not disagreeable.

In most houses there is wheat flour, with which we were sure to be treated if we stayed long enough to have it kneaded and baked. As neither yeast nor leaven are used among them, their bread of every kind is unfermented. They make only cakes and never mould a loaf.

A man of the Hebrides, for of the women's diet I can give no account, as soon as he appears in the morning, swallows a glass of whisky; yet they are not a drunken race, at least I never was present at much intemperance; but no man is so abstemious as to refuse the morning dram, which they call a skalk. The word whisky signifies water, and is applied by way of eminence to strong water, or distilled liquor. The spirit drunk in the north is drawn from barley. I never tasted it, except once for experiment at the inn in Inverary, when I thought it preferable to any English malt brandy. It was strong, but not pungent, and was free from the empyreumatic taste or smell. What was the process I had no opportunity of inquiring, nor do I wish to improve the art of making poison pleasant.

Not long after the dram, may be expected the breakfast, a meal in which the Scots, whether of the lowlands or mountains, must be confessed to excel us. The tea and coffee are accompanied not only with butter, but with honey, conserves and marmalades. If an epicure could remove by a wish in quest of sensual gratifications, wherever he had supped he would breakfast in Scotland. In the islands, however, they do what I found is not very easy to endure. They pollute the tea-table by plates piled with large slices of Cheshire cheese, which mingles its less grateful odours with the fragrance of the tea. . . .

A dinner in the Western Islands differs very little from a dinner in England, except that in the place of tarts, there are always set different preparations of milk. This part of their diet will admit some improvement. Though they have milk, and eggs, and sugar, few of them know how to compound them into a custard. Their gardens afford them no great variety, but they have always some vegetables on the table. Potatoes at least are never wanting, which, though they have not known them long, are now one of the principal parts of their food. They are not of the mealy, but the viscous kind.

Their more elaborate cookery, or made dishes, an Englishman at the first taste is not likely to approve, but the culinary compositions of every country are often such as become grateful to other nations only by degrees; though I have read a French author, who, in the elation of his heart, says that French cookery pleases all foreigners, but foreign cookery never satisfies a Frenchman.

Their suppers are, like their dinner, various and plentiful. The table is always covered with elegant linen. Their plates for common use are often of that kind of manufacture which is called cream coloured, or queen's ware. They use silver on all occasions where it is common in England, nor did I ever find the spoon of horn, but in one house. The knives are not often either very bright or very sharp. They are indeed instruments of which the Highlanders have not been long acquainted with the general use. They were not regularly laid on the table before the prohibition of arms, and the change of dress. Thirty years ago the High-lander wore his knife as a companion to his dirk or dagger, and when the company sat down to meat, the men who had knives cut the flesh into small pieces for the women, who with their fingers conveyed it to their mouths.

5

A FARMER'S DAY
(1965)

Llanbedr Women's Institute

The farmer has, of necessity, to be an early riser, between 6 and 6.30 am. If he is a dairy farmer the first job must be to do the milking. This is usually completed and the churns of milk taken to the milk-stands at the farm gate before breakfast. After breakfast the milking machine has to be washed out, and then the farmer is ready to go to work in the fields.

Today there is a ten-acre field of barley to be harvested and the local agricultural contractor will be arriving about noon with his combine harvester. It is not possible to start harvesting until the dew has risen and the sun has dried the ground. The first setback of the day occurs when it is discovered that there is a puncture in the wheel of one of the tractors. This means removing the wheel and putting it into the car trailer and bribing the long-suffering wife to run it into the garage to be repaired immediately. Following this hindrance the farmer gets on with the job of preparing his sacks for the grain, when his wife, who has returned from the garage, hurries into the shed to say that their neighbour has telephoned asking for help with a difficult calving. Having dispatched his workmen to cut hedges there is nothing else for it but for the farmer to go to his neighbour's aid. It is 10 am when he gets back to his sacks, having done his good deed for the day. Shortly after this a car is driven into the yard; it is the representative of a firm of feeding-stuffs. An order has to be given to him, and this takes up another half-hour of the farmer's precious time. Representatives are never pushed for time, and will talk indefinitely if they think they can persuade the farmer to give them an order. Without further interruption the task of sorting the sacks is completed and the tractors and trailers are prepared for carrying home the sacks of grain. Fortunately the garage proprietor has kindly brought the tractor wheel back again.

At 12 o'clock the farmer and his men go off for their dinner which must be ready for them to swallow before they set off for the barley field. While he eats the farmer scans the morning mail. A Parish Council meeting tonight. 'They'll be lucky,' he mutters. He must also ring up and postpone that delivery of fertilizer due in the afternoon.

The contractor is, as usual, late, finally arrives at 2 o'clock and at last the drone of the harvester can be heard. One man rides on the harvester, two attend to the sacks as they slowly fill with the golden grain. The other two men are employed on lifting the heavy sacks of corn on to the trailers, and when they have a full load taking it to the farm for storage. It is a slow job, and a stop is made at 4 o'clock for tea, brought to the field by the farmer's wife. Now one man must go back to the farm to do the milking, and the others must push on if they are to complete the combining before dark. At about 6 o'clock the farmer's wife is again hurrying into the field, with the cheerful information that the bull has got out of its pen and is rampaging round the yard trying to get into the field which the milking cows have just been turned into. Everything stops for half an hour while the men return to the farm, and eventually succeed in getting the bull back into its pen.

Completion of the job of combining the barley is done by the headlights of the tractors, and it is 11 o'clock when a very weary farmer returns home for his supper, and nearly midnight before he gets to bed. Tomorrow the straw must be baled and carried in, and the corn will probably have to be dried, and as he climbs into bed the farmer suddenly remembers that the vet is due in the morning to carry out his annual tuberculin test of the dairy herd. But then 'tomorrow is another day.'

6

THE BEST CHEESE OF ENGLAND
(c1724)

Daniel Defoe

In the low country, on the other side Mendip Hills, lies Cheddar, a village pleasantly situated under the very ridge of the mountains; before the village is a large green or common, a piece of ground in which the whole herd of the cows, belonging to the town, do feed; the ground is exceeding rich, and as the whole village are cowkeepers, they take care to keep up the goodness of the soil by agreeing to lay on large quantities of dung for manuring, and enriching the land.

The milk of all the town cows is brought together every day into a common room, where the persons appointed, or trusted for the

management, measure every man's quantity and set it down in a book. When the quantities are adjusted, the milk is all put together, and every meal's milk makes one cheese, and no more, so that the cheese is bigger, or less, as the cows yield more, or less, milk. By this method the goodness of the cheese is preserved and, without all dispute, it is the best cheese that England affords, if not that the whole world affords.

As the cheeses are, by this means, very large, for they often weigh a hundred weight, sometimes much more, so the poorer inhabitants who have but few cows are obliged to stay the longer for the return of their milk; for no man has any such return 'till his share comes to a whole cheese, and then he has it; and if the quantity of his milk delivered in, comes to above a cheese, the overplus rests in account to his credit, 'till another cheese comes to his share; and thus every man has equal justice, and though he should have but one cow he shall, in time, have one whole cheese. This cheese is often sold for six pence to eight pence per pound, when the Cheshire cheese is sold but for two pence to two pence halfpenny.

◆

To Take Away Freckles in the Face

Take one pint of white wine vinegar and put it into a glass with six oaken apples and a few elder leaves. Set it in the sun and wash your face therewith.

Thomas Newington, 1719

◆

7

HUNTING THE FOX
(1872)

Anthony Trollope

Lizzie was in truth delighted to have her cousin beside her. He had, at any rate, forgiven what she had said to him at his last visit, or he would not have been there. And then, too, there was a feeling of reality in her connection with him, which was sadly wanting to her – unreal as she was herself – in her acquaintance with the other people around her. And on this occasion three or four people spoke or bowed to her, who had only stared at her before; and the huntsman took off his cap, and hoped that he would do something better for her than on the previous Monday. And the huntsman was very courteous also to Miss Roanoke, expressing the same hope, cap in hand, and smiling graciously. A huntsman at the beginning of any day or at the end of a good day is so different from a huntsman at the end of a bad day! A huntsman often has a very bad time out hunting, and it is sometimes a marvel that he does not take the advice which Job got from his wife. But now all things were smiling, and it was soon known that his lordship intended to draw Craigattan Gorse. Now in those parts there is no surer find, and no better chance of a run, than Craigattan Gorse affords.

'There is one thing I want to ask, Mr Greystock,' said Lord George, in Lizzie's hearing.

'You shall ask two,' said Frank.

'Who is to coach Lady Eustace today; you or I?'

'Oh, do let me have somebody to coach me,' said Lizzie.

'For devotion in coachmanship,' said Frank, 'devotion, that is, to my cousin, I defy the world. In point of skill I yield to Lord George.'

'My pretensions are precisely the same,' said Lord George. 'I glow with devotion; my skill is naught.'

'I like you best, Lord George,' said Lizzie, laughing.

'That settles the question,' said Lord George.

'Altogether,' said Frank, taking off his hat.

'I mean as a coach,' said Lizzie.

'I quite understand the extent of the preference,' said Lord George. Lizzie was delighted, and thought the game was worth the candle. The noble master had told her that they were sure of a

151

run from Craigattan, and she wasn't in the least tired, and they were not called upon to stand still in a big wood, and it didn't rain, and, in every respect, the day was very different from Monday. Mounted on a bright-skinned, lively steed, with her cousin on one side and Lord George de Bruce Carruthers on the other, with all the hunting world of her own county civil around her, and a fox just found in Craigattan Gorse, what could the heart of woman desire more? This was to live. There was, however, just enough of fear to make the blood run quickly to her heart.

'We'll be away at once now,' said Lord George with utmost earnestness. 'Follow me close, but not too close. When the men see that I am giving you a lead, they won't come between. If you hang back, I'll not go ahead. Just check your horse as he comes to his fences, and, if you can, see me over before you go at them. Now then, down the hill; there's a gate at the corner, and a bridge over the water. We couldn't be better. By George! there they are, altogether. If they don't pull him down in the first two minutes, we shall have a run.'

Lizzie understood most of it – more at least than would nine out of ten young women who had never ridden a hunt before. She was to go wherever Lord George led her, and she was not to ride upon his heels. So much at least she understood – and so much she was resolved to do. That dread about her front teeth which had perplexed her on Monday was altogether gone now. She would ride as fast as Lucinda Roanoke. That was her prevailing idea. Lucinda, with Mrs Carbuncle, Sir Griffin, and the ladies' groom, was at the other side of the covert. Frank had been with his cousin and Lord George, but had crept down the hill while the hounds were in the gorse. A man who likes hunting but hunts only once a year is desirous of doing the best he can with his day. When the hounds came out and crossed the brook at the end of the gorse, perhaps he was a little too forward. But, indeed, the state of affairs did not leave much time for waiting, or for the etiquette of the hunting-field. Along the opposite margin of the brook there ran a low paling, which made the water a rather nasty thing to face. A circuit of thirty or forty yards gave the easy riding of a little bridge, and to that all the crowd hurried. But one or two men with good eyes, and hearts as good, had seen the leading hounds across the brook turning up the hill away from the bridge, and knew that two most necessary minutes might be lost in the crowd. Frank did as they did, having seen nothing of any hounds, but with instinctive knowledge that they were men likely to be right in a hunting-field. 'If that ain't Nappie's horse, I'll eat him,' said one of the leading men to the other, as all the three were breasting the hill together. Frank only knew that he had been carried over water and timber without a mistake, and felt a glow of gratitude towards Mr MacFarlane. Up the hill they went, and not waiting to inquire into the circumstances of a little gate, jumped a four foot wall and were away. 'How the mischief did he get a top of Nappie's horse?' said the horsey man to his friend.

'We're about right for it now,' said the huntsman, as he came up alongside of Frank. He had crossed the bridge, but had been the first across it, and knew how to get over his ground quickly. On they went, the horsey man leading on his thoroughbred screw, the huntsman second, and Frank third. The pace had already been too good for the other horsey man.

When Lord George and Lizzie had mounted the hill, there was a rush of horses at the little gate. As they topped the hill Lucinda and Mrs Carbuncle were jumping the wall. Lord George looked back and asked a question without a word. Lizzie answered it as mutely. Jump it! She was already a little short of breath, but she was ready to jump anything that Lucinda Roanoke had jumped. Over went Lord George, and she followed him almost without losing the stride of her horse. Surely in all the world there was nothing equal to this! There was a large grass field before them, and for a moment she came up alongside of Lord George. 'Just steady him before he leaps,' said Lord George. She nodded her assent, and smiled her gratitude. She had plenty of breath for riding, but none for speaking. They were now very near to Lucinda, and Sir Griffin, and Mrs Carbuncle. 'The pace is too good for Mrs Carbuncle's horse,' said Lord George. Oh, if she could only pass them, and get up to those men whom she saw before her! She knew that one of them was her cousin Frank. She had no wish to pass them, but she did wish that he should see her. In the next fence Lord George spied a rail, which he thought safer than a blind hedge, and he made for it. His horse took it well, and so did Lizzie's; but Lizzie jumped it a little too near him, as he had paused an instant to look at the ground. 'Indeed, I won't do it again,' she said, collecting all her breath for an apology. 'You are going admirably,' he said, 'and your horse is worth double the money.' She was so glad now that he had not spared for price in mounting her. Looking to the right she could see that Mrs Carbuncle had only just floundered through the hedge. Lucinda was still ahead, but Sir Griffin was falling behind, as though divided in duty between the niece and the aunt. Then they passed through a gate, and Lord George stayed his horse to hold it for her. She tried to thank him but he stopped her. 'Don't mind talking, but come along; and take it easy.' She smiled again, and he told himself that she was wondrous pretty. And then her pluck was so good! And then she had four thousand a year! 'Now for the gap! – don't be in a hurry. You first, and I'll follow you to keep off these two men. Keep to the left, where the other horses have been.'

On they went, and Lizzie was in heaven. She could not quite understand her feelings, because it had come to that with her that to save her life she could not have spoken a word. And yet she was not only happy but comfortable. The leaping was delightful, and her horse galloped with her as though his pleasure was as great as her own. She thought that she was getting nearer to Lucinda. For her, in her heart, Lucinda was the quarry. If she could only pass Lucinda! That there were any hounds she had altogether forgotten. She only knew that two or three men were leading the way, of whom her cousin Frank was one, that Lucinda Roanoke was following them closely, and that she was gaining upon Lucinda Roanoke. She knew she was gaining a little, because she could see now how well and squarely Lucinda sat upon her horse. As for herself, she feared that she was rolling; but she need not have feared. She was so small, and lithe, and light, that her body adapted itself naturally to the pace of her horse. Lucinda was of a different build, and it behoved her to make for herself a perfect seat.

'We must have the wall,' said Lord George, who was again at her side for a moment. She would have 'had' a castle wall, moat included, turrets and all, if he would only have shown her the way. The huntsman and Frank had taken the wall. The horsey man's bit of blood, knowing his own powers to an inch, had declined – not roughly, with a sudden stop and a jerk, but with a swerve to the left which the horsey man at once understood. What the brute lacked in jumping he could make up in pace, and the horsey man was along the wall and over a broken bank at the head of it, with the loss of not more than a minute. Lucinda's horse, following the ill example, balked the jump. She turned him round with a savage gleam in her eye, which Lizzie was just near enough to see, struck him rapidly over the shoulders with her whip, and the animal flew with her into the next field. 'Oh, if I could do it like that!' thought Lizzie. But in that very next minute she was doing it, not only as well but better. Not following Lord George, but close at his side, the little animal changed his pace, trotted for a yard or two, hopped up as though the wall were nothing, knocked off a top stone with his hind feet, and dropped on to the ground so softly that Lizzie hardly believed that she had gone over the big obstruction that had cost Lucinda such an effort. Lucinda's horse came down on all four legs, with a grunt and a groan, and she knew that she had bustled him. At that moment Lucinda was very full of wrath against the horsey man with the screw who had been in her way. 'He touched it,' gasped Lizzie, thinking that her horse had disgraced himself. 'He's worth his weight in gold,' said Lord George. 'Come along. There's a brook with a ford. Morgan is in it.' Morgan was the huntsman. 'Don't let them get before you.' Oh, no. She would let no one get before her. She did her very best, and just got her horse's nose on the broken track leading down into the brook before Lucinda. 'Pretty good, isn't it?' said Lucinda. Lizzie smiled sweetly. She could smile, though she could not speak. 'Only they do balk one so at one's fences!' said Lucinda. The horsey man had all but regained his place, and was immediately behind Lucinda, within hearing – as Lucinda knew.

On the further side of the field, beyond the brook, there was a little spinney, and for half a minute the hounds came to a check. 'Give 'em time, sir, give 'em time,' said Morgan to Frank, speaking in full good humour, with no touch of Monday's savagery. 'Wind him, Bolton; Beaver's got it. Very good thing, my lady, isn't it? Now, Carstairs, if you're a going to 'unt the fox, you'd better 'unt him.' Carstairs was the horsey man, and one with whom Morgan very often quarrelled. 'That's it, my hearties,' and Morgan was across a broken wall in a moment, after the leading hounds. 'Are we to go on?' said Lizzie, who feared much that Lucinda would get ahead of her. There was a matter of three dozen horsemen up now, and, as far as Lizzie saw, the whole thing might have to be done again. In hunting, to have ridden is the pleasure; and not simply to have ridden well, but to have ridden better than others. 'I call it very awkward ground,' said Mrs Carbuncle, coming up. 'It can't be compared to the Baron's country.' 'Stone walls four feet and a half high, and well built, are awkward,' said the noble master.

But the hounds were away again, and Lizzie had got across the gap before Lucinda, who indeed made way for her hostess with a haughty politeness which was not lost upon Lizzie. Lizzie could not stop to beg pardon, but she would remember to do it in her prettiest way on their journey home. They were now on a track of open country, and the pace was quicker even than before. The same three men were still leading, Morgan, Greystock and Carstairs. Carstairs had slightly the best of it; and of course Morgan swore afterwards that he was among the hounds the whole run. 'The scent was that good, there wasn't no putting of 'em off – no thanks to him,' said Morgan. 'I 'ate to see 'em galloping, galloping, galloping, with no more eye to the 'ounds than a pig. Any idiot can gallop, if he's got it under him.' All which only signified that Jack Morgan didn't like to see any of his field before him. There was need, indeed, now for galloping, and it may be doubted whether Morgan himself was not doing his best. There were about five or six in the second flight, and among these Lord George and Lizzie were well placed. But Lucinda had pressed again ahead. 'Miss Roanoke had better have a care, or she'll blow her horse,' Lord George said. Lizzie didn't mind what happened to Miss Roanoke's horse, so that it could be made to go a little slower and fall behind. But Lucinda still pressed on, and her animal went with a longer stride than Lizzie's horse.

They now crossed a road, descending a hill, and were again in a close country. A few low hedges seemed as nothing to Lizzie. She could see her cousin gallop over them ahead of her, as though they were nothing; and her own horse, as he came to them, seemed to do exactly the same. On a sudden they found themselves abreast with the huntsman. 'There's a biggish brook below there, my lord,' said he. Lizzie was charmed to hear it. Hitherto she had jumped all the big things so easily, that it was a pleasure to hear of them. 'How are we to manage it?' asked Lord George. 'It is rideable, my lord; but there's a place about half a mile down. Let's see how'll they head. Drat it, my lord; they've turned up, and we must have it or go back to the road.' Morgan hurried on, showing that he meant to 'have' it, as did also Lucinda. 'Shall we go to the road?' said Lord George. 'No, no!' said Lizzie. Lord George looked at her and at her horse, and then galloped after the huntsman and Lucinda. The horsey man, with the well-bred screw, was first over the brook. The little animal could take almost any amount of water, and his rider knew the spot. 'He'll do it like a bird,' he had said to Greystock, and Greystock had followed him. Mr MacFarlane's hired horse did it like a bird. 'I know him, sir,' said Carstairs. 'Mr Nappie gave £250 for him down in Northamptonshire last February – bought him of Mr Percival. You know Mr Percival, sir?' Frank knew neither Mr Percival nor Mr Nappie, and at this moment cared nothing for either of them. To him, at this moment, Mr MacFarlane, of Buchanan Street, Glasgow, was the best friend he ever had.

Morgan, knowing well the horse he rode, dropped him into the brook, floundered and half swam through the mud and water, and scrambled out safely on the other side. 'He wouldn't have jumped it with me, if I'd asked him ever so,' he said afterwards. Lucinda rode at it, straight as an arrow, but her brute came to a dead balk, and, but that she sat well, would have thrown her into the stream. Lord George let Lizzie take the leap before he took it, knowing that, if there were misfortune, he might so best render help. To Lizzie it seemed as though the river were the blackest, and the deepest, and the broadest that ever ran. For a moment her heart quailed – but it was but for a moment. She shut her eyes, and gave the little horse his head. For a moment she thought that she was in the water. Her horse was almost upright on the bank, with his hind-feet down among the broken ground, and she was clinging to his neck. But she was light and the beast made good his footing, and then she knew that she had done it. In that moment of the scramble her heart had been so near her mouth that she was almost choked. When she looked round, Lord George was already by her side. 'You hardly gave him powder enough,' he said, 'but still he did it beautifully. Good heavens! Miss Roanoke is in the river.' Lizzie looked back, and there, in truth, was Lucinda struggling with her horse in the water. They paused a moment, and then there were three or four men assisting her. 'Come on,' said Lord George, 'there are plenty to take her out, and we couldn't get to her if we stayed.'

'I ought to stop,' said Lizzie.

'You couldn't get back if you gave your eyes for it,' said Lord George. 'She's all right.' So instigated, Lizzie followed her leader up the hill, and in a minute was close upon Morgan's heels.

The worst of doing a big thing out hunting is the fact that in nine cases out of ten they who don't do it are as well off as they who do. If there were any penalty for riding round, or any mark given to those who had ridden straight – so that justice might in some sort be done – it would perhaps be better. When you have nearly broken your neck to get to hounds, or made your horse exert himself beyond his proper power, and then find yourself, within three minutes, overtaking the hindmost ruck of horsemen on a road because of some iniquitous turn that the fox has taken, the feeling is not pleasant. And some man who has not ridden at all, who never did ride at all, will ask you where you have been; and his smile will give you the lie in your teeth if you make any attempt to explain the facts. Let it be sufficient for you at such a moment to feel that you are not ashamed of yourself. Self-respect will support a man even in such misery as this.

The fox on this occasion, having crossed the river, had not left its bank, but had turned from his course up the stream, so that the leading spirits who had followed the hounds over the water came upon a crowd of riders on the road in a space something short of a mile. Mrs Carbuncle, among others, was there, and had heard of Lucinda's mishap. She said a word to Lord George in anger, and Lord George answered her. 'We were over the river before it happened, and if we had given our eyes we couldn't have got to her. Don't you make a fool of yourself!' The last words were spoken in a whisper, but Lizzie's sharp ears caught them.

'I was obliged to do what I was told,' said Lizzie apologetically.

'It will be all right, dear Lady Eustace. Sir Griffin is with her. I am so glad you are going so well.'

They were off again now, and the stupid fox absolutely went back across the river. But, whether on one side or on the other, his struggle for life was now in vain. Two years of happy, free existence amidst the wilds of Craigattan had been allowed him. Twice previously had he been 'found,' and the kindly storm or not less beneficent brightness of the sun had enabled him to baffle his pursuers. Now there had come one glorious day, and the common lot of mortals must be his. A little spurt there was, back towards his own home – just enough to give something of selectness to the few who saw him fall – and then he fell. Among the few were Frank, and Lord George, and our Lizzie. Morgan was there, of course, and one of his whips. Of Ayrshire folk, perhaps five or six, and among them our friend, Mr Carstairs. They had run him down close to the outbuildings of a farmyard, and they broke him up in the home paddock.

'What do you think of hunting?' said Frank to his cousin.

'It's divine!'

'My cousin went pretty well, I think,' he said to Lord George.

'Like a celestial bird of Paradise. No one ever went better – or I believe so well.'

8

THE CHARM OF THE SCYTHE
(1913)

George Bourne

In the appearance of a scythe – a whimsical friend avers, too fantastically – so slender and yet strong, so graceful, so keen and so aquiline withal about the nose, there is every mark of the aristocrat; it is the grandee among country tools; an ancient and honourable lineage is betokened in every one of its shapely curves. Upon prongs and forks and shovels you must look with suspicion – there is no telling to what base ends they have been applied. Such things as rakes and hoes you may despise for humble grubbers in the dirt, as they are; even the fag-hook and the bill lend themselves to every hand and lack exclusiveness; but there is nothing common nor unclean about the scythe, which stands apart with a sort of resemblance to the sword of chivalry.

Without indulging such far-fetched fancies, it must still be owned that scythes have a charm quite singular among tools. Their shape alone might account for it; smooth and sinuous, with deadly possibilities lurking somewhere in their aspect, they do certainly fascinate. It is a severe and simple beauty theirs, as good as that of Greek statues, unspoiled by prettiness, comparable to the exactness of natural things; such a beauty as only generations of single-minded attention to what is fit can give to any human product. But they make an even greater appeal to the imagination than to the sight; for perhaps in all the world there is no other thing so intimately associated with the summer at its best, and its best only. At sight of this tool one does not always think consciously of the deep meadows and the June days, but it is odd if some of their beauty does not find its way into one's spirit. And from the brave English weather that they recall, a feeling of kinship with the generations of men who have rejoiced in it with scythes in their hands is never very far remote.

9

WORK PERFORMED BY CHILDREN ON FARMS IN THE 1860S

Report on the Employment of Children, Young Persons and Women in Agriculture, 1867–69

January   Hop pole shaving and other coppice work in woodland countries.

February   Twitching, stone picking, bean and pea setting.

March   Potato setting, bird scaring, cleaning land for spring corn.

April   Bird scaring, weeding corn, setting potatoes.

May   Bird scaring, weeding corn, cleaning land for turnips, bark harvest, tending cows in the lanes, etc.

June   Hay making, turnip singling.

July   Turnip singling, pea picking, cutting thistles, scaring birds from ripening corn.

August   Corn harvest, gleaning.

September Hop harvest, tending sheep or pigs on the stubbles.

October   Potato and fruit gathering, twitching, dibbling and dropping wheat.

November Bird scaring from new sown wheat and beans, acorning.

December Stone picking, spreading cow droppings; in Norfolk, scaring birds from corn stacks; in Essex, helping their fathers to make surface drains; in woodland districts, coppice work; topping and tailing turnips, and cleaning roots for cattle.

10

THE HIRING FAIR
(1939)

Patrick Gallagher

When I was ten years of age I was in the second book, but until I had passed into the third book I would not be looked upon as a scholar. But I could not wait. The year before had been a bad year in Scotland, and my father had not enough money home with him to pay the rent and the shop debts. It was the same with the neighbours. A crowd of us boys were got ready for the hiring fair at Strabane. Boys, oh, boys, but we were glad. The big people warned us we would not have such a rush in our feet when we had the thirty-seven miles' tramp to Ballybofey past us, but we only laughed at them.

I'll always mind the morning I first left home to go to the Lagan; that was what we called the countryside beyond the mountains where boys went on hire. I think I see my mother as she handed me my four shillings for the journey. She was crying. She kissed me again and again. I can't say whether I was crying or not, though it's likely I was, for to this day it's easy to make me cry. It was in Irish she spoke and this is the sense of what she said: 'Paddy, son, here is four shillings. Two shillings will take you to the fair. If you hire, keep the other two shillings till you come home; if you don't hire, it will take you back to me. Wherever you go and wherever you be, say your prayers night and morning and say three Hail Marys to the Blessed Virgin that God will keep you from the temptations of the devil.' Everywhere you looked some mother was saying something to her own boy or girl, and I think they were all crying too. But anyway we got started. We were all barefooted; we had our boots in our bundles. There was not much weight in our bundles. There was nothing in mine, only two shirts, some patches, thread, buttons, and a couple of needles.

We made a lot of noise along the road but there was still plenty of walk in us when we had finished the thirty-seven miles to Ballybofey. We lodged in a sort of barn, twenty-six boys of us on shake-downs on the floor. The old-fashioned fellows who went over the roads before advised us to take off our shirts to save ourselves from vermin. In the hurry in the morning the shirts got mixed up, but the one I got was as good as the one I lost. We paid threepence each for our night's lodging. We ate what we had left over of our pieces and started for the station. The train fare for the rest of our journey was one and twopence, so I still had one two-shilling piece, a sixpence and a penny.

When we reached Strabane we all cuddled together, and were scared at first, but the big fellows told us to scatter out so as the farmers would see us. They made us walk up and down to see how we were set up and judge what mettle was in us. Anybody who looked tired or faulty in any way was passed over. The strong boys were picked up quickly, and I was getting scared I would be left. In the end two men came to me.

'Well,' said one of them. 'Wee fellow, what wages do you want for the six months?'

I said, 'Three pounds ten.'

He said, 'Get out, you would be dear at your meat. Walk up there to the market clock until I see what you are like.'

I walked up, he followed and made me walk back to where I started from. I heard him whispering to the other fellow, 'He is wee, but the neck is "good,"' and he then offered me two pounds ten.

The other man caught both our hands in his, hit our hands a slap, and said, 'Bought and sold for three pounds.'

We both agreed. My master took my bundle from me and told me to meet him there at that spot in an hour.

11

OBSERVATIONS OF THE BREAM
(1653)

Izaak Walton

The bream, being at a full growth, is a large and stately fish. He will breed both in rivers and ponds, but loves best to live in ponds, and where, if he likes the water and air, he will grow not only to be very large, but as fat as a hog. He is by Gesner taken to be more pleasant or sweet than wholesome. This fish is long in growing, but breeds exceedingly in a water that pleases him; yea, in many ponds so fast as to over-store them, and starve the other fish.

He is very broad, with a forked tail, and his scales set in excellent order; he hath large eyes, and a narrow sucking mouth; he hath two sets of teeth, and a lozenge-like bone, a bone to help his

163

grinding. The melter is observed to have two large melts; and the female, two large bags of eggs or spawn.

Gesner reports that in Poland a certain and a great number of large breams were put into a pond, which in the next following winter were frozen up into one entire ice, and not one drop of water remaining, nor one of these fish to be found, though they were diligently searched for; and yet the next spring, when the ice was thawed, and the weather warm, and fresh water got into the pond, he affirms they all appeared again. This Gesner affirms, and I quote my author because it seems almost as incredible as the resurrection to an atheist; but it may win something, in point of believing it, to him that considers the breeding or renovation of the silk-worm and of many insects. And that is considerable, which Sir Francis Bacon observes in his 'History of Life and Death,' fol. 20, that there be some herbs that die and spring every year, and some endure longer.

But though some do not, yet the French esteem this fish highly, and to that end have this proverb, 'He that hath breams in his pond is able to bid his friend welcome.' And it is noted that the best part of a bream is his belly and head.

Some say that breams and roaches will mix their eggs and melt together, and so there is in many places a bastard breed of breams, that never come to be either large or good, but very numerous.

The baits good to catch this bream are many. 1. Paste made of brown bread and honey, gentles, or the brood of wasps that be young, and then not unlike gentles, and should be hardened in an oven, or dried on a tile before the fire to make them tough; or there is at the root of docks or flags or rushes, in watery places, a worm not unlike a maggot, at which tench will bite freely. Or he will bite at a grasshopper with his legs nipped off, in June or July, or at several flies under water, which may be found on flags that grow near to the water-side. I doubt not but that there be many other baits that are good; but I will turn them all into this most excellent one, either for a carp or bream, in any river or mere. It was given to me by a most honest and excellent angler; and hoping you will prove both, I will impart it to you.

1. Let your bait be as big a red worm as you can find, without a knot. Get a pint or quart of them in an evening in garden walks or chalky common, after a shower of rain, and put them with clean moss well washed and picked, and the water squeezed out of the moss as dry as you can, into an earthern pot or pipkin set dry, and change the moss fresh every three or four days, for three weeks, or a month together; then your bait will be at the best, for it will be clear and lively.

2. Having thus prepared your baits, get your tackling ready and fitted for this sport. Take three long angling rods, and as many and more silk or silk and hair lines, and as many large swan or goose-quill floats. Then take a piece of lead made after this manner [as shown], and fasten them to the low ends of your lines; then fasten your link-hook also to the lead, and let there be about a foot or ten inches between the lead and the hook; but be sure the lead be heavy enough to sink the float or quill a little under the water, and not the quill to bear up the lead, for the lead must lie on the ground. Note, that your link next the hook may be smaller than the rest of your line, if you dare adventure, for fear of taking the pike or perch, who will assuredly visit your hooks, till they be taken out, as I will show you afterward, before either carp or bream will come near to bite. Note also, that when the worm is well baited, it will crawl up and down as far as the lead will give leave, which much enticeth the fish to bite without suspicion.

3. Having thus prepared your baits and fitted your tackling, repair to the river, where you have seen them swim in skulls or shoals, in the summer time, in a hot afternoon, about three or four of the clock, and watch their going forth of their deep holes and returning, which you may well discern, for they return about four of the clock, most of them seeking food at the bottom, yet one or two will lie on the top of the water, rolling and tumbling themselves whilst the rest are under him at the bottom, and so you shall perceive him to keep sentinel. Then mark where he plays most and stays longest, which commonly is in the broadest and deepest place of the river, and there, or near thereabouts, at a clear bottom and a convenient landing-place, take one of your angles ready fitted as aforesaid, and sound the bottom, which

should be about eight or ten feet deep, two yards from the bank is the best. Then consider with yourself whether that water will rise or fall by the next morning, by reason of any water-mills near, and according to your discretion take the depth of the place, where you mean after to cast your ground-bait, and to fish, to half an inch, that the lead lying on or near the ground-bait, the top of the float may only appear upright half an inch above the water.

Thus you having found and fitted for the place and depth thereof, then go home and prepare your ground-bait, which is, next to the fruit of your labours, to be regarded.

You shall take a peck, or a peck and a half, according to the greatness of the stream and deepness of the water where you mean to angle, of sweet gross-ground barley malt, and boil it in a kettle. One or two warms is enough, then strain it through a bag into a tub, the liquor whereof hath often done my horse much good; and when the bag and malt is near cold, take it down to the water-side about eight or nine of the clock in the evening, and not before. Cast in two parts of your ground-bait, squeezed hard between both your hands; it will sink presently to the bottom, and be sure it may rest in the very place where you mean to angle. If the stream run hard or move a little, cast your malt in handfuls a little the higher upwards the stream. You may, between your hands, close the malt so fast in handfuls, that the water will hardly part it with the fall.

Your ground thus baited and tackling fitted, leave your bag with the rest of your tackling and ground-bait near the sporting-place all night, and in the morning, about three or four of the clock, visit the water-side, but not too near, for they have a cunning watchman, and are watchful themselves too.

Then gently take one of your three rods, and bait your hook, casting it over your ground-bait, and gently and secretly draw it to you till the lead rests about the middle of the ground-bait. Then take a second rod, and cast in about a yard above, and your third a yard below the first rod; and stay the rods in the ground. But go yourself so far from the water-side that you perceive nothing but the top of the floats, which you must watch most diligently. Then when you have a bite, you shall perceive the top of your float to sink suddenly into the water. Yet, nevertheless, be not too hasty to run to your rods, until you see that the line goes clear away, then creep to the water-side, and give as much line as you possibly can. If it be a good carp or bream, they will go to the farther side of the river. Then strike gently, and hold your rod at a bent a little while. But if you both pull together, you are sure to lose your game, for either your line, or hook, or hold will break. And after you have overcome them, they will make noble sport, and are very shy to be landed. The carp is far stronger and more mettlesome than the bream.

Much more is to be observed in this kind of fish and fishing, but it is far better for experience and discourse than paper. Only thus much is necessary for you to know, and to be mindful and careful of, that if the pike or perch do breed in that river, they will be sure to bite first, and must first be taken. And for the most part they are very large; and will repair to your ground-bait, not that they will eat of it, but will feed and sport themselves among the young fry that gather about and hover over the bait.

The way to discern the pike and to take him, if you mistrust your bream-hook – for I have taken a pike a yard long several times at my bream-hooks, and sometimes he hath had the luck to share my line – may be thus. Take a small bleak, or roach, or gudgeon, and bait it, and set it alive among your rods two feet deep from the cork, with a little red worm on the point of the hook; then take a few crumbs of white bread, or some of the ground-bait, and sprinkle it gently amongst your rods. If Mr Pike be there, then the little fish will skip out of the water at his appearance, but the live-set bait is sure to be taken.

Thus continue your sport from four in the morning till eight, and if it be a gloomy windy day, they will bite all day long. But this is too long to stand at your rods at one place, and it will spoil your evening sport that day, which is this: about four of the clock in the afternoon repair to your baited place; and as soon as you come to the water-side, cast in one-half of the rest of your ground-bait, and stand off. Then whilst the fish are gathering together, for there they will most certainly come for their supper, you may take a pipe of tobacco; and then in with your three rods, as in the morning. You will find excellent sport that evening till eight of the clock. Then cast in the residue of your ground-bait, and next morning by four of the clock visit them again for four hours, which is the best sport of all; and after that, let them rest till you and your friends have a mind to more sport.

From St James's-tide until Bartholomew-tide is the best; when they have had all the summer's food, they are the fattest. Observe lastly, that after three or four day's fishing together your game will be very shy and wary, and you shall hardly get above a bite or two at a baiting. Then your only way is to desist from your sport about two or three days; and in the meantime, on the place you late baited, and again intend to bait, you shall take a tuft of green but short grass, as big or bigger than a round trencher. To the top of this turf, on the green side, you shall, with a needle and green thread, fasten one by one as many little red worms as will near cover all the turf. Then take a round board or trencher, make a hole in the middle thereof, and through the turf, placed on the board or trencher, with a string or cord as long as is fitting, tied to a pole, let it down to the bottom of the water, for the fish to feed upon without disturbance about two or three days; and after that you have drawn it away, you may fall to and enjoy your former recreation.

12

HARVESTING IN THE DELUGE
(1936)

Margaret Mary Leigh

We had nine and a half acres of corn. The first sheaf was cut on August 27, and the last came into the sawmill on October 13. That it should have taken seven weeks to secure so small a crop is a measure of the bad weather we had to contend with. There were six of us – three scythemen and three other workers – and given a dry week we could have got both fields cut, bound and stooked by the end of it, even without machinery. As it was, the long field took a fortnight (August 27–September 10), and the field below Rattray's five days (September 10–September 15). The following four and a half weeks (September 15–October 17) were spent in frantic attempts to get the sheaves dry enough for stacking, and our persistent efforts were rewarded by securing about ninety-five per cent of the crop in good condition. This was achieved only by working early and late, and handling every single sheaf of about six thousand *individually*. In no other way, I believe, could so much corn have been saved, but I do not want to do it again. It will be remembered that we had the hay on our hands at the same time; but the corn had the priority, and we made hay only when it was too wet to work in the cornfields.

I had sown White Line oats, a variety specially bred to be stiffer in the straw and less liable to lodge in bad weather. It justified its reputation, for though both fields had been fallow the previous season and yielded a long-strawed and heavy crop, the corn stood up gallantly, even to the hurricane and deluge of August 21, which caught it nearly ripe and on an exposed slope. As our oats are used for feeding in the sheaf and not for threshing, it is advisable to start cutting when the crop is on the green side, especially in such a climate, where long delayed reaping would allow the parts left last to get over-ripe. So, when the deep green field was slightly tinged with yellow, and a sunny morning promised a good day, we decided to make a beginning. At dawn the hay on all the fences was bone-dry, and we took in six large loads before leaving the hayfield and adjusting our scythes for the corn. We had barely worked for three hours when it began to rain; the sheaves were hastily stooked up and we retired to the barn to fork hay. Nothing further could be done till the 31st, and then work was once again stopped by rain in the afternoon, and haymaking resumed. The following day was fair in the morning, but nothing could be done after dinner, nor for the next two days at all. September 4, 5, and 6 were fine, and we were able to work all day; by the last evening only a small patch was left, but owing to renewed downpours this could not be cut till the 10th. The short spell of good weather had helped us forward, but as luck would have it, Peter developed a bad cold on the 4th, and on this and the following day we were one scythe short.

In addition to Murdo, I had engaged the shepherd's nephew for a few days. Both these lads were experienced scythemen, and Peter by this time had become proficient. Vivian, Mr Gordon, and I went behind to bind the sheaves, and when enough had been cut the scythemen joined us in binding and stooking. In so treacherous a climate it is risky to leave corn on the ground, and I made a practice of having everything stooked up as we went along, so that if a shower came unexpectedly we had nothing to worry about.

After a good deal of practice at Strathascaig, I had become a fairly rapid binder, and my share of the harvest work at Achnabo was mainly the tying of innumerable sheaves. To the spectator at the edge of the field, this seems a simple, and, if he is romantically minded, a beautiful task: you just gather a bundle of corn, lift it, dandle it like a baby, pull out two or three straws to form a tie, bind it, throw it aside, and gather another one. But to the devil with romance! Sheaf-binding is about the worst and most back-breaking job on the farm, and, like so many other rural operations, far less simple than it looks, even when the swathes are lying evenly; if they are in disorder, as often happens when the corn is laid or unskilfully cut, it is almost impossible to make a success of it. If the sheaves are too big, they will not dry; if too small, they will not stand up. If the butts are uneven, the stooks will be crooked, knock-kneed, and damp at the base. If the band is too tight, the straw under it will not dry; if too loose, it will slip when the sheaf contracts in drying; if unskilfully made it will come untied when the stooks are forked into the cart. Even if the crop is clean, the harsh straw frays the skin, so that a day's work leaves the hands and arms covered with a network of minute scratches. And when hemp-nettle is present, which combines the prick of a thistle with the sting of a nettle, the binder's lot is indeed a hard one, especially as prolonged stooping gives him a frightful backache. At Strathascaig I used to think that hemp-nettles were the worst weeds in corn, but since coming to Achnabo I have changed my mind. The top of the long cornfield, in which no cleaning crop had been grown since I know not when, was thick with tall bristling thistles. The sheaves could hardly be handled without gloves, and the speed of binding was slowed down by half. The stooker has the best of it, but even his task is a thankless one if sheaves are as badly made as most of ours. He walks hither and thither, picking up sheaves and setting them up in fours if the weather is quiet and settled, with butts firmly straddled out and heads together, so that the air can circulate round the base. In a high wind, ten or twelve sheaves must go to the stook: they are rapidly hurled together, embraced, and securely tied.

The stooks in the long cornfield, which lay exposed to the full force of a south-westerly gale, had a severe battering. Nearly all of those made up to date were blown down by the storm of Monday the 3rd. They were set up again the same afternoon, and stood fairly well until the even worse hurricane of Saturday the 8th destroyed the whole lot, including all those that had been erected in the interval. This day was memorable. The whole field, with the exception of the small patch mentioned above, was in the stook. We had gone out after breakfast to reset a few that had collapsed in the night, when it began to blow. The wind rose rapidly; stooks fell faster than they could be set up, and in half an hour the whole field was flat. The sky was full of rain, which would most certainly fall as soon as the wind moderated. Much of the corn had from necessity been cut wet; it had been soaked in the stook by a whole day's downpour on the 7th, and would not benefit by lying drenched on the ground over the weekend. Realising that the stooks would never stand unsupported, we rushed out three or four of the tripods and a quantity of stack rope. In ordinary weather the sheaves would have been far too damp to build into hand-ricks, but we reckoned that so strong a wind would blow right through the interstices of the newly built and as yet un-settled mass, and dry the corn better than would be possible if it were lying exposed on the ground. In this we were right, but the

difficulty was to keep the erection from blowing away in its early stages. We spread the legs of the tripod as widely as possible, and then anchored it on the windward side by a rope stay passed from the top of the tripod to a peg driven into the ground. Mr Gordon and Vivian gathered, while Peter built and I held the sheaves in position. When the hand-rick reached waist height the stay was no longer required, but we had to build and rope the top with the help of a step-ladder.

The wind roared across the field and groaned in the pine-wood behind it; tall trees lashed to and fro like saplings, while far below the hay torn from the fences was whirled high in the air. Sheaves as we handed them up were nearly snatched from our grasp and hurled far to leeward; heavy gusts struck the hand-rick, now packed and solid, making it shake and stagger; and Peter, perched on the topmost step, flung his arms about the narrowing point to keep it fast while we ran round the base with ropes, fixing it down in ever tightening spirals. We made two of these hand-ricks in the morning; after dinner the wind moderated and we built several more of various shapes and sizes. Three small ones, which had been made out of the corn cut on the first day, were found to be damp, and we took them into the sawmill to be dried on the now vacant hay rack. This job was hardly done before darkness overtook us, and we were forced to leave a fair number of fallen stooks to be set up again on Sunday. As anticipated, it poured on Saturday night, but our strenuous building of hand-ricks was rewarded by the sight of them standing undamaged by wind or rain till the end of the month. The rest of the corn in the long cornfield was gathered into large hand-ricks by September 14; the last of these was carried in good condition on the 2nd of October.

The second period of our harvest began at noon on the 10th, when we started to cut the field below Rattray's. This, though sown a week later, had overtaken the long cornfield, so that we had to work the two fields concurrently, the earlier having reached the stook and hand-rick stage when the latter was still being reaped and bound. The land, which had been well harrowed and rolled in the spring, was smooth and clean, and except at the western end, the corn was not too long in the straw. There were no stones to blunt the scythes and no thistles to delay the binders; we made fine progress until the usual afternoon deluge stopped all outdoor work for the day, and Vivian was dispatched to hunt for food in the village. Next morning we resumed cutting, but it began to rain soon after dinner, and we retired to the sawmill to fork hay. The previous year we had the corn in stacks outside, but the prolonged bad weather made me wish to have as much as possible stored under cover. We therefore decided to shift all hay from the southern end of the sawmill to the northern, thus leaving a large space that could be packed to the rafters with sheaves, and would if need be hold the whole crop.

The 13th was the finest working day of the season, and we made good use of it. There was no wind, and the corn was drenched with dew, but after so many delays we could not afford to wait for ideal conditions. So I ordered an early start, and the first sheaves were cut in a state of moisture that would have appalled a southern farmer. At the beginning of the harvest I should not have done it myself, but we were getting a little desperate, and beyond tying the sheaves loosely and stooking them in fours we left the thing to Providence. The two hired lads went at five to help a neighbour cart his hay, but the rest of us worked late, and when we finished there was not much more than a day's work left to do.

The next day was hot and oppressive. Once more we started cutting early, but soon after eleven thundery clouds were seen in the west, and just before twelve a distant peal was heard. We made a rush to the long cornfield and secured the rest of the stooks in hand-ricks. Among the hills of Skye a storm was in progress, which at any moment might drift in our direction; but after causing a commotion of curses and hasty work it passed away to the north, and the rest of the day was dry. The field below Rattray's was finished next morning, and the last sheaf carried home to Flora in the kitchen, where it was kept until defaced by mice.

From this time onwards small loads of corn began to trickle in to the sawmill. The first couple of hundred sheaves were from lack of experience stacked too damp; they heated and we had to cart them out to the fence to dry. After that we made a practice of feeling each individual sheaf as it came in; if any one showed a trace of dampness, it was put on the rack with band loosened, or in bad cases completely untied. We had cherished a faint hope that those three fine days would be the first of a spell of settled weather. But the rain came back to stay, and by the 24th it was clear that unless something were done promptly the corn in Rattray's field would sprout in the stook. The field was too sheltered for rapid drying; the stooks were sodden and drooping, grass was growing through the butt-ends, and many sheaves were already sprouting under the bands, though the heads, except where stripped by pigeons, were still in good condition. I regretted now that I had not carted off the whole crop as soon as it was cut and stooked it in the long cornfield, where there was always plenty of wind to dry the stooks, and bare stubble under them, instead of the lush undergrowth of sown grass that spoilt the drying in the other field.

The byre drain had choked, and an old man had been sent by the estate to dig a trench for new pipes. Before settling on a croft in the village, he had gained years of experience as a farm servant on the East Coast, and I thought he might have some useful suggestions. I took him up to look at the field. He agreed that the corn could not be left where it was, and advised us to cart it to the sawmill field and let the sheaves dry upon a 'soo.' This is an old device, well known in the North as an effective substitute for stooking in bad weather. It is a steeply pitched trestle-shaped erection, roughly built of old posts or odd pieces of wood lashed or nailed together; it can be extended to any length desired, and raised to the height at which a man can conveniently reach to fill it. The sheaves are put on the soo in overlapping layers, heads inward, in the manner of thatching, while the ends are left open for the air to pass through and dry the ears. The topmost layer of sheaves are inverted and tightly bound with a rope. We had a quantity of spars left over from the tripods; they were hauled out by Peter and Mr Gordon, who rapidly built them into two soos which held between them about sixteen hundred sheaves. Meantime Vivian and Murdo carted down the corn and I put it on the soo. But this was not the end of our trouble. To save marking or splitting the spars, which were new and squared, we had on the old fellow's advice used lashings of stack-rope instead of nails. The open ends of the first soo had been strengthened with wooden stays, but the weight of the sodden corn was enormous, and before long ominous groans and cracks were heard, the middle of the soo began to sag, and presently the whole erection quietly collapsed, in torrents of rain. It was soon rebuilt with nails and internal stays, and the second one to match; after that they weathered a gale and we had no further misadventure. But I do not think that we should build soos again. It is true that the sheaves, though wringing wet when put on, did not heat, and only the topmost or roofing layer sprouted. But the drying was very slow, as, apart from the ears, which were exposed to the wind passing through the tunnel, there was too little ventilation of individual sheaves.

The two soos when full would not accommodate more than half the corn from the field below Rattray's. On the 27th we decided to try the experiment of drying the remainder on the fence like hay. The south side of the long cornfield was bounded by a fence of two wires only, the lower one raised well above the ground. To this fence, the sheaves were carted and put on vertically, the butts resting in serried row upon the lower wire, which split them to the band, while the heads were tucked firmly under the upper one. Thus jammed they were secure from storms, and being unprotected and broadside on to the prevailing wind, they dried far more quickly than their neighbours on the soo, though needless to say they suffered several fresh wettings before we could get them secured in hand-ricks on October 2. All this corn was wringing wet when it came out of the stook, and most of it was put on the fence in a pitiless downpour, but it was finally saved in better condition than any other. If at the time of cutting I had been able to foresee the appalling weather that was to come, I should have put every sheaf on the fence without stooking at all, and allowed it to mature there; for I have no doubt that this method would have saved much loss of time and labour.

By the third week in September we realised that we must be ready to finish drying all the corn indoors. As we were still making hay, the barn with its rack and packing accommodation was reserved for that, leaving the sawmill free for corn. The big sawmill rack was too small for our needs, and we were busy contriving new drying-places for the sheaves that came in daily from fences, soos, or hand-ricks. We made a small rack in the stable, but the sheaves dried too slowly, and it was abandoned. The granary, a long upstairs building covering the whole length of cart-shed and dairy, was converted to corn-drying, a small space on one side being reserved for Mr Gordon and his poultry food. The window, which was in line with the door, was taken out, and light racks of sheep-netting stretched across the rafters. There was an excellent through draught, and sheaves could be unloaded into the cart-shed below and forked straight up through a trap-door. The cart-shed itself was fitted with overhead racks of wire and sheep-netting, while surplus sheaves were spread about on the wood-heap, draped over the trap, or leant in a single row against the wall. Thin planks were laid across the rafters of the sawmill, with a space between each, and a layer of sheaves one deep was spread across them. The whole farm seemed buried in half-dry corn – every place was littered with odd bits of straw, husks, and shaken grain. Peter and I would spend one or two hours daily in testing, sorting, and grading sheaves into three classes – those ready for stacking, those needing a spell on the rack, and those only fit for poultry. The second was the largest class, and the third fortunately very small – perhaps one cart-load out of twenty. Although the last load came in from the field on October 13, the sorting of sheaves was not finished till four days later.

13

SCANDAL AND GOSSIP IN THE VILLAGE
(1930)

Henry Williamson

The tales which pass on the tongues of village people rarely gain or lose in the telling. The plain narrative is told as it was heard. After twenty minds have taken it in and given it out again it remains almost the same. There may be several reasons, or a combination of reasons, for this. Lack of imagination, this faculty not having been used for inward self-searching; fear of being found out; or because most of them are naturally factful where their money is not concerned. Much of the gossip is 'news,' which usually moves in a circular path, returning to the subject of it.

That the tales pass unvarying does not always mean that they are true. Some of the stories may have been started by someone incapable, through the shallowness of personal experience or intuition, of understanding the motives of others. Thus all stories of others are steeped with the quality of the originator; but how infrequently is this recognised! Too often the facts of the story are not strung with the spirit of their origin; the motives of others are not taken into account, causing distress to the sensitive. To an intelligent and impartial listener, a story going around reveals only the quality of mind of the first speaker, just as what a man writes about his neighbours reveals his own quality and nature.

The ordinary villager does not like to express an original opinion unless he or she is certain others would agree. A man might begin with the words, 'They say,' and a woman with 'You know what they be saying up in the village? 'Tis awful what they do tell about. They be masterpieces for scandal. There's no saying what they'll be saying next. They say that – ,' and then follows the story.

It does not need much intelligence to see the beam in a neighbour's eyes, especially if a beam of similar size and nature inhabits your own. Indeed, having a beam yourself, you are made the more aware, and thereby the more irritated, by the presence of other people's beams. The beam of gossip is a most subtle one to pluck out and hold with the tweezers of truth. Are not all things relative; as many worlds as there are pairs of eyes serving the interiors of skulls? Sometimes, however, the intangible issue of Truth may be escaped by humour. Such a case occurred in the village recently.

One Sunday morning a parson preached a sermon on this very subject of gossip. The subtlety of cause and effect, the influences of remote aversions and complexes, which may have had their share in the original spite, were not touched upon, but only what he termed the 'malicious effect of thoughtless scandal.' He was suffering from some himself, and felt it keenly. Being full of trenchant generalization, it was considered a good sermon, and nearly all those who heard it were confirmed in their righteous dislike of their neighbour's shortcomings. It was talked about all the week, and the next Sunday the congregation awaited with interest another such sermon. It happened to be the Sunday when the local company of the County Territorial regiment held their annual Church Parade. The parson had something direct to say about another unpleasant aspect of village life. It appeared that a lady visitor to the village during the past week had told him that never in all her experience of English village life had she seen so much drunkenness as existed in the village of Ham. The parson said that if 'things did not improve, some people might find themselves within the arm of the law.'

It made a sensation; the good people knew whom he meant, etc. Albert Hancock, landlord of the Higher House, was a regular churchman in his neat blue serge suit, and after morning service he called upon Mr Taylor of the Lower House. Mr Taylor did not go to church; Sunday for him being the day when he could lie up a bit extra. He had just got out of bed. Together the two publicans, with the village constable, and some of the regular customers of the two inns, led by John Brown of Crowcombe Farm, called on the parson. John Brown said that he represented the considered opinion of those present with him, if his reverence would excuse him saying so. He wished to say, with all respect, that the sermon preached by his reverence the previous Sunday, dealing with malicious gossip and the evil effects of a thoughtless word, had made such an impression on them that he felt he would like to suggest that the observations of a visitor, after staying but three days in the village, might possibly fall within the meaning of the word gossip. He hoped his reverence would excuse him for telling what his reverence probably knew already, that his remarks in church would be in the local paper next Thursday, that many of the Territorials in church, strangers from Combe, Town, and Cross Tree, etc, would carry away a bad impression of the parish, and the constable would be asked by his sergeant why the alleged drunkenness had not been reported. Men had a glass or two sometimes at night, and they sang a song sometimes, but the charge of general drunkenness seemed to him, a rough and ready man, without education, to come precisely within the meaning of the term scandal.

The parson, a man of courage, who was then new to the parish, apologized during the evening service for what, he said, he then knew to be an unfounded charge; but he had made it in all good faith, and for the good of the village, as he hated trouble, and looked upon them all as good children of God. He did not say (and he may not have known) how the nervous tissue of the complaining spinster lady visitor had been wrought upon by her interpretations of what she thought was actuality when, walking down Stony Hill on the Saturday night preceding, silently on rubber soles, she had passed between two lines of men standing with faces to the ditched walls on either side of the lane, where no nettles or other weeds could grow. One of the men – it was Willy Gammon – was singing; others were talking loudly, and sometimes there was a word that had a meaning in a town different from its jovial everyday use in the country. It was a few minutes after ten o'clock, and the men had just come out of the Higher House.

What were natural acts were thought to be 'vile and beastly' in the good woman's mind, and out of her reaction and indignation – without thought – she had made her charges against the village. By her words had she revealed her limitations. In the Higher House they understood, and were not angry with her; but it is doubtful if she will ever understand the Higher House.

14

THE CARTER'S PRIDE
(1904)

Gertrude Jekyll

In the older days the country towns on market days were gay with the brightly painted farm waggons with their well-groomed teams. There was an amicable rivalry among the carters as to the dressing of their horses, for the brightly polished brass ornaments and the gay rosettes of worsted ribbons were the carter's own property, and when not on the horses were often arranged as a trophy over the cottage fireplace. Foremost among these ornaments were the ear-bells, with their upright plume of black and white, or red and yellow horsehair, that followed the top strap of the headstall and buckled in just above the blinkers. Sometimes in the place of the plume there was the ornament of three tinkling bells, or the circular brass plate, hinged at the top, that flashed as it swung, often turning right over as Dobbin tossed his head; and there was a brass plate with shaped edge, engraved with a horse and cart or some other device, that went upon the nose-band. Then there were the 'face-pieces,' in a great variety of pattern; also used below the collar, three or four one above another. Other portions of the harness were profusely ornamented with small round brass studs and heart-shaped and bossy brasses.

The love of decorating his horses is still a matter of pleasant pride to the good carter, and when I see a well-looking team, made unusually smart for the road or town, I know that the carter is a good fellow who takes a right pride in his work and cattle.

But the number of the pretty teams are few compared to those of the older days, when one still heard the pleasant music of the 'latten' bells. A few years ago I bought two sets of these at a farm sale. An old carter standing by said to me, 'I mind when we always went to market with the teams dressed and the latten bells on, and when they wore they, the horses was just as proud as the carters was.' Latten is an old English word for a kind of brass or bronze, answering to the French *laiton*. There were four rings of bells in the set, and each set had four bells, except the one with three of the largest bells of deep tone; each set made its own chord, while the whole clanged and jingled in pleasant harmonies. The leather hood was often scalloped or evenly jagged at the lower edge, and generally had a pretty running ornament of barley, incised with a small gouge in the surface of the leather. A red woollen fringe hung inside the hood all round; sometimes it came only a little way down, but generally was so long as to hide the bells completely. The two spikes passed down the two sides of the collar along the hames.

The original use of the bells on the harness was to give notice in the narrow lanes, so that a carter hearing a distant team, could either wait before entering the lane or draw to the side in good time at some wider part. There is a legend of two carters who purposely ignored the warning, met in the middle of a narrow lane, and fought the matter out. How the battle ended and how the teams and waggons were got out remains unrecorded in local history.

Ear-caps were prettily braided in gay colours, edged with brightly coloured tufts, and tied in place with worsted ribbon to match. Manes were plaited and tied with ribbons, also matching; and then Prince and Smiler, Dragon and Champion; or Diamond, Violet, Punch and Jolly, as the case might be, tossing their heads to make their pretty music, and pawing the ground to show their eagerness, went proudly on their townward way.

Some of the older harness was needlessly heavy, but it seems a pity that the great upstanding flaps that stood up above the collar, that looked so handsome and were such a comforting protection to the horse's withers when turned down in wet weather, should now be so little used.

◆

Paste for Chapped Hands

Mix a quarter of a pound of unsalted hog's-lard, which has been washed in common and then rose-water, with the yolks of two new-laid eggs, and a large spoonful of honey. Add as much fine oatmeal or almond paste as will work into a paste.

Maria Rundell, 1837

◆

15

THE SOW GIVES BIRTH
(1965)

Dunsop Bridge Women's Institute

My husband was going to the Lonk Sheep Breeders' Annual Dinner. This year it was held at Todmorden. This happened to be on a very cold night. My last-minute instructions were to 'keep a look-in at that sow,' which I did, but with several interruptions of several incoming phone calls, a neighbour to use the phone, and the grocer calling to deliver the weekly order, and getting the children to bed. It was two and a half hours or so between one look-in and the next. By this time there were nine little pigs, five of which were laid out as if dead, and quite cold, as they had not been under the infrared lamp. I gathered them up in my apron, dashed indoors, gave them a hot bath and put them in the Rayburn warming oven. In a very short time they had completely recovered, and they were all back with the sow when my husband returned. What a night!

16

AN OLD FARM KITCHEN
(1984)

Ian Niall

Early recollections are often most vivid, because they concern what are called one's impressionable years. If I think of my own I am immediately transported to the kitchen of my grandfather's house, for it was there that I took my first steps, having been sent to the country as an infant in the belief that country air and country food were essential for my survival. It turned out, of course, that I was far from frail. I grew and flourished like the green bay tree and there was no need for any molly-coddling at all, assuming that there was time for pampering in so busy a household.

There may have been times when an impression was made on me by the solemn, steady tick of the grandfather clock and the impatient buzzing of a bluebottle trying to escape at the window, but more often than not that farmhouse kitchen was as busy as the stackyard at threshing, the twenty-acre in the heat of harvest or the hayfield that, in those far-off days, had to be turned by lines of men plying wooden rakes like beings possessed, especially when the far-away mountain was half-obscured by lowering cloud.

If my grandfather held sway everywhere beyond the porch, and was ritually master at the head of the table, it was my grandmother who ran things within the threshold, and her industry and organization set the pace for everything outside. There could be no threshing without baking, cooking, brewing and churning, and no one could rise early to harvest unless at some time or other grandmother had prepared for that breakfast, salting a ham, making preserve, laying in stores. The town was a considerable distance away and it would have been a shame and a disgrace, in any case, had the humblest labourer been asked to eat anything that was not home-baked. It would have indicated a sad state of indolence had the soda-bread been buttered with anything but butter churned in the dairy across the court. To provide porridge for the man who had to be warm in order to go to the far marches to bring down a ploughing team, the pot had to be constantly on the hob and there had to be someone to stir the pot.

In the corner of the kitchen there stood an article of furniture called an ark. It was, in fact, a sort of bunker that held one quarten sack of oats and one of flour. Tea and sugar had to be stocked in similar proportions: a chest of tea, a sack of flour. The ham that hung on the ceiling hooks was salt and those who had it for breakfast needed copious amounts of tea to quench their thirst. They needed tea at breakfast time and tea in the mid-morning.

Two, or sometimes three, baskets had to be prepared and tea cans filled to be carried to the men who might be working in two or three different places. Pancakes were baked for the tea baskets, pancakes and oven scones. Large quantities of gooseberry jam, black-currant and blackberry jam were laid in at the appropriate season. For a good part of the late summer and early autumn half of the burnished iron range was taken up by the brass preserving pan. The labour in the kitchen matched the labour out of doors.

As soon as the mid-day meal was cleared away – as many as six men and sometimes more had to be fed with broth or soup, potatoes, mutton, salt beef or boiled ham, followed by whatever sweet would fill them full – the womenfolk began to prepare for their orgy of baking. Mounds of soda scones, treacle scones and scones made of potato or oatmeal were turned out and left to cool under a white linen cloth. It used to puzzle me as a small child how unconcerned the baking woman was to see so much of her labour devastated when the first wave of workers came from the harvest field to eat before lending a hand at milking.

The clock ticked, but no one heard it, except perhaps myself when the house was all at once empty, and my aunts were off somewhere in the garden picking a black-currant bush, or gathering gooseberries or apples.

I cannot think of the farm kitchen when it did not have some mouth-watering, appetising scent about it. Even when my grandmother was making mushroom ketchup the spices had a delicious aroma. Time was all she lacked, good housekeeper that she was; time to deal with a newly-slaughtered pig – she wasted nothing but the grunt – time to pickle and salt things, to make brawn, to lay up fat carefully clarified, to label and pack away every storable thing that would provide for a day to come, to make shortbread that melted in one's mouth, blackberry wine that tasted like port, and even nettle beer to clear the blood of impurities.

It seems to me that even with time so precious there was time for certain ritual, for the brass tap on that monster of iron that was called a range was polished until it shone like gold, and so did the rail, the mantel-rail that enclosed the inevitable brass candlesticks which, in my innocence, I really took to be gold until my grandmother had gone to her long home and someone remarked that the brass candlesticks had lost a little of their brilliance through neglect and that the old lady would not rest easy if she thought that things were not being kept as she had kept them for a lifetime.

The pressure on the kitchen hardly ever seemed to diminish. When harvest was over and the business of laying away fruit, preserves and all the surplus of the summer and autumn was over there would surely be a threshing on a large scale. We had our own mill but it wasn't adequate. When large quantities of straw and grain were urgently needed, the steam threshing mill would be summoned to enable the first stock of grain to be put in the granary and the strawhouse to be filled for bedding the wintering cows. The mill men were fed along with our own workers and whatever neighbours came to lend a hand.

When at length the threshing ended and the mill engine sat cooling down in the stackyard, at nightfall there was a social occasion, a sort of second harvest home, a supper of roasted spare ribs, or a hare that had been shot on the stubbles, cheese from the great tub cheese that stood on the corner of the table so that anyone could cut for himself and replace the 'lid' or crust. This was another thing that grandmother had to watch. Although there was nothing about cheesemaking that she did not know, we no longer made cheeses, and the buying of cheese was something to which some thought had to be given. In a dairying countryside people were judged by the quality of the cheese they had on their table. It had to be of exactly the right flavour, crumble as a good cheese should, and keep as no cheese will keep nowadays.

When I think about it, my grandmother must have been a most careful woman. She wasted nothing, she anticipated every need of the household. Ask her for anything from a clove to a section of honey and she could produce it, and she still found time to see that the range was burnished, the parlour fire built with peats, and honeysuckle gathered from the hedge to drench the back porch with sweet scent at nightfall. If someone came into the kitchen with a pheasant that had been beheaded by the reaper she had the bird hung. If they brought her a hare she bled it for soup. At daybreak she would be picking over mushrooms gathered on the old turf of the field behind the house, and last thing at night, by the light of the oil lamp, she would be stitching another square in her patchwork quilt, or making toddy for someone who had stayed too long in a downpour.

Things have changed beyond recognition, and I doubt whether many farm kitchens today are stocked with a crate of tea, a side of bacon, sacks of sugar, oats and flour. I am sure there are not many where every loaf or cake is baked at home. Some of those cakes were made from secret recipes and had as many as two dozen eggs in them. The deep freeze, the travelling shop, the refrigerator and the washing machine have revolutionized the life of the farmer's wife and transformed her kitchen from a place of burnished steel, shining brass and copper and hard labour, to enamel, bright chrome and comparative ease.

I have no doubt that my grandmother would have loved these things, but I have a feeling that she would still have put her salt hams on the hooks, stored away her ketchup and jams and jellies, and laid in enough stores to withstand a month-long siege, for this was the housekeeping she learned as her mother's hand-maid. The burnished metals were the symbols of industry, and nothing in life must be wasted – the little yellow apple on the most gnarled tree in the garden, the berry on the bush or the passing minute that was recorded by the steady ticking of the wag-at-the-wall clock.

17

TARKA THE GUARD DOG
(1985)

Phil Drabble

One of the risks in having a new dog is that it won't hit it off with the old one. Although I feel half-dressed without a dog, and in more than sixty years have never been without one, a roll-call of their names would be less than a baker's dozen. Once they have been accepted as members of our household, they have been part of the family for life. With the exception of Grip and Rebel, two Staffordshire bull terriers, whose ancestors had been bred for fighting, they all settled down pretty well.

Grip and Rebel, the best ratting dogs I ever saw, blew their tops because they both tried to get through a half-open door at the same time when they heard me return from work. Each thought the other was trying to reach me first and, although they were dog and bitch, they set on to fight as viciously as human prizefighters. I choked them apart before too much damage was done, but they were never again safe to leave together without supervision. When they died, I replaced them with gentler breeds.

Tick, the German short-haired pointer who shared my life for twelve years, was such a favourite that another of the same breed, bringing back too vivid memories, would not have stood a chance. So Tarka, the Rottweiler, joined the family a year ago. She was just over seven weeks old, too tiny even to climb into the dog box by the radiator in the kitchen. The police-dog trainer, who found her for me, warned that the breed are very wilful and that I would find my new pup a challenge to train. It was an understatement.

She is immensely intelligent and delightfully affectionate . . . but although it is simple to make her understand what is wanted, that is only half the battle. If I was bright enough to make Tick understand what I wanted, it was her pleasure to comply, but the same willingness is shown by Tarka only if it is what she wants too. It would, of course, have been simple enough to have knocked compliance into her or snatched it in with one of the modern choke-chains, which look less brutal than old-fashioned dog whips because they don't leave a mark, but that is not my way. I want my dogs faithful as friends, not zombies, and I find that limitless patience always does the trick in the end, and my new pup is showing every sign of being as good as my last.

There has been one serious worry. Belle, the Alsatian, is a gentle-natured, affectionate bitch but not a strong personality – except when strangers trespass. Then she stands no nonsense whatsoever. But Tick always dominated her and, although they were very good friends, there was never any doubt about which of them was top dog. Belle treated Tarka, when she arrived, like a delicate doll, to be fondled and played with. The pup could do no wrong, whether it was hanging onto her long tail, pulling her ears or nicking goodies from her dinner.

Soon the pup grew into a hefty lump of muscle, with teeth still as sharp as needles. I left the old bitch to establish the peck order and would not have remonstrated if she had put the upstart well and truly in her place, but she took everything that was coming to her without complaint. So I ticked the pup off and stopped her, but she bounced back like India rubber and the old bitch was as offended as if it was her that I had scolded. It got to the stage where the pup dominated the old lady until she was utterly demoralized, refusing to come for walks and going off her food.

Now, I am delighted to say, it is all ending happily. The turning point came when the pup got her second teeth (which are not so needle-sharp) and lost her playfulness as she matured. They have suddenly found that they have more serious interests in common, and love ratting in the yard at night, or coming for walks in the wood. They even share delicacies from the same plate.

Although Rottweilers are used as police dogs in Germany, Tarka is so good natured that she welcomed strangers at first – but that is changing too. When they are the other side of the fence, she bares her teeth, roars her defiance, and Belle joins in the chorus. It is the start of another delightful partnership.

◆

For Chapped Lips

Put a quarter of an ounce of benjamin, storax, and spermaceti, two penny-worth of alkanet-root, a large juicy apple chopped, a bunch of black grapes bruised, a quarter of a pound of unsalted butter, and two ounces of bees-wax, into a new tin saucepan. Simmer gently till the wax, &c., are dissolved, and then strain it through linen. When cold, melt it again, and pour it into small pots or boxes; or if to make cakes, use the bottoms of tea-cups.

Maria Rundell, 1837

18

THE CIDER-MAKING BUSINESS
(1887)

Thomas Hardy

In the yard between Grace and the orchards there progressed a scene natural to the locality at this time of the year. An apple-mill and press had been erected on the spot, to which some men were bringing fruit from divers points in mawn-baskets, while others were grinding them, and others wringing down the pomace, whose sweet juice gushed forth into tubs and pails. The superintendent of these proceedings, to whom the others spoke as master, was a young yeoman of prepossessing manner and aspect, whose form she recognized in a moment. He had hung his coat to a nail of the outhouse wall, and wore his shirt-sleeves rolled up beyond his elbows, to keep them unstained while he rammed the pomace into the bags of horsehair. Fragments of apple-rind had alighted upon the brim of his hat – probably from the bursting of a bag – while brown pips of the same fruit were sticking among the down upon his fine round arms, and in his beard.

 She realized in a moment how he had come there. Down in the heart of the apple-country nearly every farmer kept a cider-making apparatus and wring-house for his own use, building up the pomace in great straw 'cheeses,' as they were called; but here, on the margin of Pomona's plain, was a debatable land neither orchard nor sylvan exclusively, where the apple-produce was hardly sufficient to warrant each proprietor in keeping a mill of his own. This was the field of the travelling cider-maker. His press and mill were fixed to wheels instead of being set up in a cider-house; and with a couple of horses, buckets, tubs, strainers, and an assistant or two, he wandered from place to place, deriving very satisfactory returns for his trouble in such a prolific season as the present.

The outskirts of the town were just now abounding with apple-gatherings. They stood in the yards in carts, baskets, and loose heaps; and the blue stagnant air of autumn which hung over everything was heavy with a sweet cidery smell. Cakes of pomace lay against the walls in the yellow sun, where they were drying to be used as fuel. Yet it was not the great make of the year as yet; before the standard crop came in there accumulated, in abundant times like this, a large superfluity of early apples, and windfalls from the trees of later harvest, which would not keep long. Thus in the baskets, and quivering in the hopper of the mill, she saw specimens of mixed dates, including the mellow countenances of streaked-jacks, codlins, costards, stubbards, ratheripes, and other well-known friends of her ravenous youth.

19

BEES AND THE FAMILY
(1966)

George Ewart Evans

The close link of the bees with the household or family of their owner is a feature of northern mythology; and the custom of 'telling the bees' was practised in many north European countries until recent years. It was a common practice among the old rural community in East Anglia, and here is a typical account of it taken from a man [W. H. Thurlow] who was born at Stonham Aspal, Suffolk. 'If there was a death in the family our custom was to take a bit of crepe out to the bee-skeps after sunset and pin it on them. Then you gently tapped the skeps and told the bees who it was who had died. If you didn't do this, they reckoned the bees wouldn't stay, they'd leave the hives – or else they'd pine away and die.'

It is clear from other sources that up to sixty or seventy years

ago in East Anglia the beekeepers regarded the bees as highly
intelligent beings and treated them as such: 'the wisdom of the
bees' and 'the secret knowledge of the bees' were more than just
poetic phrases to them; they believed they were true to the letter.
In the Suffolk village of Debenham there was an old beekeeper
who regularly talked to his bees and claimed to be able to inter-
pret their response by the pitch of their buzzing. It is certain that
bees are very responsive to different tones of the human voice,
and this is probably the reason for the country belief that bees are
peace-loving beings and will not stay with a quarrelsome family.
Similarly it is likely that it is the basis of the injunction that 'you
must never swear in the hearing of your bees.' A Suffolk man
said, 'My grandfather was a bit of a rough diamond, and he wasn't
above letting a few words fly in front of us children when he felt
like it. But he would never use bad language when he was near his
bees. He'd always be on his best behaviour then!'

But to return to the old beekeeper [recalled by Leonard
Aldous]: 'James Collins treated the bees as members of the family.
He was a retired thatcher and he used to come and *work the bees*, as
he said, at the saddler's where I was apprentice. This was well
before the First World War. I used to carry the box up for him
when he was going to smoke the bees out and I was able to
observe him pretty closely. If there was a tempest about – if the
air felt thundery in any way – he wouldn't go near the bees. And
at any time before approaching the hives he'd stand back and

listen, to find out how they were getting on. Then he'd look to see which way they were travelling, so that he wouldn't get into their line of flight. He'd watch them quietly; and he often told me how he had a good idea where they'd been taking their honey. If they came to their hives low, they'd most likely have come off a field of clover. If they had been working on fruit trees they'd come in much higher. It wouldn't do to get in their line of flight: you'd be sure to get stung. The old man told me in this connection: "If the bees come near you don't start beating the air: leave 'em. Don't fight the bees; the bees will allus win."

'It's true. The bees will stop a horse. And I thought of what Jim Collins said when I heard what happened over at Stonham. Just by the Maltings there was a man cutting clover with a cutter and two horses. Everything was going on well till the machine broke down. The worst part about it was that it stopped right in the line of flight of some bees who were working the field of clover. They attacked the driver and he straightway made a bolt for it, leaving the horses standing there. Both horses were stung unmercifully. One of them died soon afterwards; and the other one – I saw it myself – was so bad and its head so swollen up with the stings that it had to be supported in its stable by a kind of sling fixed to the roof.

'But Jim Collins was the cleverest man I knew at bees. He used to talk to them quietly when he was at the hives; and he reckoned he could tell when they were about to swarm by the different sound of their buzzing: how they answered his talk. As I say, he treated the bees as members of the family, as though they were friends; and I never knew him to be stung. Although the bees and the hives really belonged to Mr Rumsey, my master, Jim reckoned that he was their owner: the bees, he said, belonged to him. He could manage them; and he used to say that if he went away and left his hat hanging on one of the trees in the garden, the bees would never leave. If they swarmed they wouldn't go farther than the garden. He wore a hat with a veil when he was working his bees but often as not the veil used to be drawn back on his hat and nowhere near his face and his neck. There is a story that another Debenham beekeeper once took a swarm of bees in his hat; and then put the hat on and walked home. And after knowing Jim Collins I can well believe the story's a true one.'

But the bees not only knew the voice of their owner but also his particular smell: one beekeeper [William Cobbold] told the writer 'Whenever I go to the barber's I've always to tell him: "Nothing on, thank you." If he were to put lotion on my hair, however nice it smelled, the bees wouldn't think much of it at all. I know from experience that if I approached their hives with scented lotion on my hair it would make them angry.' The bees in fact should be treated at all times, so is the belief, as if they were people; and people who were very ready to take offence if not treated properly. They must not be bought or sold or even taken or given as a present. A beekeeper may give away a hive, and later the recipient will find a way of unobtrusively repaying the kindness either with an appropriate gift or with some worthwhile service.

It is in this context of the close link between the beekeeper and his bees and his high opinion of their intelligence that the custom of 'telling the bees' was practised, and it is against this background that it must be regarded. But it would be difficult to explain the custom other than by treating it as a true superstition, a remnant of an ancient and complex body of belief that was active in the old rural community until the First World War. The bees in classical mythology had a close link with the Ga Mater or the Earth Mother; and Melissa (the Bee) was priestess to her under another of her titles, the Great Mother. Jupiter, also, favoured the bees for the services they had given him when he was helpless in the Cretan cave. He, the Jupiter of the Underworld, had rewarded them with a portion of the divine nature, making them souls or carriers of souls to the hereafter. 'The Zeus child of the Cretans, fed by a swarm of little creatures who were souls – the bees – had something of a God of the dead about him: his Cretan cave had the property of a place of the dead just as his other sanctuary had on Mount Lykaion.'

This special function of the bees in the old hierarchy of gods illumines a passage in the Fourth Georgic – lines 219 to 227, a passage that has been mistranslated at least since Dryden by a persistent reading of a kind of Christian pantheism into what is essentially pagan mythology. In the usual rendering of these lines there is a complete break of thought as compared with the original Latin, and the bees' function is ascribed illogically to God. But it is clear from the myth itself, and the continuity given to the passage by paraphrasing the myth into its rendering, that the bees themselves were believed to carry the delicate filament of life from heaven or the gods – life that is given at birth to all living creatures including men. And at a creature's death they bear the filament or the soul back to that country where, as Virgil says, 'there is no room for death and where the souls fly free, ranging the deep heavens to join the stars' imperishable number.' This conception, although adapted and Christianized beyond recognition during the Middle Ages so as to make the passage even now a potential source of controversy like those lines in the Fourth (or Messianic) Eclogue, has nevertheless been kept in its true, original form in the mythology of northern Europe.

In Scandinavia, for instance, the idea not only of the divine nature of the bees but also of their special function was preserved in a form identical with the old classical belief; and there is no doubt that the belief persisted in East Anglia, an area that for long periods was easily accessible to Norse influence. Osbert Sitwell has recalled how the Sitwell family's East Anglian butler used to refer to the groups of cumulus cloud passing majestically across a blue sky as 'them great big Norwegian Bishops.' The Sitwell children were probably impressed but not enlightened – at least, not until many years later when a correspondent, referring to this passage in one of Osbert Sitwell's earlier books, pointed out that Bishops was a mis-hearing for bee-ship or bee-skip (*bȳskip*), and that the phrase Henry Moat the butler had used carried the belief that 'the souls of the dead are represented as bees and were supposed to traverse the sky in what was specifically termed a bee-ship.' And it should be pointed out that the old straw-plaited beehive could easily be considered as an analogue of a well-rounded cumulus cloud. Moreover, Virgil also compares a swarm of bees to a dark cloud being drawn across the sky by the wind.

Thus when we look for the rationale or the explanation of the old custom of 'telling the bees' we can put forward the hypothesis that it stems directly from the pagan belief; and although this hypothesis is unlikely to gain general acceptance, it may serve as an example of how these apparently worthless and curious beliefs held by the old rural community – and derided by the ignorant – all had their own meaning, an ancient logic that should be material for the historian equally as relevant as a fossil, an arte-fact, an old building, or a valuable piece of parchment.

There is also another link between the bees in classical times and their discipline as observed in the old country tradition. This was the custom of tinging (or tanging) the bees. Here is an account of it from East Anglia [by W. H. Thurlow]. 'Before he went to work on a summer's morning my father often used to tell my mother, "Watch the bees today, Mother. It's a-going to be hot." And if later on there was a commotion in the garden, us children used to run into the house and say, "The bees are out, Mother!" Then she'd get the key of the door and she'd say, "Go and get the dust-pan, quick!" She'd then go after the bees a-tinging the pan with the door-key to make the swarm settle. They used to say that you could follow wherever your bees went if they swarmed across someone else's property. There was a clear right-of-way, as long as you did no damage.'

There is also another belief about the bees that should be briefly recorded; a bee-sting has curative value for those who suffer from rheumatism or arthritis. A Suffolk doctor recently told the writer, 'Mr A. spent a number of years abroad. When he returned to this village he was crippled with rheumatism. He decided to keep bees in order to get rid of it. He became a bee-keeper and, in fact, he did cure himself.'

20

RURAL POLITENESS
(1711)

Joseph Addison

The first and most obvious reflections which arise in a man who changes the city for the country, are upon the different manners of the people whom he meets with in those two different scenes of life. By manners I do not mean morals, but behaviour and good breeding, as they show themselves in the town and in the country.

And here, in the first place, I must observe a very great revolution that has happened in this article of good-breeding. Several obliging deferences, condescensions, and submissions, with many outward forms and ceremonies that accompany them, were first of all brought up among the politer part of mankind, who lived in courts and cities, and distinguished themselves from the rustic part of the species (who on all occasions acted bluntly and naturally) by such a mutual complaisance and intercourse of civilities. These forms of conversation by degrees multiplied, and grew troublesome; the modish world found too great a constraint in them, and have therefore thrown most of them aside. Conversation, like the Romish religion, was so encumbered with show and ceremony that it stood in need of a reformation to retrench its superfluities, and restore its natural good sense and beauty. At present, therefore, an unconstrained carriage, and a certain openness of behaviour, are the height of good-breeding. The fashionable world is grown free and easy; our manners sit more loose upon us; nothing is so modish as an agreeable negligence. In a word, good-breeding shows itself most, where to an ordinary eye it appears the least.

If after this we look on the people of mode in the country, we find in them the manners of the last age. They have no sooner fetched themselves up to the fashion of a polite world, but the town has dropped them, and are nearer to the first stage of nature, than to those refinements which formerly reigned in the court, and still prevail in the country. One may now know a man that never conversed in the world by his excess of good-breeding. A polite country squire shall make you as many bows in half an hour as would serve a courtier for a week. There is infinitely more to do about place and precedency in a meeting of justices' wives than in an assembly of duchesses.

This rural politeness is very troublesome to a man of my temper, who generally takes the chair that is next me, and walks first or last, in the front or in the rear, as chance directs. I have known my friend Sir Roger's dinner almost cold before the company could adjust the ceremonial and be prevailed upon to sit down; and have heartily pitied my old friend, when I have seen him forced to pick and cull his guests, as they sat at the several parts of his table, that he might drink their healths according to their respective ranks and qualities. Honest Will Wimble, who I should have thought had been altogether uninfected with ceremony, gives me abundance of trouble in this particular. Though he has been fishing all the morning, he will not help himself at dinner till I am served. When we are going out of the hall, he runs behind me; and last night, as we were walking in the fields, stopped short at a stile till I came up to it, and upon my making signs to him to get over, told me, with a serious smile, that sure I believed they had no manners in the country.

There has happened another revolution in the point of good-breeding, which relates to the conversation among men of mode, and which I cannot but look upon as very extraordinary. It was certainly one of the first distinctions of a well-bred man to express everything that had the most remote appearance of being obscene in modest terms and distant phrases; whilst the clown, who had no such delicacy of conception and expression, clothed his ideas in those plain homely terms that are the most obvious and natural. This kind of good manners was perhaps carried to an excess, so as to make conversation too stiff, formal, and precise; for which reason (as hypocrisy in one age is generally succeeded by atheism in another) conversation is in a great measure relapsed into the first extreme; so that at present several of our men of the town, and particularly those who have been polished in France, make use of the most coarse, uncivilized words in our language, and utter themselves often in such a manner as a clown would blush to hear.

This infamous piece of good-breeding, which reigns among the coxcombs of the town, has not yet made its way into the country; and as it is impossible for such an irrational way of conversation to last long among a people that makes any profession of religion, or show of modesty, if the country gentlemen get into it, they will certainly be left in the lurch. Their good-breeding will come too late to them, and they will be thought a parcel of lewd clowns, while they fancy themselves talking together like men of wit and pleasure.

As the two points of good-breeding which I have hitherto insisted upon, regard behaviour and conversation, there is a third which turns upon dress. In this too the country are very much behindhand. The rural beaus are not yet got out of the fashion that took place at the time of the Revolution, but ride about the country in red coats and laced hats; while the women in many parts are still trying to outvie one another in the height of their head-dresses.

◆

Uses of Poppies

Poppies that grow in the corne, the leaves stamped and bound unto the eyes or face that are black and blew by means of some blow or stripe, do perfictly take it away. The dry herb steeped in warme water worketh the like effect. The juyce of poppies taketh away warts if they be often rubbed therewith.

Thomas Newington, 1719

◆

21

HOW TO RUN A GYMKHANA
(1931)

Henry Hope-Murray

It is of first importance in arranging a gymkhana to arrange a day that will be likely to attract spectators. If it is a Wednesday, make certain that there is not a flower show being held on that day, or if it is a Saturday that there is not a race meeting on the same day that would be likely to distract people from the attendance. Consider whether you are in a pony or a horse district. If you are not in a polo pony neighbourhood it is of little use having bending races; similarly, if you are not in a horse district it is of little use having events that include jumping. Having decided upon your day, draft your programme, giving careful attention to the times that each item will occupy. Nothing bores spectators more than drawn-out events, or worse still, a delay between events. Consider, too, for whom you are catering – grown-ups or children. If it is between May and August you are unlikely to get sufficient entries to warrant having children's events. All the ones old enough to compete will be at school and their ponies will be at grass.

You have now to choose a site where it is to take place. If you can persuade someone with a place to lend a field for it, so much the better. There is something peculiarly attractive about a private place in summer; it is so infinitely preferable to a public place. It is attractive in itself. Advertise well beforehand in the newspapers and by posters. Keep the entry fees low; it will pay you, as even those without a chance of winning will not mind entering if the fees are low. In the same way keep the prices of admittance down as much as possible; a shilling should suffice. Programmes should not be elaborate and should cost no more than 3d.

As regards the staff necessary, get as many of your friends as possible to assist. They will enjoy it and it will cost you nothing. The officials necessary are a secretary, a collecting steward, a ring master, who announces the events and the names of the competitors, and a property master, who is responsible for producing the *property* required for the events at the right place.

As regards stabling, a rope line erected breast high will do well provided it is long enough. It is much cheaper than anything else and perfectly adequate. Money prizes should not be given. They would not be large enough to attract additional entries, and prizes in kind are infinitely more popular with ladies and children.

In choosing events the following may be found to fit the programme: 1. *Bending Race for Gentlemen.* Run in heats. The race to be run in and out of posts 9 yards apart. 2. *Jumble Race for Ladies.* Competitors to run 50 yards to a line, from which they will walk 50 yards to where their unsaddled ponies are held. Competitors must saddle-up unaided, mount, ride round a post at end of course and back over a flight of hurdles to Winning Post. 3. *Costume Race.* In pairs (Lady and Gentleman). Competitors ride 50 yards, one dismounts, dresses (without assistance) in costume (while partner holds the pony), remounts and both ride to Winning Post, which they must pass hand in hand. 4. *Polo Ball Race for Gentlemen*, either with ordinary polo ball, or if the grass is long, with one of Salter's rubber balls as used for indoor polo. Competitors start 300 yards from two goal posts and hit through the goal. Once the ball is over the back line, it cannot be brought back. To be run in heats if necessary. 5. *V.C. Race for Children.* Competitors ride 100 yards over a low fence to pick up a dummy and return carrying same to starting point. To be run in heats. 6. *Miniature Show Jumping Course.* For Children under fifteen. 7. *Handy Hunter Course.* With six jumps for Ladies. A time limit to be imposed, say, two minutes.

The last two contests might be held after tea. Start the afternoon at 2.30 pm and end not later than 6.30 pm.

If you are hoping to make money for some local charity it is imperative to take a census of the neighbourhood as to horses and riders before you embark on the venture. You will then have an idea of what to cater for and how much you are justified in spending in expenses and prizes. Gymkhanas which include children's events are undoubtedly very popular today.

22

WEAVING THE TWEED
(1936)

Margaret Mary Leigh

With a little more leisure we could have produced our own clothes. Some years ago I had learned hand-weaving from an English friend, and hand-spinning from a servant who was a native of Harris. My own wheel and loom, which had been used at Strathascaig for turning the Laird's fleeces into tweed, were stored in the lumber-room at Achnabo: but all these things take time. I have heard people complaining of the price asked for genuine hand-woven tweeds – usually 7s a yard, but often less; they would be sorry to produce tweed themselves at this figure. Having myself done the whole process, carding excepted, from the sheep's back to my own, I can claim to know something about it.

In this district sheep are not washed before clipping, and the fleeces are packed as they are, full of dirt, grease, tangles, and scraps of twig and heather. They must be washed very thoroughly with soft soap and ammonia, often in six or seven waters, and then hung up to dry. The handling and wringing of fleeces is heavy work, and drying them a slow business, for they must be kept away from livestock and from places where fodder is stored. Scraps of wool have killed many calves; they lodge in the stomach, where the hooked fibres gather food around them, until little by little a hard ball is formed which causes congestion and finally death. When the fleeces are quite dry, the worst tangles must be teased out by hand before carding. Most spinners now send their fleeces to be carded at a mill, but a few still do it at home, and the results are more pleasing and durable, especially where very soft wool such as Shetland is used. Dyeing is usually done after washing and before carding. Herself was an expert dyer, and we made many experiments with various vegetable dyes; but the commonest and perhaps most effective is that obtained from crotal – the greyish-green lichen that grows on rocks and old stone walls. A fire is built outside, and a large cauldron or boiler set over it. This is filled up with wool and crotal in alternate layers, pound for pound, and allowed to boil for about two hours, when the wool is taken out and the scraps of crotal shaken from it. The colour obtained is a rich reddish brown, which when mixed either in carding or in weaving with other colours, is the foundation of most of the well-known Harris tweed. The wool is dried once more, and then carded. The effect of this process is to tease out all irregularities and shape the mass of wool into long thin rolls that can be easily handled by the spinner.

To the beginner, spinning is the devil's own job. It takes about a fortnight to learn to spin with competence. Like many other things it cannot be taught; you must just practise till you get the knack, and try to master your temper. The wheel must be controlled with your feet and the yarn with your hands; the problem is to work them together, and the worst moment is the joining of one carded roll to another without stopping the wheel or allowing the yarn end to run out of your hand and on to the bobbin – a thing it will do every other minute; and this means tedious re-threading with a bent hairpin, and fury and despair. Or the wheel will suddenly run in reverse, with tangle and confusion, or it will slip its band, or refuse to turn the spindle at all. If the wool goes on to the bobbin too quickly, it will be thick and lumpy; if too slowly, it will overtwist and break. When the bobbin is full, the wheel must be disconnected and the yarn wound off into a ball for convenience in weaving. If knitting wool is required, two balls are taken, each put into a separate pail, both ends led to the spindle, and the wheel worked in reverse: the separate strands will thus be twisted into two-ply yarn.

Weaving is a far more skilled and complicated craft than spinning, and very few hand-looms are now to be seen on the mainland. Most local spinners send their finished yarn to a hand-weaver or a mill to be made into tweed. But if the cloth is to be woven at home, the process is roughly this. The length of tweed

desired – say twelve yards – and the number of lengthwise or warp threads – say eighteen to the inch – is decided upon. Sufficient yarn is taken to the warping-board, where it is wound on spaced pegs in such a way that when removed it will lie in the form of a woollen serpent twelve yards long, consisting of 472 separate threads arranged in a definite order – that is 18 × 27, for most hand-woven tweeds are 27 inches wide. The threads are then taken to the loom and passed in the same order through the gaps in the reed, a comb-like contrivance fixed on the beater, which keeps the warp threads evenly spaced, thus controlling the width of the cloth. If this order is once lost, the result is complete and hopeless chaos.

After passing through the reed, the yarn is threaded, still in the same order, through the heddles at the back of the reed. These are loops of wire or twine strung on pairs of sticks, which are connected with the treadles, and work in twos, fours, or sixes, according to the weaving – plain or patterned – that is desired. The ends are then tied to the roller at the back of the loom, and the weaver, helped by an assistant, slowly rolls the whole length of warp threads on to the back roller, leaving just enough length of yarn in front of the reed to tie the ends to the front roller. During the process of rolling, all threads must be kept at an even tension or they will sag or break. The warp is now ready for weaving. The rest of the yarn, or weft, is wound on a spool-winder into small bobbins for insertion in the shuttle.

The actual weaving of the material is done on the space between the front roller and the reed. At each movement of the treadle the weaver raises or depresses a set of warp threads, and through the tunnel or 'shed' thus made, the weft thread is thrown in the shuttle, and beaten hard down on its predecessor, thus making the cloth. As the weaving proceeds, the rolling process is reversed, until, when the piece is completed, the whole length of warp threads will have been gradually transferred from the back roller to the front.

The tweed is then taken from the loom, and the loose ends roughly bound over to prevent fraying. It is then washed to remove the grease left by the carders for ease in spinning. When nearly but not quite dry, we smooth it flat on a big table and roll it tightly and evenly on a wooden roller, upon which it is left to dry out completely. From this bald and imperfect description the reader will realise that the home producer of tweed deserves 7s a yard. The price of wool has little effect on the price of tweed; about three-quarters of a pound of Cheviot wool, now 1s 1d a pound, goes to a yard of fairly heavy-weight tweed, and the cost of the raw material is, as in so many other cases, very small in comparison with the cost of labour.

These tweeds give very long wear. They are not as hard as certain of the closely beaten mill-woven cloths, but they have a way of moulding themselves to the figure, and of getting shabby in a graceful and gentlemanly fashion. Vegetable dyes fade into pleasant hues; dirt blends well with crotal, and frayed edges attract no more attention than the fringe of a kilt. You may spend a good deal on your suits to start with, for they need good tailoring, but you can wear them till they fall to pieces without losing caste.

23

THE TRAITOROUS WAYS OF DECOY DUCKS
(c1724)

Daniel Defoe

The art of taking the fowls, and especially of breeding up a set of creatures called decoy ducks, to entice and then betray their fellow-ducks into the several decoys, is very admirable indeed and deserves a description, though 'tis not very easy to describe it, take it in as few words as I can.

The decoy ducks are first naturalized to the place, for they are hatched and bred up in the decoy ponds. There are in the ponds certain places where they are constantly fed, and where being made tame, they are used to come even to the decoy man's hand for their food.

When they fly abroad, or as might be said, are sent abroad, they go none knows where; but 'tis believed by some they fly quite over the seas into Holland and Germany. There they meet with others of their acquaintance, that is to say, of their own kind, where sorting with them and observing how poorly they live, how all the rivers are frozen up and the lands covered with snow, and that they are almost starved, they fail not to let them know (in language that they make one another understand) that in England, from whence they came, the case is quite altered; that the English ducks live much better than they do in those cold climates; that they have open lakes, and sea shores full of food, the tides flowing freely into every creek; that they have also within the land, large lakes, refreshing springs of water, open ponds, covered and secured from human eyes, with large rows of grown trees and impenetrable groves; that the lands are full of food, the stubbles yielding constant supplies of corn, left by the negligent husbandmen, as it were on purpose for their use, that 'tis not once in a wild duck's age that they have any long frosts or deep snows, and that when they have, yet the sea is never frozen or the shores void of food; and that if they will please but to go with them into England, they shall share with them in all these good things.

By these representations, made in their own duck language (or by whatever other arts which we know not) they draw together a vast number of the fowls and, in a word, kidnap them from their own country; for being once brought out of their knowledge, they follow the decoys as a dog follows the huntsman; and 'tis frequent to see these subtle creatures return with a vast flight of fowls with them or at their heels, as we may say, after the said decoy ducks have been absent several weeks together.

When they have brought them over, the first thing they do is to settle with them in the decoy ponds, to which they (the decoy ducks) belong. Here they chatter and gabble to them in their own language, as if they were telling them that these are the ponds they told them of, and here they should soon see how well they should live, how secure and how safe a retreat they had here.

When the decoy men perceive they are come, and that they are gathering and increasing, they fail not to go secretly to the pond's side, I say secretly, and under the cover which they have made with reeds, so that they cannot be seen, where they throw over the reeds handfuls of corn, in shallow places, such where the decoy ducks are usually fed, and where they are sure to come for it, and to bring their new guests with them for their entertainment.

This they do for two or three days together, and no harm follows, 'till throwing in this bait one time in an open wide place, another time in another open wide place, the third time it is thrown in a narrower place; that is to say, where the trees, which hang over the water and the banks, stand nearer, and then in another yet narrower, where the said trees are overhead like an arbour, though at a good height from the water.

Here the boughs are so artfully managed that a large net is spread near the tops of the trees among the branches and fastened to hoops which reach from side to side. This is so high and so wide, and the room is so much below and the water so open, that the fowls do not perceive the net above them at all.

Here the decoy man keeping unseen behind the hedges of reeds, which are made perfectly close, goes forward, throwing corn over the reeds into the water. The decoy ducks greedily fall upon it, and calling their foreign guests seem to tell them that now they may find their words good, and how well the ducks live in England; so inviting or rather wheedling them forward, 'till by degrees they are all gotten under the arch or sweep of the net, which is on the trees and which by degrees, imperceptibly to them, declines lower and lower, and also narrower and narrower, 'till at the farther end it comes to a point like a purse, though this farther end is quite out of sight, and perhaps two or three hundred yards from the first entrance.

When the whole quantity are thus greedily following the leading ducks or decoys and feeding plentifully as they go, and the decoy man sees they are all within the arch of the net and so far within as not to be able to escape, on a sudden a dog which 'till then he keeps close by him, and who is perfectly taught his business, rushes from behind the reeds and jumps into the water, swimming directly after the ducks and (terribly to them) barking as he swims.

Immediately the ducks (frighted to the last degree) rise upon the wing to make their escape, but to their great surprise are beaten down again by the arched net, which is over their heads. Being then forced into the water, they necessarily swim forward, for fear of that terrible creature the dog; and thus they crowd on, 'till by degrees the net growing lower and narrower, as is said, they are hurried to the very farther end, where another decoy man stands ready to receive them and who takes them out alive with his hands.

As for the traitors that drew the poor ducks into this snare, they are taught to rise but a little way, and so not reaching to the net, they fly back to the ponds and make their escape; or else, being used to the decoy man, they go to him fearless and are taken out as the rest; but instead of being killed with them, are stroked, made much of, and put into a little pond just by him, and fed and made much of for their services.

24

THE ANNUAL SHOW
(1965)

Bellingham Women's Institute

Bellingham and District Leek Club members held their annual show – the 32nd show of flowers, vegetables and also bread – in the Town Hall, Bellingham on Saturday, 9th October 1965. Two challenge cups are awarded for the best stand of leeks and onions in the show. It was open to the public from 2 o'clock till 6.55 pm. Total membership for the year stood at 55. An extra attraction was an Open Quoits Competition during the day. A dance was held, commencing at 9.30 pm, with music by the Shades of Blue beat group, admission 3/-. Every September, a week before Bellingham show, a fair comes, with dodgem cars. Usually a large crowd collects on the fairground, known as 'The Hoppings' by the local children, on the Saturday afternoon and evening of the Bellingham Show. Unfortunately wet weather often spoils the ground, leaving everything in a quagmire.

25

FAIR DAY
(1909)

Edward Thomas

Today is fair day. The scene is a green, slightly undulating
common, grassy and rushy at its lower end where a large pond
wets the margin of the high road, and at the upper end sprinkled
with the dwarf and the common gorse out of which rise many
tumuli, green or furzy mounds of earth, often surmounted by a
few funereal pines. The common is small; it is bounded on every
side by roads, and on one by a row of new mean houses; there is a
golf-house among the tumuli; in one place a large square has
been ploughed and fenced by a private owner. But the slope of
the sandy soil is pleasant; in one place it is broken into a low cliff
over-hanging the water, and this with the presence of the gorse
give it a touch of the wildness by which it may still deserve its
name of 'heath.' Most powerful of all in their effect upon the
place are the tumuli. They are low and smooth; one or two
scarcely heave the turf; some have been removed; and there is no
legend attached to them. Yet their presence gives an indescribable
charm and state, and melancholy too, and makes these few acres
an expanse unequalled by any other of the same size. Not too far
off to be said to belong to the heath, from which they are separated by three miles of cultivated land and a lesser beechen hill, are
the Downs; among them one that bears a thin white road winding
up at the edge of a dark wood. In the moist October air the Downs
are very grave and gentle and near, and are not lost to sight until
far beyond the turreted promontory of Chanctonbury.

Early in the morning the beggars begin to arrive, the lame and
the blind, with or without a musical instrument. King of them all
certainly is he with no legs at all and seeming not to need them, so
active is he on a four-wheeled plank which suspends him only a
foot above the ground. Many a strong man earns less money. The
children envy him as he moves along, a wheeled animal, weather-
beaten, white-haired, white-bearded, with neat black hat and
white slop, a living toy, but with a deep voice, a concertina and a
tin full of pence and halfpence.

These unashamed curiosities line the chief approaches down
which every one is going to the fair except a few shabby fellows
who offer blue sheets full of music-hall ballads to the multitude

and, with a whisper, indecent songs to the select. Another no less energetic, but stout and condescending, yellow-bearded, in a high hard felt hat, gives away tracts. The sound of a hymn from one organ mingles with the sound of 'Put me among the girls' from another and the rattle of the legless man's offertory-tin.

The main part of the fair consists of a double row, a grove, of tents and booths, roundabouts, caravans, traps and tethered ponies. A crowd of dark-clad women goes up and down between the rows: there is a sound of machine-made music, of firing at targets, of shouts and neighs and brays and the hoot of engines. Here at the entrance to the grove is a group of yellow vans; some children playing among the shafts and wheels and musing horses; and a gypsy woman on a stool, her head on one side, combing her black hair and talking to the children, while a puppy catches at the end of her tresses when they come swishing down. Beyond are coconut-shies, short-sighted cyclists performing, Aunt Sallies, rows of goldfish bowls into which a light ball has to be pitched to earn a prize, stalls full of toys, cheap jewellery and sweets like bedded-out plants, and stout women pattering alongside – bold women, with sleek black or yellow hair and the bearing and countenance of women who have to make their way in the world. Behind these, women are finishing their toilet and their children's among the vans, preparing meals over red crackling fires, and the horses rest their noses on the stalls and watch the crowd; the long yellow dogs are curled up among the wheels or nosing in the crowd.

There are men selling purses containing a sovereign for sixpence, loud, fat cosmopolitans on a cockney basis with a ceaseless flow of cajolery intermingled with sly indecency; the country policeman in the background puzzling over his duty in the matter, but in the end paralyzed by the showmen's gift of words. One man has before him a counter on which he asks you to cover a red-painted disc with five smaller discs of zinc, charging twopence for the attempt and promising a watch to the great man who succeeds. After a batch of failures he himself, with good-natured but bored face, shows how easily it is done, and raising his eyes in despair craves for more courage from the audience. The crowd looks on, hesitating, until he singles out the most bashful countryman at the back of the throng, saying, 'I like your face. You are a good sort. You have a cheerful face; it's the rich have the sad faces. So I'll treat you to a go.' The hero steps forward and succeeds, but as it was a free trial he receives no watch; trying again for twopence he fails. Another tries. 'By Jove! that was a near one.' A woman tries, and just as she is finishing,

'You're a 'cute one, missus,' he ejaculates, and she fails. Another
tries, and the showman has a watch ready to hand over, and only
at the last moment says excitedly (restoring the watch quietly to
its place), 'I thought you'd got it that time. Come along! It's the
best game in the world.' Once more he repeats the trick himself
without looking, and then exclaims as he sweeps the discs
together, 'It's a silly game, I call it!' He is like the preachers who
show the stupid world how virtue is won: he has a large audience,
a large paunch, and many go away disappointed. The crowd
stares, and has the one deep satisfaction of believing that the
woman who travels with him is not his wife.

At the upper end of the grove is the gaudy green and gold and
scarlet-painted and embossed entrance to the bioscope, raised a
few feet above the crowd. On the platform before the door stand
two painted men and a girl. The girl has a large nose, loose mouth
and a ready, but uneasy, discontented smile as if she knows that
her paint is an imperfect refuge from the gaze of the crowd; as
if she knows that her eyes are badly darkened, and her white
stockings soiled, and her legs too thin under her short skirt, and
her yellow hair too stiff. She lounges wearily with a glib clown who
wears a bristly fringe of sandy hair round his face, which tickles
her and causes roars of laughter when he aims at a kiss. The other
performer is a contortionist, a small slender man in dirty, ill-
fitting scarlet jacket with many small brass buttons, dirty brown
trousers crisscrossed by yellow stripes; his hands in his pockets;
his snub nose deep pink, and his lean face made yet leaner and
more dismal by a thin streak of red paint on either cheek. His
melancholy seems natural, yet adds to his vulgarity because he
forsakes it so quickly when he smirks and turns away if the girl
exposes her legs too much. For she turns a somersault with the
clown at intervals; or doubles herself back to touch the ground
first with her yellow hair and at last with her head; or is lifted up
by the clown and, supported on the palm of one of his hands,
hangs dangling in a limp bow, her face yet gaunter and sadder
upside down with senseless eyes and helpless legs. The crowd
watch – looking sideways at one another to get their cue – some
with unconscious smiles entranced, but most of them grimly controlling the emotions roused by the girl or the contortionist or the
clown and the thought of their unstable life. A few squirt water
languidly or toss confetti. Others look from time to time to see
whether any one in the county dare in broad daylight enter the
booth for 'gentlemen only,' at the door of which stands a shabby
gaudy woman of forty-five grinning contemptuously.

Up and down moves the crowd – stiffly dressed children carrying gay toys or bowls of goldfish or coconuts – gypsy children with scarves, blue or green or red – lean, tanned, rough-necked labourers caged in their best clothes, except one, a labourer of well past middle age, a tall straight man with a proud grizzled head, good black hat of soft felt low in the crown, white scarf, white jacket, dark-brown corduroys above gleaming black boots.

On the open heath behind the stalls they are selling horses by auction. Enormous cart-horses plunge out of the groups of men and animals and carry a little man suspended from their necks; stout men in grey gaiters and black hats hobble after. Or more decorously the animals are trotted up and down between rows of men away from the auctioneer and back again, their price in guineas mingling with the statement that they are real workers, while a small boy hustles them with whip and shout from behind, and a big stiff man leads them and, to turn them at the end of the run, shoves his broad back into their withers. The Irish dealers traffic apart and try to sell without auction. Their horses and ponies, braided with primrose and scarlet, stand in a quiet row. Suddenly a boy leads out one on a halter, a hard, plump, small-headed beast bucking madly, and makes it circle rapidly about him, stopping it abruptly and starting it again, with a stiff pink flag which he flaps in its face or pokes into its ribs; if the beast refuses he raises a high loud 'whoo-hoop' and curses or growls like an animal. For perhaps five minutes this goes on, the boy never abating his oaths and growls and whoops and flirtings of the pink flag. The horse is led back; a muttering calm follows; another horse is led out. Here and there are groups of cart-mares with huge pedestalled feet and their colts, or of men bending forward over long ash-sticks and talking in low tones. Horses race or walk or are backed into the crowd. Droves of bullocks are driven through the furze. Rows of bulls, sweating but silent and quiet, bow their heads and wait as on a frieze. Again the pink flags are flourished, and the dealer catches a horsey stranger by the arm and whispers and shows him the mare's teeth. This dealer is a big Irishman with flattened face and snaky nose, his voice deep and laughing. He smiles continually, but when he sees a possible buyer he puts on an artful expression so transparent that his merry face shines clearly underneath and remains the same in triumph or rebuke – is the same at the end of the day when he leads off his horses and stopping at a wayside inn drinks on the kerb, but first gives the one nearest him a gulp from the tankard.

26

A COUNTRY CRICKET-MATCH
(1830)

Mary Russell Mitford

I doubt if there be any scene in the world more animating or delightful than a cricket-match – I do not mean a set match at Lord's Ground for money, hard money, between a certain number of gentlemen and players, as they are called – people who make a trade of that noble sport, and degrade it into an affair of bettings, and hedgings, and cheatings, it may be, like boxing or horse racing; nor do I mean a pretty fête in a gentleman's park where one club of cricketing dandies encounter another such club, and where they show off in graceful costume to a gay marquee of admiring belles, who condescend so to purchase admiration and while away a long summer morning in partaking cold collations, conversing occasionally, and seeming to understand the game, the whole being conducted according to ballroom etiquette, so as to be exceedingly elegant and exceedingly dull. No! the cricket that I mean is a real solid old-fashioned match between neighbouring parishes, where each attacks the other for honour and a supper, glory and half-a-crown a man. If there be any gentlemen amongst them, it is well – if not, it is so much the better. Your gentleman cricketer is in general rather an anomalous character. Elderly gentlemen are obviously good for nothing; and young beaux are, for the most part, hampered and trammelled by dress and habit; the stiff cravat, the pinched-in waist, the dandy-walk – oh, they will never do for cricket! Now, our country lads, accustomed to the flail or the hammer (your blacksmiths are capital hitters) have the free use of their arms; they know how to move their shoulders; and they can move their feet too – they can run; then they are so much better made, so much more athletic, and yet so much lissomer – to use a Hampshire phrase, which deserves at least to be good English. Here and there, indeed, one meets with an old Etonian, who retains his boyish love for that game which formed so considerable a branch of his education: some even preserve their boyish proficiency, but in general it wears away like the Greek, quite as certainly, and almost as fast; a few years of Oxford, or Cambridge, or the continent, are sufficient to annihilate both the power and the inclination. No! a village match is the thing, where our highest officer, our conductor (to borrow a musical term) is but a little farmer's second son; where a day-labourer is our bowler, and a blacksmith our long-stop; where the spectators consist of the retired cricketers, the veterans of the green, the careful mothers, the girls, and all the boys of two parishes, together with a few amateurs, little above them in rank and not at all in pretension; where laughing and shouting, and the very ecstasy of merriment and good humour, prevail: such a match, in short, as I attended yesterday, at the expense of getting twice wet through, and as I would attend tomorrow, at the certainty of having that ducking doubled.

For the last three weeks our village has been in a state of great excitement, occasioned by a challenge from our north-western neighbours, the men of B., to contend with us at cricket. Now we have not been much in the habit of playing matches. Three or four years ago, indeed, we encountered the men of S., our neighbours south-by-east, with a sort of doubtful success, beating them on our own ground, whilst they in the second match returned the compliment on theirs. This discouraged us. Then an unnatural coalition between a high-church curate and an evangelical gentleman-farmer drove our lads from the Sunday-evening practice, which, as it did not begin before both services were concluded, and as it tended to keep the young men from the ale-

house, our magistrates had winked at, if not encouraged. The sport therefore had languished until the present season, when under another change of circumstances the spirit began to revive.

Half a dozen fine active lads, of influence amongst their comrades, grew into men and yearned for cricket. An enterprising publican gave a set of ribands. His rival, mine host of the Rose, an out-doer by profession, gave two. And the clergyman and his lay ally, both well-disposed and good-natured men, gratified by the submission to their authority, and finding, perhaps, that no great good resulted from the substitution of public houses for out-of-door diversions, relaxed. In short the practice recommenced, and the hill was again alive with men and boys and innocent merriment; but farther than the riband matches amongst ourselves nobody dreamed of going, till this challenge – we were modest, and doubted our own strength. The B. people, on the other hand, must have been braggers born, a whole parish of gasconaders. Never was such boasting! such crowing! such ostentatious display of practice! such mutual compliments from man to man – bowler to batter, batter to bowler! It was a wonder they did not challenge all England. It must be confessed that we were a little astounded; yet we firmly resolved not to decline the combat; and one of the most spirited of the new growth, William Grey by name, took up the glove in a style of manly courtesy, that would have done honour to a knight in the days of chivalry. 'We were not professed players,' he said, 'being little better than schoolboys and scarcely older, but, since they had done us the honour to challenge us, we would try our strength. It would be no discredit to be beaten by such a field.'

Having accepted the wager of battle, our champion began forthwith to collect his forces. William Grey is himself one of the finest youths that one shall see – tall, active, slender and yet strong, with a piercing eye full of sagacity, and a smile full of good humour – a farmer's son by station, and used to hard work as farmer's sons are now, liked by everybody and admitted to be an excellent cricketer. He immediately set forth to muster his men, remembering with great complacency that Samuel Long, a bowler *comme il y en a peu*, the very man who had knocked down nine wickets, had beaten us, bowled us out at the fatal return match some years ago at S., had luckily, in a remove of a quarter of a mile last Lady-day, crossed the boundaries of his old parish, and actually belonged to us. Here was a stroke of good fortune! Our captain applied to him instantly, and he agreed at a word. Indeed Samuel Long is a very civilized person. He is a middle-aged man who looks rather old amongst our young lads, and whose thickness and breadth give no token of remarkable activity; but he is very active, and so steady a player! so safe! We had half gained the match when we had secured him. He is a man of substance, too, in every way; owns one cow, two donkeys, six pigs, and geese and ducks beyond count; dresses like a farmer, and owes no man a shilling – and all this from pure industry, sheer day-labour. Note that your good cricketer is commonly the most industrious man in the parish; the habits that make him such are precisely those which make a good workman – steadiness, sobriety, and activity. Samuel Long might pass for the beau ideal of the two characters. Happy were we to possess him!

Then we had another piece of good luck. James Brown, a journeyman blacksmith and a native, who, being of a rambling disposition, had roamed from place to place for half a dozen years, had just returned to settle with his brother at another corner of our village, bringing with him a prodigious reputation in cricket and in gallantry – the gay Lothario of the neighbourhood. He is said to have made more conquests in love and in cricket than any blacksmith in the county. To him also went the indefatigable William Grey, and he also consented to play. No end to our good fortune! Another celebrated batter, called Joseph Hearne, had likewise recently married into the parish. He worked, it is true, at the A. mills, but slept at the house of his wife's father in our territories. He also was sought and found by our leader. But he was grand and shy; made an immense favour of the thing; courted courting and then hung back – 'Did not know that he could be spared; had partly resolved not to play again – at least not this season; thought it rash to accept the challenge; thought they might do without him.' – 'Truly I think so too,' said our spirited champion. 'We will not trouble you, Mr Hearne.'

Having thus secured two powerful auxiliaries, and rejected a third, we began to reckon and select the regular native forces. Thus ran our list: William Grey, 1. Samuel Long, 2. James Brown, 3. George and John Simmons, one capital, the other so so, an uncertain hitter but a good fieldsman, 5. Joel Brent, excellent, 6. Ben Appleton. Here was a little pause. Ben's abilities at cricket were not completely ascertained; but then he was so good a fellow, so full of fun and waggery! no doing without Ben. So he figured in the list, 7. George Harris. A short halt there too! Slowish, slow but sure. I think the proverb brought him in, 8. Tom Coper. Oh, beyond the world, Tom Coper! the red-headed gardening lad, whose left-handed strokes send *her* (a cricket-ball, like that other moving thing a ship, is always of the feminine gender) send her spinning a mile, 9. Harry Willis, another black-smith, 10.

We had now ten of our eleven, but the choice of the last occasioned some demur. Three young Martins, rich farmers of the neighbourhood, successively presented themselves, and were all rejected by our independent and impartial general for want of merit – *cricketal* merit. 'Not good enough,' was his pithy answer. Then our worthy neighbour, the half-pay lieutenant, offered his services – he, too, though with some hesitation and modesty, was refused – 'Not quite young enough' was his sentence. John Strong, the exceeding long son of our dwarfish mason, was the next can-didate; a nice youth, everybody likes John Strong; and a willing, but so tall and so limp, bent in the middle – a thread-paper, six feet high! We were all afraid that, in spite of his name, his strength would never hold out. 'Wait till next year, John,' quoth William Grey, with all the dignified seniority of twenty speaking to eigh-teen. 'Coper's a year younger,' said John. 'Coper's a foot shorter,' replied William. So John retired; and the eleventh man remained unchosen, almost to the eleventh hour. The eve of the match arrived, and the post was still vacant, when a little boy of fifteen, David Willis, brother to Harry, admitted by accident to the last practice, saw eight of them out and was voted in by acclamation.

That Sunday evening's practice (for Monday was the important day) was a period of great anxiety and, to say the truth, of great pleasure. There is something strangely delightful in the innocent spirit of party. To be one of a numerous body, to be authorised to say *we*, to have a rightful interest in triumph or defeat, is gratify-ing at once to social feeling and to personal pride. There was not a ten-year-old urchin, or a septuagenary woman in the parish, who did not feel an additional importance, a reflected consequence, in speaking of 'our side.' An election interests in the same way; but that feeling is less pure. Money is there, and hatred, and politics, and lies. Oh, to be a voter, or a voter's wife, comes nothing near the genuine and hearty sympathy of belonging to a parish, breathing the same air, looking on the same trees, listening to the same nightingales! Talk of a patriotic elector! Give me a parochial patriot, a man who loves his parish! Even we, the female partisans, may partake the common ardour. I am sure I did. I never, though tolerably eager and enthusiastic at all times, remember being in a more delicious state of excitation than on the eve of that battle. Our hopes waxed stronger and stronger. Those of our players, who were present, were excellent. William Grey got forty notches off his own bat; and that brilliant hitter Tom Coper gained eight from two successive balls. As the evening advanced, too, we had encouragement of another sort. A spy, who had been despatched to reconnoitre the enemy's quarters, returned from their practising ground, with a most consolatory report. 'Really,' said Charles Grover, our intelligence – a fine old steady judge, one who had played well in his day – 'they are no better than so many old women. Any five of ours would beat their eleven.' This sent us to bed in high spirits.

Morning dawned less favourably. The sky promised a series of deluging showers, and kept its word as English skies are wont to do on such occasions; and a lamentable message arrived at the headquarters from our trusty comrade Joel Brent. His master, a great farmer, had begun the hay-harvest that very morning, and Joel, being as eminent in one field as in another, could not be spared. Imagine Joel's plight! the most ardent of all our eleven! a knight held back from the tourney! a soldier from the battle! The poor swain was inconsolable. At last, one who is always ready to do a good natured action, great or little, set forth to back his petition; and, by dint of appealing to the public spirit of our worthy neighbour and the state of the barometer, talking altern- ately of the parish honour and thunder showers, of lost matches and sopped hay, he carried his point, and returned triumphantly with the delighted Joel.

In the meantime we became sensible of another defalcation. On calling over our roll, Brown was missing; and the spy of the preceding night, Charles Grover – the universal scout and messenger of the village, a man who will run half-a-dozen miles for a pint of beer, who does errands for the very love of the trade, who, if he had been a lord, would have been an ambassador – was instantly despatched to summon the truant. His report spread general consternation. Brown had set off at four o'clock in the morning to play in a cricket-match at M., a little town twelve miles off which had been his last residence. Here was desertion! Here was treachery! Here was treachery against that goodly state, our parish! To send James Brown to Coventry was the immediate resolution; but even that seemed too light a punishment for such delinquency. Then how we cried him down! At ten on Sunday night (for the rascal had actually practised with us, and never said a word of his intended disloyalty) he was our faithful mate, and the best player (take him for all in all) of the eleven. At ten in the morning he had run away, and we were well rid of him; he was no batter compared with William Grey or Tom Coper; not fit to wipe the shoes of Samuel Long, as a bowler; nothing of a scout to John Simmons; the boy David Willis was worth fifty of him. 'I trust we have within our realm, five hundred good as he,' was the universal sentiment. So we took tall John Strong, who, with an incurable hankering after the honour of being admitted, had kept constantly with the players, to take the chance of some such accident – we took John for our *pis-aller*. I never saw anyone prouder than the good humoured lad was of this not very flattering piece of preferment.

John Strong was elected, and Brown sent to Coventry; and, when I first heard of his delinquency, I thought the punishment only too mild for the crime. But I have since learned the secret history of the offence (if we could know the secret histories of all offences, how much better the world would seem than it does now!) and really my wrath is much abated. It was a piece of gallantry, of devotion to the sex, or rather a chivalrous obedience to one chosen fair. I must tell my readers the story.

Mary Allen, the prettiest girl of M., had it seems revenged upon our blacksmith the numberless inconsistencies of which he stood accused. He was in love over head and ears, but the nymph was cruel. She said no, and no, and no, and poor Brown, three times rejected, at last resolved to leave the place, partly in despair, and partly in that hope which often mingles strangely with a lover's despair, the hope that when he was gone he should be missed. He came home to his brother's accordingly; but for five weeks he heard nothing from or of the inexorable Mary, and was glad to beguile his own 'vexing thoughts,' by endeavouring to create in his mind an artificial and factitious interest in our cricket-match – all unimportant as such a trifle must have seemed to a man in love. Poor James, however, is a social and warm-hearted person, not likely to resist a contagious sympathy. As the time for the play

THE COUNTRYSIDE COMPANION

advanced, the interest which he had at first affected became genuine and sincere; and he was really, when he left the ground on Sunday night, almost as enthusiastically absorbed in the event of the next day as Joel Brent himself. He little foresaw the new and delightful interest which awaited him at home, where, on the moment of his arrival, his sister-in-law and confidante presented him with a billet from the lady of his heart. It had, with the usual delay of letters sent by private hands, in that rank of life, loitered on the road, in a degree inconceivable to those who are accustomed to the punctual speed of the post, and had taken ten days for its twelve miles' journey. Have my readers any wish to see this *billet-doux*? I can show them (but in strict confidence) a literal copy. It was addressed,

> For mistur jem browne
>   blaxmith by
>   S.

The inside ran thus: 'Mistur browne this is to Inform yew that oure parish plays bramley men next monday is a week, i think we shall lose without yew. from your humbell servant to command, Mary Allen.'

Was there ever a prettier relenting? a summons more flattering, more delicate, more irresistible? The precious epistle was undated; but, having ascertained who brought it, and found, by cross-examining the messenger, that the Monday in question was the very next day, we were not surprised to find that *Mistur browne* forgot his engagement to us, forgot all but Mary and Mary's letter, and set off at four o'clock the next morning to walk twelve miles, and play for her parish, and in her sight. Really we must not send James Brown to Coventry, must we? Though if, as his sister-in-law tells our damsel Harriet he hopes to do, he should bring the fair Mary home as his bride, he will not greatly care how little we say to him. But he must not be sent to Coventry – True-love forbid!

At last we were all assembled, and marched down to H. common, the appointed ground, which, though in our dominions according to the map, was the constant practising place of our opponents, and *terra incognita* to us. We found our adversaries on the ground as we expected, for our various delays had hindered us from taking the field so early as we wished; and, as soon as we had settled all preliminaries, the match began.

But, alas! I have been so long settling my preliminaries that I have left myself no room for the detail of our victory, and must squeeze the account of our grand achievements into as little compass as Cowley, when he crammed the names of eleven of his mistresses into the narrow space of four eight-syllable lines. *They* began the warfare, these boastful men of B. And what think you, gentle reader, was the amount of their innings? These challengers – the famous eleven – how many did they get? Think! Imagine! Guess! You cannot? Well! – they got twenty-two, or rather, they got twenty; for two of theirs were short notches, and would never have been allowed, only that, seeing what they were made of, we and our umpires were not particular. They should have had twenty more, if they had chosen to claim them. Oh, how well we fielded! and how well we bowled! our good play had quite as much to do with their miserable failure as their bad. Samuel Long is a slow bowler, George Simmons a fast one, and the change from Long's lobbing to Simmons's fast balls posed them completely. Poor simpletons! they were always wrong, expecting the slow for the quick, and the quick for the slow.

Well, we went in. And what were our innings? Guess again! – Guess! A hundred and sixty-nine! In spite of soaking showers, and wretched ground, where the ball would not run a yard, we headed them by a hundred and forty-seven; and then they gave in, as well they might. William Grey pressed them much to try another innings. 'There was so much chance,' as he courteously observed, 'in cricket, that advantageous as our position seemed, we might, very possibly, be overtaken. The B. men had better try.' But they were beaten sulky, and would not move – to my great disappointment; I wanted to prolong the pleasure of success. What a glorious sensation it is to be for five hours together winning – winning – winning! always feeling what a whist-player feels when he takes up four honours, seven trumps! Who would think that a little bit of leather, and two pieces of wood, had such a delightful and delighting power?

The only drawback on my enjoyment was the failure of the pretty boy, David Willis, who injudiciously put in first, and playing for the first time in a match amongst men and strangers, who talked to him, and stared at him, was seized with such a fit of shame-faced shyness that he could scarcely hold his bat and was bowled out without a stroke, from actual nervousness. 'He will come of that,' Tom Coper says. I am afraid he will. I wonder whether Tom had ever any modesty to lose. Our other modest lad, John Strong, did very well; his length told in fielding, and he got good fame. Joel Brent, the rescued mower, got into a scrape and out of it again, his fortune for the day. He ran out his mate, Samuel Long, who, I do believe, but for the excess of Joel's eagerness, would have stayed in till this time, by which exploit he got into sad disgrace; and then he himself got thirty-seven runs, which redeemed his reputation. William Grey made a hit which actually lost the cricket-ball. We think she lodged in a hedge, a quarter of a mile off, but nobody could find her. And George Simmons had nearly lost his shoe, which he tossed away in a passion, for having been caught out, owing to the ball glancing against it. These, together with a very complete somerset of Ben Appleton, our long-stop, who floundered about in the mud, making faces and attitudes as laughable as Grimaldi, none could tell whether by accident or design, were the chief incidents of the scene of action.

Amongst the spectators nothing remarkable occurred, beyond the general calamity of two or three drenchings, except that a form, placed by the side of a hedge, under a very insufficient shelter, was knocked into the ditch, in a sudden rush of the cricketers to escape a pelting shower, by which means all parties shared the fate of Ben Appleton, some on land and some by water; and that, amidst the scramble, a saucy gipsy of a girl contrived to steal from the knee of the demure and well-apparelled Samuel Long, a smart handkerchief, which his careful dame had tied around it, to preserve his new (what is the mincing feminine word?), his new – inexpressibles; thus reversing the story of Desdemona, and causing the new Othello to call aloud for his handkerchief, to the great diversion of the company. And so we parted; the players retired to their supper, and we to our homes; all wet through, all good-humoured, and all happy – except the losers. Today we are happy too. Hats, with ribands in them, go glancing up and down; and William Grey says, with a proud humility, 'We do not challenge any parish; but if we be challenged, we are ready.'

◆

To Make Conserve of Roses

Take a quart of red rose-water, a quart of fair water, boil in the water a pound of red rose leaves, the white cut off, the leaves must be boiled very tender; then take three pounds of sugar, and put to it a pound at a time, and let it boil a little between every pound, so put it up in your pots.

A Queen's Delight, 1695

◆

27

THE HARVEST HOME DINNER
(1939)

Flora Thompson

On the morning of the harvest home dinner everybody prepared
themselves for a tremendous feast, some to the extent of going
without breakfast, that the appetite might not be impaired. And
what a feast it was! Such a bustling in the farmhouse kitchen for

days beforehand; such boiling of hams and roasting of sirloins; such a stacking of plum puddings, made by the Christmas recipe; such a tapping of eighteen-gallon casks and baking of plum loaves would astonish those accustomed to the appetites of today. By noon the whole parish had assembled, the workers and their wives and children to feast and the sprinkling of the better-to-do to help with the serving. The only ones absent were the aged bedridden and their attendants, and to them, the next day, portions, carefully graded in daintiness according to their social standing, were carried by the children from the remnants of the feast. A plum pudding was considered a delicate compliment to an equal of the farmer; slices of beef or ham went to the 'better-most poor'; and a ham-bone with plenty of meat left upon it or part of a pudding or a can of soup to the commonalty.

Long tables were laid out of doors in the shade of a barn, and soon after twelve o'clock the cottagers sat down to the good cheer, with the farmer carving at the principal table, his wife with her tea urn at another, the daughters of the house and their friends circling the tables with vegetable dishes and beer jugs, and the grandchildren, in their stiff, white, embroidered frocks, dashing hither and thither to see that everybody had what they required. As a background there was the rickyard with its new yellow stacks and, over all, the mellow sunshine of late summer.

Passers-by on the road stopped their gigs and high dog-carts to wave greetings and shout congratulations on the weather. If a tramp looked wistfully in, he was beckoned to a seat on the straw beneath a rick and a full plate was placed on his knees. It was a picture of plenty and goodwill.

It did not do to look beneath the surface. Laura's father, who did not come into the picture, being a 'tradesman' and so not invited, used to say that the farmer paid his men starvation wages all the year and thought he made it up to them by giving that one good meal. The farmer did not think so, because he did not think at all, and the men did not think either on that day; they were too busy enjoying the food and the fun.

After the dinner there were sports and games, then dancing in the home paddock until twilight, and when, at the end of the day, the farmer, carving indoors for the family supper, paused with knife poised to listen to the last distant 'Hooray!' and exclaimed, 'A lot of good chaps! A lot of good chaps, God bless 'em!' both he and the cheering men were sincere, however mistaken.

28

MISHAPS ON THE ICE
(1871)

Reverend Francis Kilvert

New Year's Day, 1871
When Perch came back from skating at Draycot last night, he amused us with an account of Friday's and Saturday's doings on the ice. On Friday they had a quadrille band from Malmesbury, skated quadrilles, Lancers, and Sir Roger de Coverley. Then they skated up and down with torches, ladies and gentlemen pairing off and skating arm in arm, each with a torch. There were numbers of Chinese lanterns all round the water, blue, crimson and green lights, magnesium riband, and a fire balloon was sent up. Maria Awdry, forgetting herself and the passage of time, inadvertently spoke to Perch calling him 'Teddy' instead of 'Mr Kilvert.' Having done which she perceived her mistake, turned 'away and smote herself on the mouth,' while Perch 'looked at her with a face like a stone.' While people were standing about in groups or skating up and down gently, young Spencer skated up suddenly with oustretched arm to shake hands with Teddy. At the critical moment his skate hitched and he lost his balance and made a deep but involuntary obeisance before Perch, describing 'an attenuated arch,' with his fingers and toes resting on the ice. People hid their faces, turned and skated away with a sour smile or grinning with repressed laughter. Perch stood still waiting for the 'attenuated arch' to unbind itself and retrieve its erect posture, 'looking on with a face like a stone.' Gradually the 'arch' rose from its deep obeisance. The arch was the arch described by an attenuated tom cat. During the torch skating Harriet Awdry hurled her half-burned torch ashore. Lord Cowley was walking up and down the path on the bank watching with great impatience the skaters whom he detests. The fiery torch came whirling and flaming through the dark and hit the noble diplomatist sharply across the shins, rebounding from which it lay blazing at the foot of a tree. Lord Cowley was very angry. 'I wish these people wouldn't throw their torches about here at me,' grumbled his lordship.

SOURCES AND ACKNOWLEDGEMENTS

The Publisher has made every effort to contact all copyright holders, but wishes to apologise to those he has been unable to trace. Grateful acknowledgement is made for permission to reprint the following:

Part I Country Reflections

1 Richard Jefferies *Wild Life in a Southern County* (first published 1879; reprinted Moonraker Press, Bradford-on-Avon, 1978)
2 Robert Gibbings *Lovely is the Lee* (J. M. Dent & Sons, London, 1945). Reprinted by permission of Laurence Pollinger Ltd and the Estate of Robert Gibbings.
3 Gilbert White *The Essential Gilbert White of Selborne* ed H. J. Massingham (Breslich & Foss, London, 1983)
4 Charles St John *A Sportsman and Naturalist's Tour in Sutherlandshire* (Simpkin, Marshall, London, 1891)
5 Clement W. Scott *Poppy-Land. Pages Descriptive of Scenery on the East Coast* (Jarrold & Sons, London, 1897)
6 Jan Morris *The Matter of Wales. Epic Views of a Small Country* (Oxford University Press, Oxford, 1984). Copyright © Jan Morris. Reprinted by permission of Oxford University Press.
7 Stewart Dick *The Cottage Homes of England* (Edward Arnold, London, 1909; reprinted Bracken Books, London, 1984)
8 Wilson Stephens *The Changing Year* by 'Proteus' of *The Field* (Frederick Muller, London, 1983)
9 Dorothy Wordsworth *Journals of Dorothy Wordsworth* ed William Knight (Macmillan, London, 1925)
10 Giraldus Cambrensis (Gerald of Wales) *The History and Topography of Ireland* trans John J. O'Meara (Penguin, Harmondsworth, 1982)
11 Samuel Johnson *A Journey to the Western Islands of Scotland*, text of 1785 edition as reprinted in *A Journey to the Western Isles, Johnson's Scottish Journey Retraced* by Finlay J. Macdonald (Macdonald, London, 1983)
12 Mary Webb *The Spring of Joy* (J. M. Dent & Sons, London, 1917) as reprinted in *The Essential Mary Webb* ed Martin Armstrong (Readers Union, London, 1951)
13 Ernest C. Pulbrook *The English Countryside* (first published 1914; 2nd ed Batsford, London, 1926)
14 Stewart Dick *op. cit.*
15 Gwyn Jones *A Prospect of Wales* (Penguin, Harmondsworth, 1948) as reprinted in *A Book of Wales* selected by Meic Stephens (J. M. Dent & Sons, London, 1987)
16 *The First Cuckoo. Letters to The Times, 1900–1980* chosen by Kenneth Gregory (Times Books/Allen and Unwin, London, 1981)
17 Fred Archer *Under the Parish Lantern* (Hodder & Stoughton, London, 1966; Coronet, London, 1973)
18 William Cobbett *Rural Rides* vol 2 (first published 1830; reprinted J. M. Dent & Sons, London, 1912)
19 Robert Gibbings *Sweet Thames Run Softly* (J. M. Dent & Sons, London, 1940). Reprinted by permission of Laurence Pollinger Ltd and the Estate of Robert Gibbings.
20 W. M. Thackeray *The Irish Sketch-Book* ['by M. A. Titmarsh'] (Chapman & Hall, London, 1868)
21 Giraldus Cambrensis *The Itinerary Through Wales* trans R. C. Hoare (this edition first published 1806; reprinted J. M. Dent & Sons, London, 1976)
22 Gilbert White *op. cit.*
23 Oscar Wilde 'The Decay of Lying' in *Intentions* (James R. Osgood McIlvaine & Co, London, 1891)
24 W. H. Hudson *A Shepherd's Life* (Methuen & Co, London, 1910)
25 Nathaniel Hawthorne, *Passages From The English Notebooks* (Strahan, London, 1870)
26 Charles St John *op. cit.*
27 Celia Fiennes *Through England on a Side Saddle in the Time of William and Mary, Being the Diary of Celia Fiennes*, Introduction by Hon Mrs Griffiths (Simpkin, Marshall, London, 1888)
28 John Prioleau *Enchanted Ways* (J. M. Dent & Sons, London, 1933)
29 H. J. Massingham *In Praise of England* (Methuen & Co, London, 1924)
30 Richard Jefferies *op. cit.*

Part II Country People

1 Wilson Stephens *op. cit.*
2 Ronald Blythe *Akenfield, Portrait of an English Village* (Penguin, Harmondsworth, 1969)
3 Reverend Sabine Baring-Gould *Old Country Ways* (Methuen & Co, London, 1890)
4 See 2 above
5 Richard Jefferies *op. cit.*
6 Edward Thomas *The South Country* (first published 1909; reprinted Hutchinson, London, 1984)
7 Dion Clayton Calthrop *The Charm of Gardens* (A. C. Black, London, 1910; reprinted as *The Charm of the English Garden* by Bracken Books, London, 1985)
8 Walter Raymond *The Book of Crafts and Character* (first published 1907; reprinted J. M. Dent & Sons, London, 1934)
9 William Cobbett *Political Register* as reprinted in *Cobbett's Country Book* selected by Richard Ingrams (David & Charles, Newton Abbot, n.d.)
10 Jack Hargreaves *Out of Town* (Dovecote Press, Wimborne, 1987)

Part III Country Ways

1 J. H. B. Peel *Small Calendars* (Arthur Barker, London, 1948). Reprinted by permission of D. E. and H. J. Musche.
2 *The Open Air Year* (Times Publishing, London, 1932)
3 E. W. Martin (ed) *The Countryman's Chap-Book* (Dennis Dobson, London, 1949)
4 Samuel Johnson *op. cit.*
5 Paul Jennings (ed) *The Living Village* (Hodder & Stoughton, London, 1968)
6 Daniel Defoe *A Tour Thro' the Whole Island of Great Britain* . . . (first published 1724–26; reprinted Peter Davies, London, 1927)
7 Anthony Trollope *The Eustace Diamonds* (first published 1872; reprinted Oxford University Press, London, 1973)
8 George Bourne *Lucy Bettesworth* (first published 1913; reprinted Caliban Books, Firle, 1978)
9 Raphael Samuel (ed) *Village Life and Labour* (Routledge & Kegan Paul, London, 1975)
10 Patrick Gallagher *My Story* [by 'Paddy the Cope'] (Jonathan Cape, London, 1939)
11 Izaak Walton *The Complete Angler* ed G. Christopher Davies (Warne, London, 1878)
12 Margaret Mary Leigh *Highland Homespun* (G. Bell and Sons, London, 1936). Reprinted by permission of Unwin Hyman Ltd.
13 Henry Williamson *The Village Book* (Jonathan Cape, London, 1930). Reprinted by permission of A. M. Heath Ltd.
14 Gertrude Jekyll *Old West Surrey* (Longmans, Green, London, 1904). Reprinted by permission of Lady Freyberg.
15 See 5 above
16 Ian Niall *Country Matters* (Victor Gollancz, London, 1984)
17 Phil Drabble *Country Moods* (Michael Joseph, London, 1985). Copyright © Phil Drabble. Reprinted by permission of Michael Joseph.
18 Thomas Hardy *The Woodlanders* (first published 1887; reprinted Macmillan, London, 1974)
19 George Ewart Evans *The Pattern Under the Plough* (Faber and Faber, London, 1966)
20 *The Spectator*, No. 119, 17 July 1711 as reprinted in *Essays of Joseph Addison* ed J. R. Green (Macmillan, London, 1892)
21 *The Field*, 20 June 1931
22 Margaret Mary Leigh *op. cit.*
23 Daniel Defoe *op. cit.*
24 See 5 above
25 Edward Thomas *op. cit.*
26 Mary Russell Mitford *Our Village* vol 1 (Whittaker, Treacher, London, 1830)
27 Flora Thompson *Lark Rise* (Oxford University Press, Oxford, 1939). Reprinted from *Lark Rise to Candleford* by Flora Thompson (1945) by permission of Oxford University Press.
28 Reverend Francis Kilvert *Kilvert's Diary 1870–1879* ed William Plomer (Jonathan Cape, London, 1938; Penguin, Harmondsworth, 1977). Reprinted by permission of Jonathan Cape Ltd.

◆

The items by Thomas Newington on pages 150 and 195 are from *A Butler's Recipe Book, 1719* edited by Philip James (Cambridge University Press, Cambridge, 1935), and those by Maria Rundell on pages 179 and 186 are from her book *A New System of Domestic Cookery* (John Murray, London, 1837). The item on page 218 from *A Queen's Delight* of 1695 is reprinted from *Flowers as Food* by Florence White (Jonathan Cape, London, 1934).

◆

Illustration Sources

Half title, pages 25, 98, 180, 189, 192, 204: from *Country Days and Country Ways* by Margaret Cameron (Blackie & Son, London, n.d.)

Title page, pages 21, 48, 55, 58, 63, 83, 89, 103, 140, 147, 153, 208: from *The Picture Pleasure Book* (Abbey and Co., London, c1852)

Pages v, 27, 37, 61, 184, 211: from *Our Village* by Mary Russell Mitford (Sampson Low, Marston, Searle and Rivington, London, 1879)

Pages 11, 59: from *The Landscapes of Thomas Hardy* by Donald Maxwell (Cassell & Co., London, 1928)

Pages 13, 109: from *Wild Life in a Southern County* by Richard Jefferies (Moonraker Press, Bradford-on-Avon, 1978); wood engravings by C. F. Tunnicliffe

Page 26: from *Poppy-Land* by Clement W. Scott (Jarrold & Sons, London, 1897)

Page 31: from *Cotswold Stone* by Freda Derrick (Chapman & Hall, London, 1948)

Page 38: from *The Topographical, Statistical and Historical Gazetteer of Scotland*, vol 2 (A. Fullarton & Co., Glasgow, 1843)

Page 41: from *The History and Topography of Ireland* by Gerald of Wales (Penguin, Harmondsworth, 1982); National Library of Ireland, Ms 700

Pages 45, 117: from *Leaves From Gerard's Herball* edited by Marcus Woodward (Gerald Howe, London, 1931)

Pages 47, 53, 65, 137: from *Small Calendars* by J. H. B. Peel (Arthur Barker, London, 1948); wood engravings by Cuthill

Pages 68, 70, 150, 164: from *The Complete Angler*, vol 2 by Izaak Walton (Nattali and Bond, London, 1860)

Pages 71, 95, 171: from *A Source Book of French Advertising Art* compiled by Irving Zucker (Faber and Faber, London, 1964)

Page 73: from *The Essential Gilbert White of Selborne*, edited by H. J. Massingham (Nonesuch Press, London, 1938; Breslich and Foss, London, 1983); wood engravings by Eric Ravilious, copyright © Estate of Eric Ravilious

Page 79: from *The Story of Some English Shires* by Right Reverend Mandell Creighton (Religious Tract Society, London, 1897); engraving by Thomas Hearne

Pages 84, 156, 201: from *A Memoir of Thomas Bewick, written by Himself*, edited by Iain Bain (Oxford University Press, London, 1975)

Page 85: from *Country Voices* by Charles Kightly (Thames & Hudson, London, 1984)

Pages 93, 97: Mary Evans Picture Library, London

Page 106: from *The Hardy Country* by Charles G. Harper (Adam & Charles Black, London, 1904)

Pages 116, 135, 142, 161, 187: from *The Original Poems and Others* by Ann and Jane Taylor and Adelaide O'Keeffe, edited by E. V. Lucas (Wells Gardiner, Darton & Co., London, n.d.)

Pages 121, 219: from *Our Village* by Mary Russell Mitford (Macmillan, London, 1893); drawings by Hugh Thomson

Page 127: from *Old Christmas from The Sketch-Book* by Washington Irving (Dodge Publishing Co., New York, n.d.)

Page 141: from *Second Collection of Pictures & Songs* by Randolph Caldecott (Frederick Warne & Co., London, n.d.)

Page 175: from *Old West Surrey* by Gertrude Jekyll (Longmans, Green, London, 1904)

Pages 198, 199: from *The Book of Animal Tales* told by Stephen Southwold (George Harrap & Co., London, 1929)